Cave Dwellers and Citrus Growers

Cave Dwellers and Citrus Growers

A Jewish community in
Libya and Israel

HARVEY E. GOLDBERG

Associate Professor of Anthropology
University of Iowa

CAMBRIDGE

At the University Press 1972

Published by the Syndics of the Cambridge University Press
Bentley House, 200 Euston Road, London NW1 2DB
American Branch: 32 East 57th Street, New York, N.Y.10022

Library of Congress Catalogue Card Number: 70 – 174260

ISBN: 0 521 08431 8

Printed in Great Britain
at the University Printing House, Cambridge
(Brooke Crutchley, University Printer)

Preface

'A man must be grateful to a place from which he has benefited'
Midrash Rabbah, Genesis 33:18

This Rabbinical exegesis is cited by Avraham Hai Addadi in the introduction to his pamphlet on the customs of the Jews of Tripoli, whom he served as Head Rabbi in the middle of the last century. It is a most fitting expression of my sentiments toward the small Jewish community that formerly lived in the Gharian Mountains of Tripolitania, and whom I encountered in my field research in an Israeli village in 1963–5. As any service that I might have performed for members of this community does not compare with that of Addadi's, my indebtedness to them is correspondingly greater. I hope that by telling their story, I partially pay that debt.

I also wish to apologize to my hosts and informants for following the current version (or inversion?) of values among social scientists, by not calling their village by its true name. The names of all living individuals are also fictitious, with the exception of the two officials of the Immigration Department mentioned in Chapter 3.

The field research in Israel was supported by a U.S. Public Health Fellowship (grant number MH-07876) from the National Institute of Mental Health. A small amount of additional data was collected during the tenure of a post-doctoral fellowship from the same agency (grant number MH-15,902–01) in 1968–9. An Old Gold Summer Faculty Fellowship from the University of Iowa allowed me to complete the initial manuscript in the summer of 1970.

While in Israel, I profited from discussions with Henry Rosenfeld, Ovadia Shapira and Dov Weintraub, while much of my understanding of 'Even Yosef' (as I call the village) grows out of

[v]

conversations with Yosef Hefner. Robert Attal's personal assistance in library matters has been most helpful, no less than his bibliography of Libyan Jewry. The Manuscript Department of the National and University Library in Jerusalem permitted me to photocopy portions of the work of Rabbi Mordechai Hacohen, a keen and dispassionate observer of his co-religionists in the Tripolitanian mountains. Thanks are also due to Meira Hermoni who drew the pictures for the 'projective test' (Appendix A), and to Michael Malina for assisting in coding my field notes for the 'public opinion poll' (Chapter 3).

Portions of this work were initially prepared as part of a doctoral thesis which was written with the guidance of John Whiting. I am indebted to Talcott Parsons for stimulating my overall interest in social structural matters. Specific suggestions were made to me by Haim Blanc and Shlomo Deshen, as indicated in footnotes, and Frank Kohout provided assistance in some statistical matters. The penultimate version of the manuscript benefited from the critical comments of my father, Michael Goldberg.

My wife, Judy, served as a silent partner throughout the whole enterprise. It is difficult to think of an aspect of the research in which she did not participate. Planning a field trip, interviewing female informants, playing hostess to interviewees, and editing and typing are all lovingly appreciated, but more importantly, her encouragement forms an essential ingredient of the finished product.

Part of the material presented here has appeared in articles in the *American Anthropologist, Ethnology, Folklore Research Center Studies* (Jerusalem), *Human Organization,* and the *Jewish Journal of Sociology,* and are included with permission. Permission has also been given by the Department of Geography, University of Durham and *Man* to reproduce the diagrams in Figure 4.

The transcription of Arabic and Hebrew words is mixed. With regard to the former, I have attempted to give a faithful representation of the dialect of the Gharian Jews, but have discarded diacritical markings after the first appearance of proper nouns. With regard to the latter, the orthography intends to correspond to modern standard Hebrew. I trust that those with a special interest in these matters will find the system satisfactory, and forgive the remaining inconsistencies.

Contents

Figures

Tables

Plates

1. Introduction

The years of 1948 through 1951 were a time of mass immigration to Israel. This migration included more than 30,000 Jews from Libya, where, as in several countries of the Arab East (Iraq and Yemen), there had been a virtual exodus of all the Jewish communities from the country. As part of a mass migration, the individuals and communities involved were dealt with *en masse*. The hurried transportation to, and reception in, Israel did not allow for administrative procedures that were sensitive to cultural variations and situational exigencies. As the immigrants began to settle in the country, the members of the receiving society utilized gross ethnic categories to classify the diversity of social backgrounds from which they came. On the negative side, opprobrious terms such as 'primitive' were attached to whole groups possessed of exotic customs, or who were unfamiliar with items of Western technology.

The tendency toward mass-categorization was also reflected in intellectual reactions to the immigrants. Ethnically, the newcomers from the Middle East were often called 'oriental' Jews and they were divided, socially, under rubrics like 'modern' and 'traditional'. The latter label was applied to immigrants from Kurdistan, Yemen, and rural areas of North Africa such as the hinterland of Tripoli in Libya.

The study I am about to present, by contrast, is an ideographic account of a particular group of Middle Eastern immigrants in Israel. This Jewish community originated from two hamlets of the Gharian Mountain district of Tripolitania, Libya. The inhabitants of the Gharian, both Moslem and Jewish, have attained some fame for the underground dwellings that characterize the region. This exotic aspect of the community's background accounts, in part, for the surprising number of written materials that refer to it. Most of my data on the Gharian Jews, however, derive from field research in an Israeli village in 1963–5. The majority of the former Jewish 'cave-dwellers' of the Gharian are currently settled in this village which lies in the fertile citrus belt of the Sharon Plain.

It often happens, in anthropological research, that a field-worker sets aside the 'problem' that he originally came to study and, for a time at least, lets the events around him dictate the course of his research. This was my experience in the Israeli village of Gharian Jews to which I have given the fictitious name of Even Yosef. My original intent, when selecting an immigrant community for study, was to investigate aspects of the process of socialization in a situation of pronounced culture-conflict. In order to do this I sought a homogeneous community whose culture was very different from the dominant European culture of Israel. The community of Gharian Jews, who had been 'transplanted' to the Israeli *moshav* (small-holders' cooperative village) of Even Yosef appeared to meet this requirement. I was mistaken, however, in assuming that the degree of objective difference between the culture of Even Yosef and that of Israeli society at large was pro-portionately reflected in the extent of social conflict between the community and the wider society, or in the severity of intra-psychic tension of its members. On the contrary, it became clear after a short stay in the village that most of the adult villagers ignored the cultural differences between themselves and the 'out-side world' and for the most part were content in this ignorance.

The children and youth of Even Yosef, also, did not seem to be growing up in a situation of pronounced culture conflict. Rather they were exposed to a relative homogeneous cultural environ-ment in which the main values and role models that they en-countered were those of their parents and other villagers. In terms of my projected study, this meant that I had to temporarily discard my original research plan. Instead, I assumed the explorer's role of discovering what was going on in the new cultural world about me.

In the course of my inquiries into the social life of Even Yosef, I also began to gather data on the community's history. The more I learned about the past of the community, the more I saw its imprint on the social structure of contemporary Even Yosef. Anthropological procedure justly urges great caution in accepting people's testimony about the events of the past. I have therefore utilized written materials (which also must be viewed critically) whenever possible and appropriate. Moreover, the fact that about ninety percent of the Gharian Jewish community has been 'transplanted' in Even Yosef meant that I could cross-check the reports of informants and evaluate the statements of individuals in their social contexts. Still it should be kept in mind that my reconstruction of the Tripolitanian past is heavily influenced by what I observed in the Israeli moshav.

Chapter 2 consists of a reconstruction of communal life in the Gharian. After describing the natural, economic, political and cultural 'environments' of the community, an analysis of its internal structure is presented. The main features discussed are the prominence of a single community leader, the *sheikh*, and the place of the lesser community elite. There are no important political sub-groups between the levels of the community and the family.

The sheikh was the pre-eminent political 'broker' linking the community to the world around it. This pattern persisted for a century (and continues in Even Yosef) though the precise role played by the sheikh changed with the changing political situation of the small Jewish community.

The sheikh was the single important representative of the community in its external affairs while internally he was the senior member of the community elite. The latter were distinguished from the non-elite in wealth, knowledge of the wider society, and in religious and social propriety. In the occupational realm, all members of the community, from the poor itinerant peddlers to the wealthy merchants, were accustomed to cope with changing economic conditions, such as the economic growth brought about by Italian colonization. The elite, however, with a stronger orientation to the wider society, adapted more quickly than the non-elite. Their economic success, in turn, reinforced their elite position.

In analyzing the place of the elite of the community, I have found it useful to view this aspect of Gharian Jewish social history with concepts borrowed from natural history. For example, biological evolution depends on the existence of genetic variation within species that phenotypically exhibit a single structural form. Similarly, the evolution of the Gharian Jewish community cannot be understood without reference to the internal variation in orientations to the 'outside world' which is linked to the elite/non-elite distinction. This view implicitly criticizes attempts to over-typify the Jews of the Gharian or any other 'traditional' community.

Consider, for instance, the following statement about the Jews of rural Morocco, many of whom, like the Gharian Jews, travelled widely as peddlers and tinkers:

The 'traditional' man is deeply rooted in his place of birth. When, in 1950, the residents of Balgat, Turkey were asked where they would like to live if they had to leave their country, a shepherd answered that he would rather kill himself than live outside his native hamlet (Lerner 1958). In this deep-rooted mentality, the Jew of the Atlas, despite his geographic mobility,...is perhaps not far removed from the shepherd of Balgat (Bensimon-Donath 1968: 39).

While it is true that strong 'localism' was characteristic of many of the Gharian Jews, to ignore that there also existed more 'cosmopolitan' individuals among them is to overlook the potentiality for adaptation, not only for the individuals concerned, but for the community to which they were affiliated. An examination of the community elite, viewed as a mechanism for coping with a changing environment, is one of the main themes of the discussion of community life in Israel (Chapters 4 through 6).

The cultural repertoire of the Gharian Jews, then, included orientations that allowed them to develop ties with the wider society. Simultaneously, however, it also included symbols which could potentially emphasize more particular loyalties within the community. A number of studies have claimed that patrilineality was an important principle in the organization of the more traditional communities of the Middle East, just as it is politically important in many Moslem communities. This was not the case among the Gharian Jews, however, where the community and the family were the most significant structural units. On the other hand, their long history in a Middle Eastern milieu meant that these Jews shared much of the cultural heritage of their neighbors, and they were *aware* of patriliny as a potential symbol of group loyalty. The social expression of patriliny within the Jewish community, however, was circumscribed, appearing only in minor family rituals and some leisure and synagogue activities. Returning to a biological analogy, just as a single genotype may assume various forms in its actual expression, so there is a variable relation between the existence of the principle of patriliny within the cultural inventory of a community, and its realization in social life.

The migration of the Gharian Jews to Israel, and the first dozen years of development in the moshav of Even Yosef, are the subjects of Chapter 3. Like other participants in mass migrations, the Gharian Jews experienced the rupture of their communal ties along with physical and psychological privation. They were exposed to the demoralizing influences of life in immigrant camps and had to deal with the uncertainty of radically new conditions in their new 'home'. Throughout these events, however, the Gharian Jews preserved a sense of community and their internal social ties, though strained, were never completely dissolved.

Most importantly there was a continuity of community leadership, both in principle and personnel, which functioned in an attenuated form throughout this period. Just as the sheikh had been the main link between the community and its political environment in the Gharian so a single community leader, the *mazkir* (external secretary), became the primary intermediary between the immigrants and the various Israeli agencies of immigrant absorption and village development. Within the course of a few years the cultural principles that had structured communal life in the Gharian, proved adaptable to the economic and social framework of the Israeli moshav. With a stable and effective communal organization thus achieved, the individual village farmers were free to devote their energies and concerns to economic matters, that is 'to cultivate their own gardens'. With the guidance of the agricultural settlement administrators, and the resources extended by the land settlement agencies, they met this task with considerable technical and economic success.

A synchronic analysis of the community, as I encountered it in 1963–5, is presented in Chapter 4. The focus here is on the economic, administrative and cultural environments of Even Yosef, and the internal leadership arrangements featuring the mazkir and the lesser elite, which guide the Gharian Jewish community in its new surroundings. The formal structure of a moshav calls for executive powers to be vested in an elected moshav committee which in turn hires a mazkir to implement its decisions. While communal decision making in Even Yosef officially follows this format, the mazkir in fact behaves as a single chief executive while the moshav committee defers to his decisions in most matters. The members of the moshav committee, like the elite in the Gharian, are differentiated from the non-elite in wealth, orientation to the wider society and religious knowledge and practice. And like their predecessors in the Gharian, they see their major obligation in dealing with internal 'social problems', of the community, and not the management of moshav affairs.

The continuity that links the Gharian and Even Yosef does not appear only in the structural principles that shape the roles of the mazkir and the moshav committee members. It may be seen also in the matter of personnel. The individuals elected to the moshav committee in Even Yosef very often come from the same families who formed the elite in the Gharian. Nevertheless, Even Yosef is not a highly stratified community. One factor that works against the emergence of rigid strata is the existence of marriage links between the elite and 'rank-and-file' families of the community.

The place of the family within the political life of the community is discussed in Chapter 5. Many of the villages in Israel, that have been settled by Middle Eastern immigrants, have organized themselves into factions in which family ties appear to be the primary basis of allegiance. This did not occur in Even Yosef. There are, however, a minority of villagers who claim that the politics of Even Yosef are influenced by political-kinship groups, and, as in small communities everywhere, family loyalties do have an effect on political processes. A consideration of the political aspects of daily interaction in the village reveals that, against the background of a pervasive egalitarian ethos, moshav families vie for economic advantage, and social prestige. However, as in the Gharian, individual families do not group themselves into larger corporate political units.

Viewed as a whole the community of Even Yosef exhibits a remarkable continuity in internal values and social-structural principles, coupled with its relatively rapid adjustment to the economic and administrative realities of moshav life. The interpretation offered here is that the conjoining of stronger orientations toward the wider society with elite status within the community's structure constitutes an *institutionalized mechanism for coping with change*. The members of the elite, and pre-eminently the mazkir (as the sheikh before him), are the first to contact the sources of change in the community's environment. They are, at the same time, the best equipped among the members of the community to meet the demands of new situations. Insofar as they meet these demands successfully, and in particular maintain their economic position, they preserve their elite status. The non-elite of the community may subsequently learn new forms of adaptive behavior from their more cosmopolitan 'peers', but are buffered from direct contact with the world outside the community. In a word, the principles of social organization which had evolved in the Gharian proved adaptive in the environment of Even Yosef and thus survived.

It has often been remarked that the natural selection dictum explains everything in general and nothing in particular. Its application to the case of Even Yosef then, calls for a detailed account of the imputed selective mechanisms. As outlined, Chapters 4 and 5 show how the linkage of elite status and positive orientations to the wider society proved adaptive in Even Yosef, as they had before in the Gharian. Chapter 6 discusses (*a*) how the vital 'resource' of cosmopolitan orientations is transmitted intergenerationally within the community, and is thus preserved, and (*b*) how its linkage to individuals of elite status is maintained. This discussion enables us to return partially to my original interest in socialization in the moshav.

The discussion of the intergenerational transmission of orientations to the wider society begins with an ethnographic account of the male youth of the village. Ideally, a discussion of socialization should comprehend children and youth of both sexes. The community mores concerning heterosexual contacts, however, barred me from spending time with the female adolescents, just as it prevented me from systematic observation of the children, which would have involved extensive contacts with their mothers. My data on the male adolescents derive from participant observation and a systematic interview of a sample of youths. I also interviewed the fathers of the adolescents in my sample (the interviewing procedures are discussed in Appendix A).

A comparison of the responses to the two sets of interviews yields disarmingly straightforward results: the families in which the father is more strongly oriented toward the wider society (which includes most of the 'elite' families), 'produce' adolescent sons who are similarly predisposed. The main importance of this finding is the implication that the varying degrees of 'acculturation' among the youth cannot be explained simply by citing differential exposure to external agents of culture change, such as school or army, but must take into account the pre-existing and traditional variation within the community. Also, there is evidence that the intergenerational reproduction of orientations to the wider society stems from differences in the organization of family life and child-rearing practices among the village families, and is not a result of the simple attitudinal imitation of fathers on the part of their sons. In sum, the family is the locus of the mechanism which insures an adequate 'supply' of positive orientations to the wider society in each generation.

The final link in the chain of our argument is to assert that those adolescents possessed of a more positive orientation to Israeli society, will be selected as the village leaders in the next 'generation'. Whether this is so, or not, can only be determined by a 'restudy' at a future time. Some prognosis may be made, however, on the basis of the contemporary 'adolescent society' in Even Yosef which appears to be organized according to the same principles as the total community. The features of egalitarianism, the absence of factions, and the vesting of leadership in the hands of a few 'cosmopolitan' individuals may all be discerned in the social organization of the male youth. Thus, the youth insist that 'they are all friends with one another', and their sociometric choices and observable behavior, indicate that clique formation is weakly developed among the adolescents of the village. The sociometric 'stars', or leaders of the youth, are those who are most familiar with Israeli society at large. Moreover, these 'elite' youths have already begun to play their predicted adult roles in that they, having learned new forms of behavior outside the community, serve as models for the transmission of these new patterns to the more local-oriented youth within the moshav. While many of the activities and concerns of the youth of Even Yosef differ widely from those of their parents, it is nevertheless clear that their parents' political values and models have already been successfully inculcated. This being so, and assuming that external factors remain relatively unchanged, the Gharian Jewish community, now settled in Even Yosef, should maintain its current internal structure for some time to come.

2. The Gharian Jewish Community

At the beginning of 1949 there were about 35,000 Jews living in Libya: approximately 30,000 in Tripolitania and 5,000 in Cyrenaica.[1] Within the former province, more than 22,000 lived in the city of Tripoli, while just under 8,000 lived in towns and villages of the Tripolitanian coastal plain and mountain interior. These 'rural' Jews were distributed in 17 settlements ranging in population from 1,502 in 'Amrus on the outskirts of Tripoli to 25 in Nalut in the Western Jebel Nefusa.[2] The present study is concerned with the Jews from the Gharian Mountain region who numbered about 500.

THE GHARIAN REGION AND ITS JEWS

As depicted in Figure 1, the Gharian Mountain region lies due south of Tripoli. Gharian-town, its administrative and commercial center, is located about 100 kilometers from Tripoli, and is reached by traversing the desert of the Jefara Plain and ascending the Gharian mountains which tower about 700 meters above the plain. In pre-motorized days the trip from the Gharian to Tripoli took two and a half days. Alternatively, Tripoli could be reached by the longer route through Terhuna, Mesallata and Homs if one did not wish to cross the desert.[3]

The rainfall at Gharian-town averages about 325 millimeters per year and decreases as one moves away from the vicinity of the

---

[1] In 1949 Libya was under the rule of the British Military Administration. It had formerly been the Italian Colony of Libya and later became the independent United Kingdom of Libya (Khadduri 1963).

[2] These figures are from 1943 (Comunità 1943: A. Guweta' 1960a: 25). A fuller discussion of the demography of rural Tripolitanian Jewry may be found in Goldberg (n.d.).

[3] Further descriptive material on Gharian-town may be found in Khuja (1960).

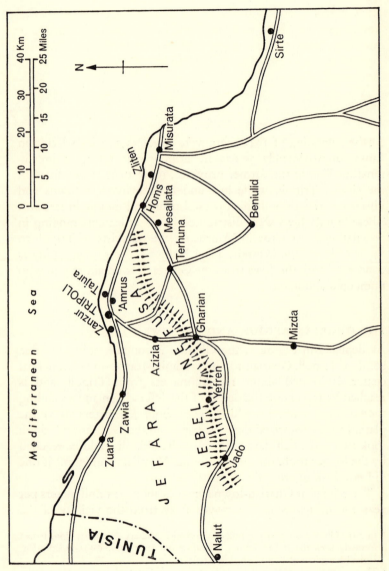

Figure 1. Tripolitania: major roads and towns.

town in any direction. There are three perennial springs in Wadi Teghessat on the outskirts of the town. The subsistence base of the Gharian district consists of the raising of barley, olives, figs and grapes, combined with sheep and goat husbandry. The region has long been known for the quality of its saffron.[1] Over one-quarter of the population may be classified as nomadic or semi-nomadic.[2]

The age of the Jewish community of the Gharian is unclear, though it is fairly certain that there has been continuous Jewish settlement there since at least the sixteenth century. It is believed that some Jews, fleeing the Spanish conquest of Tripoli in 1510, migrated to the Gharian (Hacohen ms: 34a). If this is so, it is possible that these refugees selected an extant Jewish community. Hacohen (1969: 69) reports seeing a plaque on a broken Torah case in a Gharian synagogue dating from 1559. The Jews of the Gharian are mentioned in a mythical account of an historical Mahdist revolt against Ottoman control of Tripoli toward the end of the sixteenth century.[3] In Tripoli, in 1711, the government executed a Jewish servant named Lavi el Ghariani (Féraud 1927: 206). The Gharian Jews are mentioned by several nineteenth century explorers of Africa such as Lyon (1821: 28–32), Barth (1858: 59–65), and Rohlfs (1874: 32–8); and more detailed descriptions of the community are available from the present century.[4]

---

[1] In the sixteenth century Leo Africanus (1847: 743) reported: 'Of Mount Gharian. This high and cold mountaine, containing in length fortie and in bredth fifteene miles, and being separated from other mountaines by a sandie desert, is distant from Tripolis almost fiftie miles. It yeeldeth great plentie of barly and of dates, which vnlesse they be spent while they are new, will soon prooue rotten. Heere are likewise abundance of oliues: Wherefore from this mountaine into Alexandriia and other cities there is much oil conueighed. There is not better saffron to be found in any part of the world besides, which in regard of the goodnesse is solde very deere. For yeerely tribute there is gathered out of this mountaine three-score thousand ducates, and as much saffron as fifteene mules can carrie.'

[2] The 1936 census (Italy 1939) lists 26% of the 'present population' (those actually present on the census date) as nomadic or semi-nomadic. The 1954 census lists 42% as nomadic or semi-nomadic (Libya 1959).

[3] For details see Hirschberg (1965a: 175–7; 1965b: 420, 425, 457). The distance and terrain separating Tripoli from the Gharian encouraged tribal revolts which frequently took place after a change in the ruling government (Féraud 1927: 57, 77, 81–2, 137–8, 194, 207–9, 250, 254–65, 349).

[4] See Hacohen (ms: 226a–230a; 1969: 68–70), Slouschz (1927: 115–63), Brandenburg (1911), Raccah (1938), Elmaleh (1943), Kimche (1948b), Norris (1953) and Goldberg 1967b; n.d.).

The Gharian region is reputed to consist of 100 villages (*qabail*, sing. *qbīla*) and had a population of about 56,000 in 1954.[1] During the present century Jews were found in three settlements, Tighrinna (4–5 kilometers south of Gharian-town), Ben'abbās (about 14 kilometers north of the town), and Gharian-town itself (Figure 2). Table 1 shows the population of these settlements according to different written sources. As may be seen from Table 1, the Jewish population of Gharian-town is not as old as that of the other two villages. Most of the Jews of Gharian-town came from Tripoli or Zanzur (12 kilometers to the west of Tripoli) after 1922 when the Gharian was conquered by the Italians.

TABLE 1. *Population of the Gharian Jewish settlements in the past century*

Year	Tighrinna	Ben'abbas	Gharian-town	Total	Source
1853	—	—	none	120 (families)	Benjamin 1859
1886	—	—	none	550 (people)	Ish S.D.H. 1886
1902	—	—	none	300	Alliance 1902
1914	200	100	none	300	Agostini 1917
1931	256	85	a few	341 +	Italy 1935
1936	322	97	a few	419 +	Italy 1939
1943	343	87	90	520	Comunità 1943
1948	—	—	—	464	Landshut 1950

Under Turkish rule Gharian-town did not have a large population. The term *Gharian* referred to the region as often as it did to the market town. The latter was normally called Teghessat, the name of the settlement closest to the town. The Jewish hamlet of Tighrinna was variously called *ḥarit il yhūd*, *ḥush il yhūd* (Barth 1858: 63), or *arḍ il yhūd* (Great Britain 1920: 334) by the Moslems, and was separated by several hundred meters from the Moslem settlement of Menzel Tighrinna. The hamlet of (Yhūd) Ben'abbas was similarly separated from the neighboring Moslem settlement of Errahba.

Ben'abbas, Gharian-town and Tighrinna all lie near the main road connecting the Gharian to Tripoli in the north, the Jebel

---

[1] The population of the region in 1936 was 42,011 including 2,369 Italian nationals, most of whom were probably agricultural colonists (Italy 1939: 4).

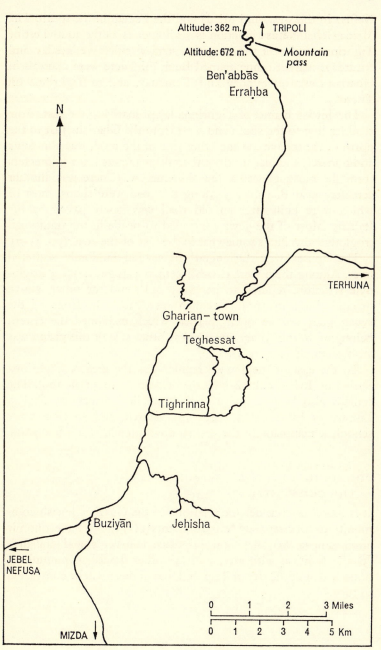

Figure 2. Gharian-town and vicinity.

Nefusa in the west, and Mizda and the Fezzan in the south. The Mizda–Jebel Nefusa junction is 5 kilometers to the southwest of Tighrinna and was the site of a semi-weekly (Wednesday and Saturday) market center named Buziyān. There were markets in Gharian-town on Sunday and Thursday, and in Tighrinna on Tuesday.

The Jewish hamlet of Tighrinna lay primarily to the east of the road leading to the south and west from the Gharian. Just to the north of the village, on the other side of the road, was a mosque and minaret, and just south of the village (about 1.5–2 kilometers from the mosque) was a Jewish cemetery. (There was another cemetery near Ben'abbas.) Along the road were shops, most of which were built after an old road was newly paved by the Italians. Most of the Jews continued to reside in the traditional troglodyte dwellings somewhat to the east of the road (pp. 35–7).

The houses were 'arranged' in several randomly scattered lines. Among them were two adjacent synagogues; one a troglodyte structure reputed to be 'very old', and the other, above ground, built in 1885 (Hacohen ms: 230a). In front of the synagogues was an open 'piazza' which contained the cistern belonging to the synagogue. On the other side of this piazza was a refuse dump (Figure 3).

To the east of the Jewish hamlet was the area of Tighrinna settled by Italian colonists in 1931 (Despois 1935: 98–100). The Italians also built a police station, medical dispensary (Italian Library of Information 1940: 46), church, and an elementary school, which many of the Jewish boys attended for a few years.

THE SOCIOCULTURAL ENVIRONMENTS OF THE COMMUNITY

It is useful to consider the relations of the Gharian Jewish community to four separate 'environments': (1) the technoeconomic environment, (2) the local populace (Moslems and Italians), (3) the political authority, and (4) other Jewish communities, notably that of the city of Tripoli. Each of these will be considered in turn.

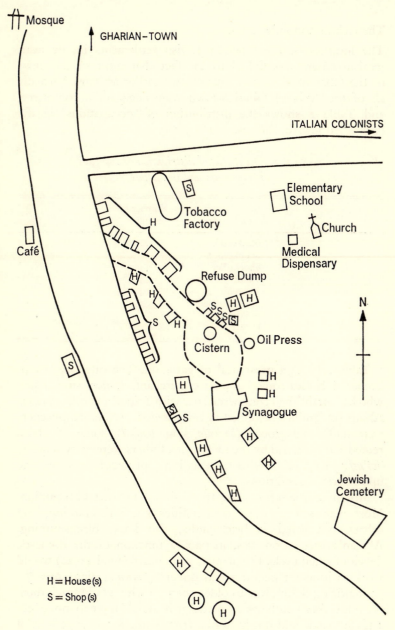

Figure 3. Sketch-map of Tighrinna.

The technoeconomic setting

The location of the Gharian Jewish settlements in, or near, market-centers was linked to the fact that most of the Jews of the Gharian were petty merchants and/or artisans. Virtually all of the Jews of Gharian-town were engaged in commerce, and Table 2 shows the distribution of 'occupations' in the two older Jewish villages.

TABLE 2. *Occupational distribution of the Jews of Tighrinna and Ben'abbas*

Occupation	Number of families
Blacksmith	24
Shopkeeper	17
Shoemaker	5
Tailor	5
Tinsmith	4
Itinerant Peddler	2
Builder	1
Driver	1

Table 2 hides a great deal of variation. The category 'shop-keeper' includes some large-scale merchants (*tujjār*, sing. *tājir*), who had established commercial ties with Tripoli and other towns. About six families belonged in this category. Other shopkeepers were traditional grocers (*baqqāla*, sing. *baqqāl*), some of whom rented shops owned by the merchants. Others were petty retailers (*ibī'ushrī*) who might also trade as itinerant peddlers, depending upon current conditions.

Moreover, the term 'occupation' should be used with caution. Most members of these communities knew tinsmithing, and others, not listed as blacksmiths, also knew blacksmithing. A man's occupation was, in part, a function of the domestic developmental cycle. Frequently, young men (aged 12–20) would work as itinerant peddlers and tinkers (*ṭawwāfa*, sing. *ṭawwāf*), apprenticing themselves to older ṭawwāfa who would teach them the trade. As a youth neared marriage he would hope to move into a trade that would not keep him from home for long periods of time. Some ṭawwāfa, utilizing modern means of transportation, would travel as far as the Fezzan. They might remain away from home for months, returning only to celebrate the religious festivals.

Geographic mobility in search of income was characteristic of all economic 'classes'. One family moved to Mizda, more than 100 kilometers south of the Gharian, to operate a 'post exchange' for the Italian troops there. Others had more or less permanent shops in the Jebel Nefusa region. A few of the families of Ben-'abbas owned or rented shops in Gharian-town where they would spend the week, returning home for the Sabbath. Some of the shopkeepers of Gharian-town would similarly return home to Tripoli where their families continued to reside.

The Jews were not prohibited from owning land, and a few families owned land and flocks. Some families worked the land themselves, but the flocks were invariably tended by Moslems who paid a portion of the profit to the Jewish owners. Frequently, the Jewish owner and herdsman would have their agreement written down by a Moslem scribe (*fqih*), and a copy was given to each of the contracting parties. The Jews who owned land observed the biblical injunction of *leqeṭ* (Leviticus 19: 9), namely, leaving the remains of the gleanings in the fields, which were normally collected by the poorer Moslems.

As already indicated, the economic survival of the Jews demanded flexibility in response to changing conditions. The wide-ranging ṭawwāfa would seek word as to which regions had ample rain in a given year, and then select their routes so as to visit villages which had produce to sell or barter. Further economic change took place in the wake of the Italian conquest. Large military garrisons were then established in the Gharian, and in the 1930s Italian farmers were settled in Tighrinna as part of the colonization program. The influx of Italians provided new economic opportunities, and many of the ṭawwāfa were able to establish themselves as 'sedentary' shopkeepers. In sum, there was a tradition of adaptibility with regard to economic pursuits.

The Jews and the local populace

The relationship of the Jewish community to the Moslems and Italians conformed to the 'mosaic pattern' depicted by Coon (1958: 5–6). In this system the cultural and social autonomy of ethnic groups is coupled with economic interdependence. One indicator of the social distance between the Jews and their neighbors was the preservation of a Jewish–Arabic dialect, differing somewhat from the dialect of the local Moslems. As was the case in Tripoli, the /t/ of Old Arabic was pronounced [t] by the Moslems and [č] by the Jews; the /q/ of Old Arabic was pronounced [g] by the Moslems and [q] by the Jews (Cesaro 1939: 24). As in other instances in which groups that are socially distant maintain economic relationships, it is useful to view these relationships in their structural contexts.

The Jewish blacksmiths made and/or maintained the agricultural implements, housewares and weapons of the Moslems. Jewish tinsmiths periodically tinned the interiors of brass utensils. When dealing with Moslems with whom they were long familiar, Jewish artisans might be paid in kind at harvest time, rather than in cash for each piece of work. In this manner, it was reported to me, the Jews would receive produce whose monetary equivalent was greater than the amount they would have collected if paid on a piece-work basis throughout the year. If this is correct, these artisans were implicitly functioning as money-lenders. Transactions with non-familiar customers were carried out on a cash or barter basis.

A Moslem with whom a Jew had long-standing economic ties was known as a ṣaḥab, a term which might be translated 'friend', but was not applied to informal acquaintances, Jewish or non-Jewish. In the case of the ṭawwāfa, the ṣaḥab was a man with whom the Jew might find lodging during his search for trade. Slouschz (1927: 108) mentions (but does not describe) 'blood brotherhoods' of the Jewish merchants in Africa with their clients. In the absence of a ṣaḥab in a certain region, the ṭawwāfa might be provided hospitality by the sheikh of the qbīla. They sometimes were called to entertain their hosts by telling stories.

Much of the peddler trade involved barter and apparently fulfilled the function of bringing produce and manufactured items to regions where they were not available. Because of their geographical mobility, kinship and commercial ties to Jews in Tripoli and other communities were important to the ṭawwāfa. Another social–ecologic niche exploited by them was the sale of cosmetics, jewelry and materials to the Moslem women. The low-status Jew was allowed to enter the house of a Moslem and trade with the women, while this would not be permitted to another Moslem (Hacohen ms: 204a).

The settlement of Italians in the Gharian, which lasted about 10 years, did not alter the 'mosaic pattern'. The Italians did not constitute an important reference group to the Gharian Jews, although they had a greater affect on the Jews of Tripoli. Almost all of them continued to wear the traditional garb,[1] and, except for the 'urban Jews' who lived in Gharian-town, they kept their homes in their own hamlets. Many of the men attended an Italian school for one or two years, but they learned to speak Italian more through their commercial contacts than through formal schooling. There were few friendships between Italians and Jews.

The Jews of Tripolitania were accorded a separate communal status. In many matters they followed the decisions of Rabbinic courts, as the Moslems did with respect to the *Shari'a* courts. In the context of a small community such as the Gharian, most matters of internal social control were managed without recourse to official Italian government offices.

The political environment

Just as the Jews of the Gharian had to deal with changing economic conditions, they also had to adapt to rapid political change. In the first third of the nineteenth century, Tripoli was ruled by the independent Qaramanli dynasty, nominally loyal to the Ottoman Empire. During this period some Gharian Jews served as local tithe collectors (Lyon 1821: 32–3). In 1835, direct Ottoman control was re-established in Tripoli (Féraud 1927: 366–71). From 1839 to 1858 the inhabitants of Gharian were intermittently involved in revolts against Ottoman rule led by tribal leaders of the Tripolitanian Jebel, notably Ghoma of Yefren (Féraud 1927: 380–2, 388, 411; Slouschz 1908: 433–53). The Jews were drawn into these conflicts when Ghoma impressed local Jewish physicians into treating his men, and Jewish blacksmiths into mending weapons. Upon the Ottoman conquest of the Gharian, the local Moslems informed to the authorities that the Jews had been loyal to Ghoma. The Jews pleaded, of course,

---

[1] The retention of the traditional clothing was not only the simple inertia of a culture trait. One merchant who travelled frequently to Tripoli suggested that more Jews might have adopted European attire, but that they were afraid of hostile reactions by the Gharian Moslems to this indicator of pro-Italian orientation.

that they had no choice but to comply, and the Ottoman Pasha accepted their plea (Hacohen ms: 80b–82a; Slouschz 1927: 151–2).

During the present century the Ottoman regime gave way to the Young Turks in 1908. This change had repercussions among the Gharian Jews, as several of them were conscripted into the Turkish Army (Cachia 1945: 82). The Turks lost Tripolitania to Italy, which 'pacified' the Gharian in 1922. During World War II, German troops were stationed in the Gharian at the same time that there were deportations of Libyan Jews to camps in Jado, and to a few places in Gharian (Rennel 1948: 270; Ḥakmon 1960). Several thousand Jews from Tripoli took refuge in Gharian-town during the British bombardment of the capital. Similarly, many Torah-scrolls were sent there to escape damage. These Jews returned to Tripoli after its capture by the British.[1]

During the British military occupation, Tripolitanian Jewry faced violent riots in 1945 and 1948 (Rennel 1948: 466). There was no loss of life in the Gharian, but there was some loss of property. Troops were stationed to guard the homes of the Jews of Ben-'abbas. These riots undoubtedly helped crystallize the decision of the Gharian Jews to participate in the mass migration to Israel that began in 1949 and emptied rural Tripolitania of its Jewish population.

Other Jewish communities

The fourth significant environment of the Gharian Jewish community consisted of the other Jewish communities in Tripolitania. The most important of these, of course, was the community of Tripoli, which was linked by economic, kinship and religious ties to the small rural communities. The shopkeepers and merchants of the Gharian had both direct and indirect commercial ties to the merchants of Tripoli. The latter were important suppliers of the ṭawwāfa of the Gharian. Commercial links similarly existed

---

[1] The majority of the Jews, because of the vulnerability of their position, chose to keep away from political involvements, as far as possible. This was sometimes difficult as the Gharian was the scene of important activities connected with Tripolitanian opposition to the Italians (Khadduri 1963: 22). One Jewish man from Tighrinna was imprisoned by the Italians for 10 years because of his support of Arab resistance. A Jewish merchant from Gharian-town, by virtue of his extensive commercial contacts, unwittingly became involved in a British intelligence ring prior to the British victory.

among the smaller communities. A ṭawwāf, in his travels, would attempt to stay at the home of a Jew rather than a Moslem.

While the communities of Tighrinna and Ben'abbas were highly endogamous (Goldberg 1967*a*), there were some marriage ties to other small communities, such as Zliten and Terhuna. Migration was always a feature of rural Tripolitanian life (Goldberg 1971) so that people had siblings and cousins in other villages. Annual or occasional visits to kinsmen and affines might result in further marriages, which encouraged further visits, and so forth.

From the point of view of Rabbinic law, the Gharian had to be linked to the city of Tripoli. Local religious specialists might perform marriages, but divorces could be granted only by the Rabbinic court in Tripoli. The same is true for disputes over inheritance, if these could not be resolved by local mediation.[1] Frequently teachers for the synagogue school would be recruited from other communities. A *shuḥīt* (Hebrew: *shoḥeṭ*, ritual slaughterer) or a *muhīl* (Hebrew: *mohel*, ritual circumcisor) would have to undergo training and receive certification in Tripoli before being allowed to practice in the Gharian. In 1923 there were 32 Torah scrolls in the synagogues of Ben'abbas and Tighrinna (Elmaleh 1943), which must have been brought from Tripoli or even further away. Printed religious books were obtained from Tripoli, which might have been printed there, in Jerba or Leghorn in Italy. The Gharian would be visited periodically by emissaries of religious institutions in Palestine, who assessed the community their due of charity (cf. Ben-Zvi 1964). During the present century the Gharian Jews began to contribute to the Zionist movement (Elmaleh 1943), and modern Hebrew textbooks from Palestine reached the synagogue school in the late 1930s.

---

[1] When I asked the Gharian Jews about local inheritance practices they said that the first born son receives a double portion (cf. Deuteronomy 21: 17), and that daughters do not inherit. This is at variance with Rabbinic Law, however, which grants more rights to the daughters of the deceased, and which was authoritative in the courts in Tripoli. While within Moroccan Jewry, there were traditional differences between the 'Castilian' laws and the native 'Mosaic' laws of inheritance practiced in many rural areas (Malka 1952; Jacobs 1956: 26–7), the customary practices of the Gharian Jews could not be considered a comprehensive legal system alternative to the Law represented by the Rabbis of Tripoli.

THE INTERNAL STRUCTURE OF THE COMMUNITY

The preceding sketch of the sociocultural environment of the Gharian Jews allows a sounder analysis of the internal social arrangements of the community. This will be discussed under four headings: (1) the status and role of the sheikh, (2) the status and role of the lesser elite, (3) communal institutions, and (4) the family.

The status and role of the sheikh

One of the important sociocultural mechanisms that facilitated the adaptation of the small Jewish minority to its unstable political environment was the concentration of political interchanges with the environment into one status (and role),[1] that of the sheikh. The sheikh was the main political 'broker' (Wolf 1956: 1075) of the community. The following discussion will deal with the office of sheikh under Turkish, Italian and British rule, and will indicate how the changing role of the sheikh was a function of the changing relationship between the Jewish community and its political environment. Three aspects of this problem, while interrelated, should be kept analytically distinct, namely, (1) the political relationship of the community to its environment, (2) the role of the sheikh, and (3) the personality of the sheikh. The discussion will conclude by outlining structural characteristics of the status of sheikh that have persisted throughout the changes hereafter to be described.

The Turkish period

During the period of Turkish rule the most salient political problem was that of physical security. The members of the Jewish community considered themselves surrounded by 'thousands of Moslems' who, under certain circumstances, might be incited to acts of anti-Jewish violence. The maintenance of order was the responsibility of the Ottoman Empire, whose seat of power, however, was in Tripoli, a distance of two and a half days across the desert. (The old men of Even Yosef, in explaining the term *osmanli*, that is Ottoman, liken it to 'the police'.) The sheikh,

---

[1] The following analysis utilizes the distinction between *status* and *role* (Linton 1936: 113–14), which seems to hint at Firth's (1951: 35–6) more systematically developed distinction between *structure* and *organization*.

therefore, had to be a skilled diplomat, sensitive to threatening changes in relationships among the groups. He had to be well-informed about the 'outside world', and to be able to present, convincingly and eloquently, the case of his people to the wielders of power. Financial resources were important so that the sheikh could devote time to communal affairs (he received no salary), and could put forth bribes in the form of cash or lavish hospitality, if necessary.

The sheikh was appointed by the *kaymakam* of the Gharian (who was called the *Bey* by the local populace). It was his duty to collect the poll tax from the members of the community, which, according to the Ottoman Laws of 1855, was imposed in lieu of military service (Lewis 1968: 116, 337; Cachia 1945: 81). The sheikh himself was not obligated to pay the tax (Hacohen ms: 213a). He was also formally empowered to imprison members of the Jewish community for 24 hours, although this right was rarely, if ever, exercised.

Because the community was dependent on the political skill of the sheikh, he had to be a person who could be entrusted with the community's interests. This trust was grounded in the fact that the sheikh upheld the social and religious values of the community. The last sheikhs under the Turks were also the religious leaders of the community and, according to Slouschz (1927: 152) held the title of *Ḥakham Bashi* (Head Rabbi) of the Gharian (see Hirschberg 1969: 203).

There are data available on two sheikhs under Turkish rule. During the time of Ghoma's revolt, Ḥumāni Ḥajjāj, who was a physician, was required to administer to Ghoma's soldiers. After the suppression of the revolt, Humani was appointed sheikh of the Gharian Jews and physician to the local Turkish garrison (Hacohen ms: 816; Slouschz 1927: 152). Humani also is mentioned by a European visitor to Tripoli (Benjamin 1859: 243), and probably was the Gharian sheikh whom the religious emissary from Palestine met there in 1872 (Ben-Zvi 1964: 81). More data is available on a successor of Humani's, Sheikh Khalīfa.[1]

---

[1] I do not know whether there were any sheikhs between Humani and Khalifa. Contrary to Slouschz (1927: 152), it is unlikely that Khalifa was Humani's descendant. Khalifa came from the Zubit 'family group' (p. 39) which was separate from Humani. It is much more likely that Ya'aqub Humani (p. 24) was a descendant of Sheikh Humani. Indeed, the 'segmentation' of a separate Humani family-group within the Hajjaj patronymic group may have originated with

Sheikh Khalīfa Zubīṭ Ḥajjāj served as leader of the community from approximately 1885 to 1913 (Hacohen ms: 229a–b). He is described in some detail by both Hacohen (ms: 228b–230a) and Slouschz (1926: 37–40; 1927: 132–53), the former stressing his skill as a physician, and the latter his talent as a poet. He was granted a license to practice medicine by modern Turkish doctors who visited Tripoli in 1885. In the same year he was instrumental in securing permission from Istanbul to build a new synagogue in Tighrinna (Hacohen ms: 230a). He was 'wealthy' thanks to his medical practice. Khalifa had one son, named Ḥuatu, who died while still a young man. Sheikh Khalifa died about 1913.

After the death of Huatu, Khalifa brought an orphan from Tripoli, named Berkhāni Zigdūn (who had French citizenship by virtue of his Tunisian origin), to work in his household. Berkhani married one of Khalifa's daughters. Another daughter was married to a local Gharianite, an older individual named Ya'aqūb Ḥumāni Ḥajjāj. A few years after this latter marriage, Khalifa passed away, and the sheikhship devolved upon Ya'aqub Humani, who served as sheikh for about seven years.

During the period of 1912 to 1922 the Gharian was controlled by local Arab leaders, as Italian power was confined to the coastal towns. Ya'aqub's sheikhship more or less coincides with this period. Few memories of him survive among the people of Even Yosef except the recollection that he was a physician, as was Khalifa. Ya'aqub Humani died without male offspring and afterward the sheikhship passed on to Berkhani.[1]

One characteristic that was shared by Khalifa Zubit, Ya'aqub Humani and Berkhani Zigdun was that they all entered into polygamous marriages. In order for them to do so they had to obtain the permission of the Rabbinic Court in Tripoli (Hacohen

Sheikh Humani. That Khalifa and Humani shared the patronym Hajjaj is very weak evidence of kinship between them.

Humani and Khalifa were residents of Tighrinna as were all the Gharian Jewish sheikhs. The community of Ben'abbas had its own informal leadership pattern which I have largely ignored.

[1] The Turkish–Italian 'interregnum' in the Gharian is a period about which memories are unclear, and often contradictory, among the people of Even Yosef. It is possible that there were other 'temporary' sheikhs during this time. Insofar as there was no stable government, there could be no stable position of sheikh. This period saw an epidemic, a sea blockade, drought and famine. Many people died. It is reported that the whole community of Ben'abbas abandoned their village about 1915 and moved to Tripoli. After two years, part of the community returned.

ms: 9a). In the cases of Khalifa and Ya'aqub, permission was granted because their first wives did not bear male offspring. In the case of Berkhani permission was granted to take a second wife because his first wife became crippled and was unable to carry on her normal domestic-conjugal activities. The only other case of polygamy of which I am aware also involved one of the community elite.

The Italian period

During Italian rule the political situation of the Gharian Jews grew more secure. The government went to great lengths to secure civil order and was quick to execute political insurgents. Tripolitanian Jews describe the improvement of their security under the Italians, as due to the fact that they 'ruled with a strong hand'. Older people of Even Yosef relate that they could no longer bribe local officials, as they did under the Turks. The stability during Italian rule also is frequently contrasted to the insecurity during the successor British administration.

The sheikh, therefore, during this period, did not have to be as skilled a diplomat as his predecessors. However, he still was the main link between the government and the community. He advised the government in assessing the taxes of individual families, and in general, was consulted in all instances when members of the community were involved with the administration.

Berkhani was appointed sheikh at the beginning of the period of Italian rule and retained the position until the British occupation. In accordance with the changed role of the sheikh, resulting from the strong Italian administration, Berkhani's performance of that role differed from Khalifa's. He hardly learned to speak Italian, and did not excel intellectually in either the religious or secular realm.

In the early years of Italian rule the local officials imposed a corvée on the Jewish community, forcing them to work on the construction of public buildings. Berkhani did nothing to oppose this corvée, even though it had no legal basis. The corvée was eventually abolished through the efforts of another member of the community. No attempt was made to replace Berkhani, however, despite his yielding nature toward the administration, because, for the most part, the rights of the Jews were insured and there was no need for a 'strong' sheikh.

In other ways the status of community leader remained the same. For example, Berkhani upheld the religious values of the community even though he was not a religious specialist. In his role as sheikh he played an important part in encouraging members of the community to study at the religious academies in Tripoli in order to acquire the skills of shoḥeṭ or mohel, if these specialties were lacking in the Gharian. He maintained contact with the Jewish communal institutions in Tripoli, to make sure that the Gharian was provided with teachers for the synagogue school. Thus he worked for the religious welfare of the community despite his lack of special religious training.

Berkhani had no relatives in the Gharian other than his affines and children. None of the families, nor any of the patronymic groups, could claim that he showed favoritism.

Berkhani also was fairly well off. He had a shop in which he sold spices and dried goods. Financial resources were necessary to entertain 'official' visitors to the community (e.g. government officials, local Moslem leaders, or Rabbis from Palestine). Funds were also important in fulfilling another function of the sheikhship, namely the resolution of disputes between members of the community.

The organization of the sheikhship during the Italian period throws into relief another important task of the sheikh, that of a mediator of conflicts. It is in this aspect of his role as sheikh that Berkhani primarily is remembered by the Gharian Jews today. There are a number of stories relating that Berkhani would give his own money to disputants in order to settle minor conflicts. The community exerted pressure on its members not to resort to the government courts but to submit disputes to the arbitration of the sheikh and other community notables. Once a person had sought Berkhani's arbitration it would be an insult to the honor of the sheikh to dispute his decision (cf. Willner and Kohls 1962: 228). The people of Even Yosef point out that his yielding nature made Berkhani a successful mediator. This is the same quality which made him a 'weak' representative to the Italian government.

At the end of 1942 the British army entered the Gharian. British officers approached Berkhani, who was then old and infirm, and asked him to name a successor. He first named Ḥai Khalifa, the present external secretary of Even Yosef. Hai, under pressure, accepted the office for a number of months, but afterwards transferred the responsibility to Khlāfu Hūga Ḥassān, who was married to Berkhani's daughter, and who remained sheikh until the members of the communities migrated to Israel.[1]

The British Military Administration

During the British occupation the political position of the Jewish community reverted to the pre-Italian situation. The relationships between British, Moslems and Jews were aggravated by contemporary political events involving corresponding groups in Palestine. Many Tripolitanian Jews claim that the British were ambivalent in their attempts to stem the anti-Jewish riots of 1945 (Zuaretz *et al.* 1960: 207–13). Because of this situation, the Gharian Jewish sheikh, though maintaining the same formal status as during the Italian period, was called upon to make his primary contribution in the role of diplomat.

Khlafu Huga Hassan was one of the more educated members of the community. He was a gifted speaker and spoke Italian fairly well. He had connections with the government before his appointment to the sheikhship as a supplier to the British Army. In his home he set up a small restaurant where he would entertain British officers and sell them handicraft items made by members of the community. Subsequent to his appointment he became a locally important political figure. Jews and Moslems would seek his intervention with the authorities and he served as a go-between for bribes extended to local officials. As his ties with the British grew stronger, his power within the community also increased. For example, he took the liberty of using the synagogue's funds (p. 33) in carrying out his political role.

Khlafu's power, however, was not without legitimation in the eyes of the community. He was the son of one of the local religious specialists. His father, Rebbi[2] Huga, read from the Torah

[1] Berkhani had been sheikh of the three Jewish settlements in the Gharian. The British, however, made their initial approaches to the Gharian Jews through the more citified Jewish leaders of Gharian-town. Thus, Khalifa Huga was appointed sheikh by the British after consultations with these leaders. As discussed below (pp. 27–8) Khalifa then became a more prominent leader in his own right.

[2] The Jews of the Gharian, and other Tripolitanian communities, commonly accord the general title *rebbi* to anyone who assumes a special religious function such as a ritual slaughterer, circumcisor, or synagogue school teacher. An older man deserving of the title would generally be *addressed* as rebbi, while a younger religious specialist would be so addressed solely in the context of his religious duties. Normally, males were addressed by their given names (except for terms of respect to older relatives), a usage that included the sheikh with the other members of the community.

and delivered sermons in the synagogue. He led prayers on *Kibbūr* (Hebrew: *Kippūr*, the Day of Atonement) and was called upon to write marriage contracts. As Rebbi Huga grew older some of these activities devolved upon Khlafu, who thus served as a religious leader simultaneously with his fulfilling the duties of sheikh.

Khlafu had but one sister and his father had no siblings, so there were few close relatives who could press him for favors not extended to other members of the community.

Khlafu's political activities were more or less known to the members of the community. His use of communal funds was justified by the good ties he maintained with the British and local Moslem leaders. During the 1945 riots he was instrumental in preserving Jewish life in the Gharian, and property losses were also minimal. This political skill was sensed by a visitor to the Gharian in 1948 who reported:

Sheikh Khlafu's authority remained undisputed even in the widespread anti-Jewish rioting of 1945. Probably this had something to do with the diplomatic qualities of the sheikh. When I asked what he thought of the events in Palestine he did not appear to hear the question and showed me some of the attractive carpets woven by his wife and selling for about £3. (Kimche 1948 *b*.)

Despite the changes in the role of sheikh, there were a number of structural characteristics which persisted throughout the various periods discussed: (1) The sheikh was the main political link between the community and the 'outside world', (2) There were few attempts to transfer leadership to another individual, once a person formally attained the status of sheikh; that is, the sheikh maintained his position throughout his life, (3) The sheikh was much more knowledgeable about the world outside than other members of the community, (4) The sheikh upheld and exemplified the religious values of the community, (5) The sheikh did not have close personal or kin links with other individuals or groups in the community, (6) The sheikh was relatively wealthy so that: (*a*) He had free time to devote to community affairs; (*b*) he could acquire and maintain those symbols of social rank appropriate to his position as representative of the community to the outside (e.g. hospitality); (*c*) he could be free from financial dependence on other individuals or groups within the community; (*d*) he would not be tempted to excessively misuse his power for personal gain, and (*e*) he could muster resources, in times of need, to bolster the community and aid individuals. I will later consider the history of the sheikhship in the context of life in Even Yosef.

The status and role of the community elite

The primary distinction in the political life of the community was between the status of sheikh and 'ordinary villager'. A different, but related, social distinction was drawn between the 'elite' and 'non-elite'. The successful recruitment of an individual to the role of sheikh presupposes a 'manpower reserve' of people capable of meeting the demands of that role. As will be discussed at length later, the elite of the community seems to have constituted that reserve, as the elite share, to a lesser degree, some of the social and personal characteristics of the sheikh.

There are three general areas in which the elite of the Gharian Jews were distinguished from the non-elite: (1) wealth, (2) knowledge of the outside world, and (3) religious specialty and social propriety.

The first criterion of elite status needs little elaboration. A man had to be wealthy, in local terms, in order to be considered among the prominent members of the community. This meant that there was a high overlap between the occupational category 'large-scale merchant' and the social category 'elite'. Some of the well-to-do shopkeepers were also counted among the elite.

The criteria of wealth and of 'knowledge of the outside world' were interrelated. Those individuals who were more perceptive and prescient about changing economic conditions were able more readily to take advantage of new opportunities. Then, as one established more commercial links within and outside of the Gharian, one came to know more about the world outside. Being a successful merchant was seen as an indicator of worldly wisdom (cf. Willner & Kohls 1962: 227–8). Any wealth gained from new commercial ventures, of course, helped reinforce an individual's elite status.

The worldly wisdom of the elite was also recognized in that they would be called upon to mediate in minor conflicts, such as family squabbles and disagreements between partners. In order for them to serve as mediators, the members of the elite were expected to behave with propriety. Social propriety was, of course, closely linked with religious propriety.

In addition to meeting the normal religious requirements of daily life, the elite might seek to enhance their prestige and reinforce the legitimation of their status by having a member of the family learn a special religious skill, such as shoḥet or mohel. Poorer families could not afford to send a son or a brother to Tripoli to learn these skills, nor could they devote time to practicing them in the Gharian. Slaughterers and circumcisors received no remuneration for their services but a shoḥet was entitled to a small portion of each animal he slaughtered. The main reasons for learning these special religious skills, however, were that it was a *miṣwa* (religious duty) to do so, and that it served the needs of the community. The only religious specialist who was paid was the synagogue school teacher, and the pay was generally low. Consequently there was a rapid turnover of teachers, and they were often recruited from outside the community.

Wealth and religious merit also were linked, in that the wealthy were in a position to make larger donations to the synagogue during sabbaths, festivals and other celebrations. A wealthy family might purchase a Torah-scroll from Tripoli, which there-after bore the name of the family, and would contribute the Torah-scroll to the synagogue. Also, the wealthy were in a position to close their shops at mid-day and congregate at the synagogue for the *minḥa* (afternoon) prayer, while the poorer and itinerant traders could not do this (cf. Chouraqui 1968: 58). It is also possible that the stronger interest in the 'great tradition' shown by the elite reflected, and in part accounted for, their positive orientation to the 'outside world'.

While the organization of the Jewish community of Tripoli was highly formalized (Colòsimo 1917), this did not greatly effect the Gharian Jews. The elite group was known technically in some other rural communities as 'comisione della comunità', but this term was unknown to most of the Gharianites and not used by those who were aware of it.

The following account of the 'cave dwellings' of the Gharian Jews, provided by a traveller to the region in the late 1920s (Kleinlerer 1929), gives evidence that status differentiation was manifest in domestic furnishings and consumption habits.

The owner of one of these 'apartments', a Jewish artisan, invited me to inspect his rooms and to see how they were furnished. Numerous holes of various sizes along the walls contained some simple objects necessary to the frugal life of the inhabitants: a few kettles, some earthenware jugs and drinking-cups, fruit, eggs, bags and wallets. In a corner is a mat of rushes covered by a woolen blanket or by a carpet: it is the bed. One sees very little else: a few jars of baked clay, heaps of wool for spinning, an oil lamp, some empty bottles.

But I have also visited in Garian the cave-dwelling of another Jew who is regarded as a wealthy man. Here were elegant furniture and rich carpets and the house did not have the bare and desolate aspect of the former one.

The elite was not a rigidly bounded group, and some mobility in and out of the elite category existed. One important factor here was the absence of elite-group endogamy. Also, it seemed to be part of the prevailing ethos that unpredictable natural and political events could completely change a man's position overnight (cf. Bensimon-Donath 1968: 20). However, there does seem to have been a certain amount of intergenerational stability in the composition of the elite group: the children of elite families had a good chance of attaining elite status themselves.

A sketch of one of the elite families will serve to illustrate some of these points. Shmuel Ḥassān was born approximately in 1887. He married at about the age of 20, and had two sons and two daughters.

In 1913 he spent two months in Tripoli receiving certification as a shoḥeṭ, earning him the title of *rebbi* among the Gharian Jews. He reports that the first time he saw an automobile was in 1913 near Tunis, during a trip to purchase merchandise.

In 1925 he began to operate as a sutler to Italian troops. Shortly after that he was given the franchise to operate the 'post exchange' for the large garrison at Mizda. For four years his wife and children lived in Mizda, but most of the time they lived in Tighrinna. During this period, his eldest son drove a large truck, purchased by the family, from Tripoli to the Fezzan. His younger son says that he learned (to sell in) several Ethiopian languages while working in Mizda.

In 1939 Rebbi Shmuel and his sons returned to Tighrinna (the post exchange was maintained until the Italian defeat), where they had built a private bakery, an oil press, a flour mill and three shops, two of which they rented to other Jews. They also built a well. This complex of structures faced the open 'piazza' in front of the synagogues, which came to be known as *shara' rebbi shmuīl* by the Jews and *mṭraḥ rebbi shmuīl* by the Moslems. At first the oil press and mill were powered by camels, but later diesel engines were imported from Italy. (Two other Jewish 'family firms' also imported diesel engines.)

Rebbi Shmuel's sons were the only Jews of Tighrinna and Ben'abbas to wear European clothing, which they donned in pursuing their commercial affairs outside the Gharian. They continued to wear the traditional garb within the community when attending the synagogue on sabbaths and festivals. The eldest son was the individual who interceded on behalf of the community to have the corvée lifted during the period of Berkhani's sheikhship (p. 25). In the 1940s part of the extended family moved their domestic quarters from the troglodyte dwellings into the new buildings, while the other Jews continued to live in their traditional homes.

Rebbi Shmuel and his family are invariably mentioned if one asks the Gharian Jews about the prominent members of their community in Tripolitania. His younger son married a daughter of Sheikh Berkhani, while his other children married less notable community members. I will further describe the 'history' of this family in the context of community and family life of the Gharian Jews in Israel (pp. 103–4).

The community

Until now I have referred to 'the community' in the loose sense of all the Jews living in the Gharian region. Some of the data already cited, together with others now to be presented, may be analyzed to yield a clearer picture of the community as a corporate entity.

The community was viewed as a single political entity by the ruling political power. Usually the person appointed sheikh of Tighrinna was the sheikh of all the Gharian Jews. Only under the British did the military authorities initially approach leaders from Gharian-town to advise them with regard to the total Jewish population. Under Turkish rule the community was taxed as an entity, and the sheikh was responsible for assessing the members of the community and delivering the tax to the government.

Similarly, a *shaliaḥ kullīl* (Rabbinic emissary) from Palestine would assess a religious tax on the community, and might threaten with religious sanctions those who would not pay. The Jewish community in Tripoli recognized 'heads' of the three different settlements of the Gharian with regard to matters which were within Jewish communal jurisdiction. In addition to the unity imposed from outside, however, there were bases of solidarity within the community itself.

Goitein's (1955: 17) statement concerning the Jews of al-Gades in Yemen that 'the abstract idea of the community was replaced by the concrete image of the synagogue' is equally true of the Gharian Jews.[1] The synagogue(s), synagogue cistern, *miqwa* (ritual bath), and cemetery were the property of the community as a whole. A man could bequeath funds to the synagogue, or the synagogue could inherit from a man who died without heirs.

Current funds were raised by the synagogue primarily through the sale of *miṣwūt* (religious honors), such as being called to the reading from the Torah-scroll. The second most important source of funds was the *gābīla*, a tax paid to the community whenever an animal was brought to a shoḥeṭ to be slaughtered. Occasionally, the sheikh might punish someone for a religious transgression, such as non-attendance at the synagogue (Elmaleh 1943). The transgressor received ritual stripes and concluded his penitence by contributing to the synagogue.

The collection of the funds was the responsibility of the *semmās* (sexton) a duty which rotated fairly frequently. The semmās, who was entitled to a percentage of the funds collected, kept the synagogue clean[2] and made sure it was provided with oil for lamps. The main expenditure of the synagogue was paying the rebbi, or school teacher who conducted daily lessons in the synagogue.

At the Thursday market in Gharian-town, some members of the elite would approach other Jews, asking for contributions to help the poorer members of the community celebrate the Sabbath. These funds were distributed to the needy with the greatest discretion to avoid embarrassment to the poor families. Other occasions for collecting and disbursing funds were funerals (p. 111), the onset of winter, and at the approach of the Passover holiday in the spring. Community funds were kept by the *gabbāi*,

---

[1] Often the villagers asked me if it were possible for me to visit the Gharian. Once, when I replied that I might, one man said 'If you go there, let us know about the synagogue and the cemetery; that's all we care about.'

[2] Frequently women, wishing to perform a miṣwa, might help clean the synagogue on the eve of the Sabbath or Festival. The semmās was also entitled to certain ritual honours in the synagogue.

while decisions regarding their disbursement were made primarily by the sheikh.

The sense of community solidarity was enhanced by the communal worship at the synagogue (which, as indicated above, was also the setting for the dramatization of differences in wealth and prestige). The high point of the ritual year, from this point of view, was probably the eve of Kibbūr (cf. Deshen 1965: 72). The miṣwa of holding the first Torah-scroll on this night was 'highest-priced' miṣwa of the year. Everyone was supposed to pay their outstanding pledges to the synagogue on the morning before Kibbūr, and would not be given any further ritual honors if they failed to make good their vows.

Community solidarity was also reinforced by the high rate of endogamy, which was close to ninety percent in both Tighrinna and Ben'abbas. The celebration of weddings, of religious majority, of circumcisions and funerals were generally attended by the total community. Inside the hīkhal (cabinet in which the Torah-scrolls were housed) in the old synagogue of Tighrinna was a decree, signed by communal leaders of an earlier generation, that no one was allowed to leave his home for work on the day of a funeral till after the burial. This was to insure adequate attendance by members of the community. The ordinance also provided that anyone who violated it should be fined that day's earnings. The necessity for such a decree, which formalizes traditional religious values, suggests that 'community solidarity' was not always something which could be taken for granted.

The family

Bensimon-Donath (1968: 56) notes the absence of a sociological or ethnological study of the traditional North African Jewish family. The present study does not pretend to correct this deficiency, but will primarily discuss relationships among families in terms of the place of the family within the family group,[1] the patronymic group, and the community.[2]

A patronymic group may be defined as a group of families sharing a patronym, without assuming anything about the nature of the social relations among them. The village of Tighrinna had

[1] A definition of 'family-group' will be given below (p. 39).
[2] Most of the discussion that follows is found in Goldberg (1967b) where additional details may be found.

two main patronymic groups; about 50% of the families were Hajjaj and about 35% were Hassan. About 75% of the families of Ben'abbas were named Guweta'. We may begin the consideration of the social importance of these name-groups by describing the traditional residence pattern of the region.

The Gharian district of Tripolitania has achieved some fame as 'the country of the cave dwellers'. The majority of habitations in the region were (and are) troglodyte dwellings dug into the sandy-clay soil. While this house-type seems exotic, mere inspection of the structure and domestic arrangements indicates that the Gharian cave-dwellings are a specialized adaptation of the general Middle Eastern 'courtyard pattern' (Norris 1953: 82–3).

Each cave-pit, or ḥūsh, consists of a central courtyard, open to the sky, from which radiate six to eight diyār (sing. dār), or dwellings. Each dār houses a nuclear family. Other rooms radiating from the central courtyard serve as kitchens, store rooms, workshops and stables. One reaches the central courtyard through a long, twisting tunnel entrance located at some distance from the ḥūsh (see Figure 4).[1] Water was normally attained from cisterns dug near each house. This house-type was common to the Moslems and Jews of the region. The houses were built by specialists from the Fezzan.

In Tighrinna there were 22 ḥiyāsh (plural) and six in Ben'abbas. Often Hajjaj families and Hassan families lived in the same ḥūsh. The owner of a ḥūsh might rent a dār within the ḥūsh to a non-relative. Although sons usually lived in the same ḥūsh as their fathers, this was by no means the universal pattern. Moreover, a son living in the same ḥūsh as his father might be the head of an independent family. The wives of the various families in the ḥūsh would cooperate for certain tasks, such as cleaning the long entrance-way, but they were not supervised by a single 'head of the house'.

Related families might signal their independent status by building a separate kitchen, placing a dog to guard the entrance to an individual dār, or by building a separate sukka (ritual booth) on the festival of Tabernacles. On the other hand, independent

---

[1] Detailed descriptions, diagrams, and photographs of the troglodyte dwellings of the Gharian are found in Lyon (1821), Brandenburg (1911), Kleinlerer (1929), Norris (1953), and Suter (1964: 223, 264–5). While Slouschz (1927) has imbued these dwellings with romantic antiquity, they most likely are fairly 'recent' development in home construction in the region (Norris 1953: 83; Suter 1964).

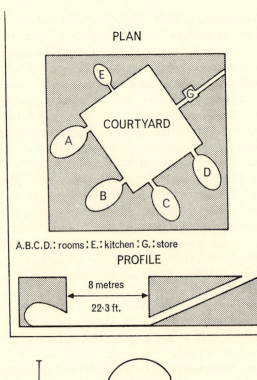

PLAN

COURTYARD

E

G

A

D

B

C

A.B.C.D.: rooms : E.: kitchen : G.: store

PROFILE

8 metres

22·3 ft.

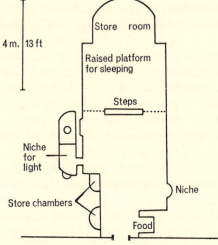

4 m. 13 ft

Store room

Raised platform for sleeping

Steps

Niche for light

O

Niche

Store chambers

Food

Plan of a Jewish 'Dār,' Tigrinna

Figure 4. Troglodyte dwellings of the Gharian.

families living in the same ḥūsh might celebrate their kin ties by
eating together on Sabbaths and holidays. Norris notes that the
centers of the Jewish ḥiyāsh in which refuse was discarded, tended
to be divided into sections, with each section belonging to a
different household. This division was not found in the Moslem
ḥiyāsh that he examined (1953: 82–3). This suggests that the
individual household among the Jews of the region was more
independent of a wider kinship group than was the individual
household among the Moslems.

Among the Gharian Jews there were no land or water rights
vested in the patronymic group but, instead, these rights were
vested in the individual family heads. The patronymic group as
such had no inheritance rights in the estate of a deceased 'member'.
In the memory of the people of Tighrinna there were no major
conflicts that divided the community along Hajjaj–Hassan lines.[1]
Finally, there was no preferred marriage within the patronymic
group; the village was the important endogamous unit.

Further evidence of the sociological unimportance of the
patronymic group may be gleaned from linguistic data. The
lineage among the Tripolitanian Moslems was known as the 'aila
(Norris 1953: 82–3). The family was known as the bēt. The term
'aila was also found among the Jews, but it referred to the
'nuclear' family and not to any larger group. When a Gharian
Jew said 'ailat Ḥajjāj (the family of Hajjaj) he was referring to one
particular family and not to all the Hajjaj families. If he wished to
refer to all the Hajjaj families he would use the plural form of
'aila and speak of 'ayāl Ḥajjāj (the families of Hajjaj). There seems
to be no term, in the Jewish dialect, that corresponds to 'lineage',
as the term 'aila did among the Moslems.

While the patronymic groups were not relevant to the main
economic and political activities of the community, it would be
incorrect to say that they played no part at all in the social life of
the villagers. There are several contexts in which patronymy was
considered relevant by the villagers themselves.

[1] This is not to say that individual families were not involved in conflicts. Slouschz
(1927: 144) describes a dispute over the qualifications of a shoḥeṭ. Hacohen
(ms: 228a) states: 'Everyone has a Mohammedan friend to stand at his (right) side
to take vengeance from his fellow Jew who opposes him. If a boy falls in love with
a girl, but her father refuses to give her to him, then the Mohammedan boy-friend
will intervene to obtain the girl against the father's will.' In neither instance,
however, is there evidence that the patronymic group was the unit involved in the
dispute.

In the first instance, different patronymic groups were believed to have had different historic origins. It was thought that the Hajjaj originated from further west in North Africa, and that one family group within the Hassan came from Spain. Two old men (both close to 80 years old), named Hassan, provided me with telescoped genealogies in which their patrilineal great-great-grandfathers came from Spain. These traditions, however, were known to only a handful of old men.

Of more general knowledge was the fact that the Hajjaj were the senior inhabitants of the village of Tighrinna. One family group of the Hassan had originally lived in another village, several kilometers to the south, named Jehisha (Figure 2; cf. Hacohen ms: 227b). It seems that the Hassan moved from Jehisha to Tighrinna some time during the first third of the nineteenth century. One old man told me that at Jehisha the Moslems used to put frogs in the pots of the Jews when the Sabbath meal was cooking. It would thus be ruined. Eventually the Jews decided to leave and come to Tighrinna. Another man told me that at Jehisha the Arabs would *steal* the meal, and leave Jews without food for the Sabbath. The Jews then decided to trick the Arabs and one Sabbath they placed frogs in the pots. The Arabs ran off with the pots only to find, later, that they had stolen nothing but frogs. Curiously enough, the narrator of the first version of this tale was a Hajjaj while the second version was related by a Hassan.

Moreover, one of the oldest men of the village related that at first there was some conflict, in Tighrinna, between the 'native' Hajjaj and the 'immigrant' Hassan. This conflict expressed itself in a dispute over rights to use the water from the synagogue's cistern. It is required that one wash one's hands before entering the synagogue. The Hajjaj used the water of the cistern that belonged to the synagogue but claimed that the Hassan had no right to this water. The latter were forced to wash their hands at home before coming to the synagogue. Eventually, the old man said, there was a reconciliation and everyone was given access to the synagogue's water.

The fact that some of the Hassan, but not all of them, were thought to have come from Jehisha indicates that there is no belief in eponymous ancestors of the patronymic groups. However, within the category of Hassan and Hajjaj are groups of families who are known to be descended from a single patrilineal ancestor, usually a few generations back, and these may be called *family groups*. Hajjaj encompasses such family groups as Humani (p. 23), Dada and Zubīṭ. Within Hassan there are the Ḥassān-Elūf and Ḥassān-Jarmūn.

Family group names have a certain currency within the daily life of the village. Within the Hassan-Eluf there was one family group named Buṣaba'. This name had been given to one individual by virtue of a permanent injury to one of his fingers. Even though the descendants of Buṣaba' have perfectly normal fingers, they continue to be known by that name (cf. Peters 1960: 33). The name serves a classificatory function. There may be several individuals in the community named Raḥmīn and even several named Rahmin Hassan; by referring to a person as Rahmin Busaba' the speaker is sure of conveying an unambiguous reference to the listener. At the same time, everyone in the village knows that Rahmin is a Hassan as well as a Busaba'. The patronyms of Hassan, Hajjaj, and Guweta' may have great depth, while the family group names are only a few generations deep.

Secondly, there are some minor customs which differentiate the patronymic groups and/or family groups. For example the different patronymic groups prepare different foods on the seventh day of the festival of Tabernacles (the day known as *Hosha'na Rabba*). At the beginning of the Hebrew month of Nisan (during which Passover is celebrated), the Guweta' and Hassan prepare a sweet dish called *besīsa* (Slouschz 1927: 203–4), while this is not prepared by the Hajjaj. During the days of the *'ūmer* (the 50-day period between Passover and Pentecost), the Hassan are more fastidious in observing the restrictions of this semi-mourning period than are the Hajjaj. While all these variations are minor, and within the framework of Rabbinic law, they are recognized by the villagers as traditional differences among the patronymic (and family) groups.

Finally, we may ask if there are any situations in which the villagers spontaneously act, or speak about interaction, in terms of patronymic groups. These situations, based on observation in Even Yosef, are few, but nevertheless suggestive. I once approached a group of four men playing cards, and began to inquire about the nature of the game; in the course of the explanation one man jokingly said 'Two of us are Hajjaj and two of us are

Hassan'. On another occasion, some young married men were joking with a bachelor friend about the possibility of his marrying a certain girl. 'What do you care about his getting married?', I asked. 'We have to help him, he is a Hajjaj', was the reply.

On the occasion of a wedding, at the conclusion of the cere-mony, everyone will attempt to take a sip from the cup of wine used during the wedding ritual. At one wedding a certain man, named Hajjaj, was eager to take a sip from the cup of wine, and he shouted across the room to another Hajjaj, 'Hey, Hajjaj, bring it over here'.

When asked if the villagers ever discussed the question of Hajjaj and Hassan, a number of people said, 'Some old men talk about it in the synagogue, but that's all'. Another reply was 'When it's raining and people have nothing to do, they may sit around and talk about it, but as soon as there is work to do they forget it'. One person told me that the patronymic groups might compete in terms of ritual honors within the synagogue. None of these patterns were observed by me directly.

The data presented thus far indicates that the patronymic groups had significance as social categories in three contexts: (1) in relation to historical origins,[1] (2) in relation to leisure-type activities and activities centered in the synagogue, and (3) in relation to some minor customs. The following discussion will suggest some lines of analysis which may be pertinent to the data presented.

Historical origins

It seems safe to conclude that the Hassan originated from outside Tighrinna. However, it is impossible at this point to verify whether or not they are descended from Spanish Jews. Given the fact that they do originate from outside Tighrinna, we may ask if the variation in ritual customs simply reflects diverse geographical origins. There are many data to support the contention that each Jewish town (or village) in Tripolitania was distinguished by virtue of some customs not found in other groups.

This geographical-cultural variation may be easily seen by

---

[1] The association of patronymic and historic origin is implied in the writings of Mordechai Hacohen. He mentions the 'tribe' (sheveṭ) Hassān coming from Jeḥisha (ms: 227b), and the Jarmūn coming from the Gharian (ms: 170a). He also gives a list of common Tripolitanian Jewish patronyms and lists the place of origin of the patronym if it is believed to be outside of Tripolitania (ms: 156a–158a).

comparing the villages of Tighrinna and Ben'abbas. These villages were separated by only 14 kilometers, but, nevertheless, they were distinguished by a number of traits. The villagers of Even Yosef could cite dialectal differences which set off the *Ghaina* (people of Tighrinna) from the *'Abbāsīya* (people of Ben'abbas). These differences were phonetic and lexical, and there also may have been minor grammatical differences. Along with this linguistic variation was some variation in synagogue customs, synagogue melodies, and the family rituals described above. The Ghaina and the 'Abbasiya now live in one village in Israel, where some of the food and ritual variation still persists. It is clear, therefore, that the differences in custom between the Hajjaj–Hassan and the Guweta' are related to their diverse geographical origins.

Leisure, synagogue, and prestige

An explanation in terms of historical origins is only a partial explanation. The Hassan probably came to Tighrinna in the first part of the nineteenth century, and in 1965, in Israel, they were still practicing certain rituals that distinguished them from the Hajjaj. How may we explain the persistence of this ritual differentiation? Evidence has already been cited to indicate that the original move of the Hassan from Jehisha to Tighrinna was accompanied by a certain amount of conflict and tension. This should be seen as conflict between two communities, originating from distinct localities, rather than conflict between two descent groups. Again, an analogous situation may be seen in the merging of the Ghaina and the 'Abbasiya in present-day Even Yosef.

When I came into contact with Even Yosef there were no signs of overt conflict between the Ghaina and the 'Abbasiya. Nevertheless, it is clear that the villagers recognized these two distinct groups as having a *potential* for political opposition. Under certain conditions this tension might be expected to erupt, but during the period of my field research it was given no concrete expression.[1] Moreover, it was considered desirable by all members of the community that the village display an image of unity toward the outside.

There is evidence, however, that there was a certain amount of

[1] The relations between the Ghaina and the 'Abbasiya in Even Yosef will be discussed later (pp. 127–8).

tension between the two groups in the early years of their settlement on the moshav. One issue, relating to the role of ritual
honors on Kibbūr seems to have had the potential of becoming a
cause célèbre, polarizing the community into Ghaina and 'Abbasiya.
The issue, however, was quickly resolved. There are three
synagogues in Even Yosef, and Ghaina and 'Abbasiya pray at
each of them. When I asked about ritual differences between the
two communities of origin, people would frequently say, 'We
forgot all that', implying that it was wrong of me to bring up
'dead' issues. Similar criticism was directed toward my inquiries
about possible conflicts between the Hajjaj and the Hassan in the
history of Tighrinna. Whatever conflicts may have existed in
the past were relatively quickly forgotten. It is possible that the
building of a new synagogue in Tighrinna at the end of the last
century was related to the 'reconciliation' of the Hajjaj and the
Hassan, and their decision to live as one community. Each of the
two synagogues in Tighrinna was attended by both Hajjaj and
Hassan.

It seems, then, that the Gharian Jews recognize the opposition
of descent or locality groups as a possible type of political
arrangement,[1] but they clearly prefer a system in which these
groups, as such, are politically quiescent. Moreover, there may have
been, historically, a conscious transfer of political power from
these subgroups of the community to the status of the sheikh.
Still, it is suggested, there lingers the *awareness* of an alternative
form of sociopolitical organization and this awareness is in some
way made manifest in sociocultural action.

It is from this perspective that I interpret the social significance
of the patronymic group categories. I have already pointed out
that these categories are explicitly recognized primarily in the

[1] In his study of the saintly lineages of the central High Atlas (Morocco), Gellner
(1969) shows how these groups, possessed of greater religious and social rank
than the Berber lay tribes among whom they lived, were not themselves organized
into opposing and 'equal' lineage-segments, though this was the prevalent
political arrangement in the region as a whole. Assuming that segmentary
organization characterized the Moslem communities of the Gharian (I only have a
little data to back this assumption), it is interesting that the Jewish community,
which was socially and religiously 'below' the Moslem majority, also lacked
patrilineal political segmentation. Both the saintly Berbers, and the Jewish traders,
were specialized, non-combatant groups that complemented, rather than opposed,
the lay Moslems. Just as the saintly Berbers competed with one another for the
'wages of sanctity' (Gellner 1969: 274), so the Jewish merchants competed with
one another (and were differentially successful) for the wages of trade.

context of leisure-type activities, and in activities centering on the synagogue. The competition between groups, within the synagogue, should be recognized as a matter of prestige, that is not directly related to political power. It might even be said that because these groups have relinquished their claim to power, they have become insistent on retaining their due share of prestige. It is as if the Gharian Jews, within the context of leisure and the synagogue, have given 'symbolic forms to the institutions they might have had in reality'.[1]

Family-group rituals

The above interpretation, which is admittedly speculative, fails to address itself to the problem of the subdivision of the patronymic groups into family groups. I shall take a different approach in attempting to give a sociological interpretation of the ritual differentiation of family groups.

It is commonplace in anthropological analysis to contrast the 'family' with a corporate descent group, with respect to the question of continuity over generations. A family is a unit that is dissolved through the biological growth and death of its members, while a corporate descent group survives the death of individual members. This analytic distinction is particularly important in cases where there is concrete overlap between the family and the corporate descent group, such as one finds in Japan (Plath 1964). In this case it is easy to confound the 'household corporation' with the biological family because there may be 100 percent coincidence in the living membership of the two groups. Taking this cue from the Japanese material, one might ask if among the Gharian Jews there is any sense in which families, or family groups, are considered to be characterized by an existence beyond the life of individual members. It is difficult to give an unequivocal answer to the question, but it may prove useful to follow this line of inquiry in an attempt to order certain facts.

The Gharian Jews show the well-known Middle Eastern cultural emphasis on progeny, in particular on male progeny – for daughters will not perpetuate the fathers 'name'.[2] Men who have

---

[1] Here I paraphrase Levi-Strauss' interpretation of Caduveo art, where he suggests that their art is a symbolic form of social institutions that the Caduveo might have had but did not adopt (1964: 180).

[2] I once showed a rebbi (shoḥeṭ and teacher) from Yefren a published book, written by a Rabbi from Jerba (Ben-Zion Cohen, *Bnei Zion*, Jerba, 'Aidan & Haddad,

fathered only (or even mostly) girls are considered to be dissatisfied with their procreative accomplishments and those of
their wives. A man who has no sons is said to have no 'children'
(*zghār*), and is considered unfortunate by the other villagers.
Among the four men, mentioned above (p. 24), who had two
wives, two of them fathered girls through their first wives, but not
boys (cf. Hacohen ms: 228a). Sometimes an older couple who have
no male children are informally 'given' a young boy by one of
their close relatives. It is clear that a man has fulfilled the duty and
need of procreation only if he has fathered a male child.

Perpetuation of the family may also be seen in the custom of a
man naming a son after a dead grandfather. In certain cases, when
the grandfather is very old, a grandson may be given the grandfather's name during the latter's life; this is only done at the
request of the grandfather.

Zenner (1965 a: 482) has called attention to the fact that traditional Jews (both European and Middle Eastern) desire sons so
that memorial rituals, such as the recitation of the *qadīsh* (prayer of
sanctification), will be performed after their passing. It is probably
true, as he suggests (1965 a: 483), that the 'departed souls' belong
to the community, as much as they do to the families of their
living descendants. Thus, in Even Yosef, I once observed an
'arbīt (evening) service, in which the father of the secretary of the
moshav was memorialized on the anniversary of his death, even

1928), in which were listed the names of all the Jews of Yefren who had given
donations toward the publication of the book (cf. Deshen 1966: 37). This man saw
that the name of one of his friends had been misspelled and he promptly took a
stylus and ink (that he normally used to correct blurred or worn letters in Torah-
scrolls) and corrected the misspelling so that the name would be 'perpetuated'
correctly. Hacohen (ms: 228b) states that with respect to most of their customs the
Jews of Gharian are similar to those of Yefren.

The following incident, from Even Yosef, also reveals the importance of
family-name continuity. Several of the male youths of the village have considered
changing their names so that they will be more 'modern' and 'Israeli' (below,
p. 157). One young man, from a family named Hassan, thought of changing his
name to the Hebrew *Hazzan* (a synagogue functionary), which would maintain
phonetic ties to the past. His younger brother, who was one of the few boys to
complete High School, wanted to change his name to *Sapir*, which would have
had the following merits. The Arabic stem Ḥ S N means beautiful, and the particular form *ḥassān* is the word for barber. The Hebrew stem S P R takes on one
from (*sappar*) which means barber, while *sapir* (English sapphire) also has a
connotation of beauty. When I asked the father of these boys his reaction to the
prospect of his sons' changing the family name, he replied that he did not mind if
the name were changed, so long as everyone decided on the *same name*.

though his son could not attend the service because he was away from the village. Nevertheless, with respect to an orientation toward *future descendants* (cf. Benedict 1949), the Gharian Jewish family exhibits a kind of supra-generational continuity.

The importance of family continuity and tradition may be seen in another way. Whenever I asked villagers about patronymic groups, or other aspects of the community's past, there usually were only a few old men who were interested, or who knew much about the community's history. This was particularly true of the village youth who had little first-hand knowledge of life in Tripolitania. When I sat at some public place and inquired about various aspects of the community's history, the youth never took any interest in my inquiries. They did show some interest, however, in a different context. On many occasions I interviewed adults in their homes and similarly asked questions about community history. Most of the adults could not empathize with my concern with the history of the community, but were quite eager to tell me about the 'history' of their own *family*. Frequently, young men were active participants in these family-centered sessions, listening to their family history, and also attempting to provide information.

It is hypothesized, then, that it is useful to look at the ritual customs that differentiate family groups in the light of the emphasis on supra-generational aspects of the family. Here we treat the family and the family group as the same because both are known to be the offspring of a single male progenitor. The performance of these rituals serves to emphasize the continuity of the family, over time, giving the individual family member a sense of connection with his past. The 'past' referred to is not the remote past of the great tradition, which is shared by all members of the community, but the more personal past of a man's immediate forebearers.[1]

---

[1] Another perspective on traditional Jewish life in rural Tripolitania is provided by M. Ohel's (1962) novel *Ish Nidham* (Overwhelmed), which deals with the communities of Mesallata and Homs.

3. From the Gharian to Even Yosef: the first dozen years

The present chapter tells the story of the migration of the Gharian Jews to Israel, and of their first 12 years in Even Yosef. Throughout this period, the Jews of the Gharian came into contact with many large-scale organizations, mostly linked to the World Zionist Organization and Government of Israel. In particular, they became involved in the land settlement and development programs in Israel, which has been described and analyzed in a number of different works.[1] In the description that follows, I will not concern myself with these organizations and their programs, except with reference to their impact on the social life of the community under discussion. My account begins with a discussion of the traditional attachment of the Gharian Jews to the Land of Israel.

I

The following story was told to me by a former resident of the Gharian:

Once, (Theodor) Herzl came to visit the Gharian, accompanied by a Rabbi from Tripoli (Herzl, the story assumes, was dressed in the traditional garb of a Tripolitanian Rabbi). At that time the Jews of the Gharian prepared a festive meal and brought a sheep to be slaughtered. Herzl said: 'Give me the sheep, I will slaughter it.' The Gharian Jews refused to rely on the importance and 'sanctity' of their guest and said: 'Show us your certificate that you are a shuḥīṭ.' Herzl did not have such a certificate and the sheep was slaughtered by the local shuḥīṭ.

[1] Immigration and the World Zionist Organization are discussed in Halpern (1961: 23–4). Description and analysis of the land settlement program, from both diachronic and synchronic perspectives, may be found in Darin-Drabkin (1962), Ben-David (1964), Weingrod (1966), Weitz and Rokach (1968), Willner (1969), Weintraub et al. (1969) and Kushner (1971). Various sections of the present chapter depend heavily on these works.

This folk-tale was explained to me by another Gharianite as exemplifying the devotion of the Jews of the Gharian to the details of the Law. In spite of their 'isolation in the mountains', they resisted possible profanation of the Law, even by a sanctified person such as Herzl. The tale also demonstrates how the secular Zionist ideology was readily absorbed into the older religious values of the Tripolitanian Jews (cf. Zuaretz and Rubin 1960: 133–41). Conversely, the tale shows how adherence to the Law, by the Gharian Jews, proved to the almost-messiah, Herzl, that they were worthy of redemption.

The ancient notion of the 'Return to Zion' had both spiritual and temporal referents. One man from Ben'abbas stated that, as a child, whenever he heard the traditional blessing 'next year in Jerusalem' he thought that Jerusalem was in the 'world to come'. On the other hand, the periodic visits of Rabbinic emissaries who collected hard-earned funds for the religious institutions in Palestine, could not but call the attention of the Gharianites to the contemporary Jewish population settled there. In 1923, the Gharian was visited by a representative of the Jewish National Fund (which was established by the World Zionist Organization in 1901); he found that a collection box for the Fund had preceded him, having been brought to the Gharian by a man from Zawia (Elmaleh 1943: 8). He states: 'When I spoke to the Gharian Jews about the Land of Israel, and of the great work of building that was progressing there, they wept aloud and asked me to take them there with me.'

In 1945 these Messianic-like expectations were complemented by the shock of the anti-Jewish riots, as well as the rapid economic decline resulting from the Fascist racial laws (Perlzweig 1949), and the Italian withdrawal from Libya (Kimche 1948a). Many Tripolitanian Jews have said that were it not for the riots, they might not have joined the migration to Israel. As it was, in 1949, the Gharian Jews left their villages and migrated to Tripoli to prepare for immigration to Israel.

II

In January 1949, the British government decided to allow the Jews of Libya to emigrate. After several months of negotiations, the Immigration Department of the Jewish Agency for Palestine was empowered to organize immigration to Israel, and the first immigrant ships sailed in early April. There was a great deal of popular pressure to increase the rate of emigration, particularly because of the uncertainty of the future of the Jewish community in independent Libya, the creation of which was currently being considered in international circles (Khadduri 1963, Chap. 5).[1] Y. Refael, the Head of the Immigration Department of the Jewish Agency, visited Tripoli in June of that year to press for an accelerated rate of emigration, and his request was granted. Shortly after that, B. Duvdvani, who was in charge of the immigration operations in Tripoli, decided to bring the Jews of Cyrenaica and of the interior of Tripolitania to the city of Tripoli to await immigration. He persuaded the American Joint Distribution Committee and the OSE (Jewish Health Organization) to provide food, clothing and medical services to these 'rural' Jews. During the months of July–November the interior of Tripolitania, including the Gharian, was emptied of its Jews.

As the Gharian Jewish community began to 'liquidate itself', people sold most of their belongings for cash. The droughts of 1946 and 1947 undoubtedly had brought economic suffering to a number of families. Selling their property was fairly simple for a majority of the Jews, but it involved a considerable loss for the wealthy merchants. Most of the community arrived in Tripoli with little cash or belongings, and were supported there by the relief organizations.

III

Various individuals, all of whom were actively involved in organizing the immigration to Israel, have described the emotional atmosphere among Tripolitanian Jews at that time as one of messianic enthusiasm (Zuaretz 1960: 291–3; Duvdvani 1960; Shilon 1960). A number of events in the immigration process were

[1] The leaders of the Jewish community publicly supported the demand for Libyan independence (Khadduri 1963: 122), while 'privately', their central political aspiration had become immigration to Israel. Various 'outside' observers have commented that Zionism was not much of an issue in Libya (Kimche 1948a: 11; Landshut 1950: 90; Daniels 1945), whereas Tripolitanian Jewry first responded to the Zionist movement before World War II (Zuaretz and Rubin 1960). The dilemma of the Tripolitanian Jews, in pre-independence Libya, was not unlike that of Jews of the Jebel Nefusa a century earlier, who supported the rebel leader Ghoma at the same time that they secretly paid their tax to the Ottoman governor in Tripoli (Slouschz 1927: 193).

imbued with religious meaning, by applying traditional elements of the synagogue ritual to the current procedures (cf. Deshen 1970). For example, after permission to migrate to Israel had been granted, the privilege of obtaining the first visa was auctioned in public, as if it were a ritual honor in the synagogue. When Y. Refael first appeared in public among the Tripolitanian Jews, many threw rosewater at him as they might at the celebrant of a wedding, or of religious majority. Jews from the Gharian and other rural communities organized processions in which Torah-scrolls from their former villages were presented to Y. Refael or other people representing Israel. As the Israel-bound ships sailed from the harbor at Tripoli, the immigrants frequently sang Moses' song of redemption at the sea (Exodus 15: 1–19) (cf. Duvdvani 1960).

IV

All the Gharian Jews left for Tripoli during the months of July–August 1949. In the city, Sheikh Khlafu and other community leaders met with representatives of the Jewish Agency to help arrange food and housing for the Gharian Jews. All the potential immigrants underwent medical checkups and, if necessary, treatment.[1] Individual families were given visas for immigration in accordance with the number of visas available, the health of the family, and so forth. Thus, individual families, rather than the community, were the main operative units of the immigration process. Some of the families sailed for Israel shortly after reaching Tripoli; others waited till the end of 1951, when the emigration from Libya came to an end. Most of the Gharian Jews had left Tripoli by the early months of 1950.

While in Tripoli, the Gharianites first began to learn about their future life in Israel. They heard that the 'government would give you a farm, a house and cow'. This was credible, in part, because they had observed the program of agricultural settlement implemented in Tighrinna for the Italian colonists there. Many people informally decided among themselves to try to keep together in Israel and settle as one community.

As some families moved to Israel, and were located in immigra-

[1] The physicians of the OSE found that 80% of the rural Jews suffered from trachoma (Agar 1960: 189). My own casual estimate is that 10% of the household heads in Even Yosef were blind in one eye as the result of eye diseases. Other common diseases were tuberculosis and ringworm of the scalp.

tion camps there, they sent letters to Tripoli describing life in Israel as they met it. They enclosed samples of Israeli money, cigarettes, and so forth. A frequent suggestion was that those yet to come bring with them a certain type of pepper which they said was not grown in Israel. Sheikh Khlafu twice visited Israel while helping to organize the immigration of the Gharianites and other Tripolitanians. While registering the Gharianites with the Jewish Agency, he began the process of 'Israelization' by assigning them Hebrew names in place of traditional ones (e.g. Zākki became Yitzḥaq, Wīya became Ḥai). Khlafu himself, however, was one of the less than 4,000 Jews who remained in Tripoli after January 1952.[1]

V

When the immigrants arrived in Haifa they were first sent to an immigration processing center in the vicinity. From there, the first Gharianites were sent to a transit camp (*ma'abara*) near Binyamina. These first arrivals wrote to friends and relatives in Tripoli to insist on being placed in the Binyamina ma'abara, and to refuse being sent elsewhere. The large majority of the Gharian Jews thus reached the Binyamina camp.

At the time of their arrival, Israel was in the midst of its mass-immigration reception phase. By the end of 1949, the Jewish population of the country had grown by more than 50 percent (cf. Matras 1965: 32–5). At first, many of the immigrants were settled in the houses of Arabs who had fled the country, and in immigration camps. In 1950 the government initiated a program of ma'abarot (plural) which differed from the immigration camps in that the former were placed at locations which the authorities hoped would grow into permanent settlements. Also, as far as possible, the immigrants in the ma'abarot were given work opportunities in the vicinity. Thus, in the Binyamina ma'abara, many of the Gharian Jews began to work. Some of them attended night classes to learn Israeli Hebrew. A few were given basic training in the army. It was in the Binyamina camp, as well, that concrete plans for settling on a moshav began to develop.

[1] Sheikh Khlafu was one of the few Gharianites to remain in Tripoli. It is not clear whether he was 'caught' by the cessation of emigration after Libyan independence or whether he simply decided to stay. If the latter was the case he fell into the general category of the well-to-do who remained, perhaps because of the reluctance to lose their capital (and prestige). He eventually emigrated to Israel after the 1967 war.

VI

The moshav is one of the forms of agricultural settlement that resulted from the interaction of the Zionist-socialist pioneering ideology with the ecologic and economic realities of Palestine. A pamphlet, published by E. Yaffe in 1919,[1] enunciated the main principles that guided the establishment of the first *moshav ovdim* (Workers' settlement) two years later. These principles of (*a*) individual farms, (*b*) national land, (*c*) self-labor, (*d*) cooperative organization, and (*e*) mutual aid, were largely realized in the economic organization of the 60-odd moshavim founded before Israeli independence in 1948.

The 'classical' moshav is a corporate community, constituted by individual families, usually numbering 50 to 100. Each family is allotted an equal amount of land, and equity is maintained also with regard to resources, such as water and credit. The land is not owned by the settler, but is leased on a long-term basis from the Jewish National Fund. Often, a portion of the land is farmed co-operatively. The land may not be transferred without the permission of the Jewish National Fund, nor may it be parcelled upon inheritance. Work on the land is performed by each family, as there is a ban on hired labor.

On a day-to-day basis, the farmer obtains his agricultural supplies from a general store where his account is debited with the value of what he has taken. Later, after the produce is co-operatively marketed, his account is credited with the amount for which the produce sold, the value of the credit advanced him is deducted, and he receives the remainder in cash. Also, payments for taxes, 'municipal services', insurance and so forth are deducted from the cash sum received by the settler.[2]

Mutual aid, in the case of illness, military call-up and other emergencies, may be provided in the form of financial assistance from the moshav and/or from labor donated by individual members of the community.

The high degree of economic interdependence of the moshav families, and the fact that the moshav is linked to a modern and developing economy, call for continual community decisions at

---

[1] *Liisud moshavei ovdim* (Toward the establishment of workers settlements).

[2] Detailed examples of daily economic transactions and moshav accounting are found in Weingrod (1966: 81–4).

both the policy and implementation levels. Policy decisions are made by the *general assembly*, consisting of the adult members of the moshav, which also elects a *moshav committee* (and other committees), to make specific decisions throughout its term of office. The decisions of the moshav committee are implemented by a salaried *mazkir ḥutz* (external secretary), usually aided by a *mazkir pnīm* (internal secretary) and other lesser administrators.

The moshav is closely tied to a number of national institutions, among which the Settlement Department of the Jewish Agency, and the *Histadrut* (General Federation of Labor), along with its subsidiaries, are the most important. Each moshav is affiliated with one of several moshav federations which, like the Jewish Agency and the Histadrut, cross-cut the partisan political structure of Israel. The two largest of these federations are the ones affiliated with MAPAI (now merged within the Israel Labor Party) and the National Religious Party.[1]

It was this generalized 'model' of the pre-state moshav that served to guide the planners of the large-scale immigrant agricultural settlement program that began after independence.

VII

During the period of the British Mandate the *kibbutz* (collective settlement) had been the main form of pioneering agricultural settlement, but the collectivism of kibbutz life was not congenial to the majority of the new immigrants. The moshav, on the other hand, provided a generalized set of principles which could be modified extensively by immigrant-settlers coming from diverse cultural backgrounds. The post-statehood land settlement program, that concentrated on immigrant moshavim, met a number of needs: it provided housing and employment for a significant portion of the new immigrants; it increased agricultural production which had suffered from the 1948–9 war and from the flight of Arab farmers, and settled border areas for security purposes.

The period from independence till 1952 has been characterized as the 'phase of improvisation' (Willner 1969: 144–68) with regard to land settlement in Israel. During this period many sites of

[1] The National Religious Party is made up of the *Po'el Mizraḥi* and the smaller and less socialist *Mizraḥi*.

future villages were selected, sometimes with little consideration given to the economic viability of the envisioned communities. The task of recruiting settlers to the administratively created villages fell to the politically-linked moshav federations. In order to protect the nascent communities from the brunt of the fierce competition among Israel's political parties for the votes of the new immigrants (cf. Willner 1969: 307–18; Weingrod 1966: 51–7), the allocation of the villages to the various federations was made before settlement actually took place. Thus, a group of settlers could select only a site that had been assigned to the federation that had succeeded in recruiting that group. The *Po'el Mizrahi* (Workers' Religious party), claiming that many of the Middle Eastern immigrants were 'religious' (having come from traditional backgrounds or having no involvement with secular ideologies), were successful in having a greater proportion of moshavim allotted to them than was reflected by their strength at the polls (cf. Marmorstein 1969: 142–3).[1]

Within the partisan structure of the Jewish Agency, the head of the Immigration department of the Agency had always been a member of a religious party. As indicated above, Y. Refael and B. Duvdvani were two of the key figures in organizing the mass emigration from Libya,[2] and both were prominent in religious parties. These parties, therefore, from the beginning, were able to exercise a strong claim to the loyalty of the Libyan Jews. Out of fifteen groups of Libyan immigrants settling on moshavim from 1949–52, seven affiliated themselves with the Moshav Federation of the Po'el Mizrahi. One of these seven settling groups was composed of the former residents of the Gharian.

[1] Out of approximately 91 moshavim established in 1950–1, 21 (23.1%) affiliated with religious parties out of which 17 (18.7%) were linked to the Po'el Mizrahi. Of these 17, 15 were settled by Middle Eastern groups (Zionist Organization 1960: 52–70). The National Religious Party usually obtains about 10% of the vote in parliamentary elections (Eisenstadt 1967: 291–5).

[2] The importance of these individuals was given popular recognition by the Tripolitanian Jews as indicated by their incorporation into current folk poetry. The following examples, loosely translated, are given by Zuaretz (1960: 293):

    (*a*) Duvdvani! How unfair!
          You put me on the second steamer.
    (*b*) We relaxed, slept through the night,
          After Yiṣḥaq Refael saw our plight.

VIII

As mentioned earlier, the Gharian Jews first heard of the land settlement program while still in Tripoli. They were contacted by, and agreed to join with, the moshav movement of the Po'el Mizrahi soon after the first families had arrived in the Binyamina camp. The contacts between the moshav federation and the community were made via the community elite who had helped in organizing the immigration process in Tripoli (p. 49). According to the accounts I heard, however, these 'lesser' leaders informed the representatives of the federation that they were only handling this task temporarily. Their 'real' leader, they asserted, would soon arrive from Tripoli. In saying this, they referred to Hai Khalifa who had briefly served as the sheikh in the Gharian (p. 26). Upon Hai's arrival in the Binyamina camp in December 1949, he assumed the main responsibility as the intermediary between the community and the federation along with the other agencies involved in the settlement program.

About the same time that the first Gharian Jews arrived in Binyamina camp, several families from the coastal Tripolitanian town of Misurata (see Slouschz 1927: 50–8 and Blake 1968) also were sent there. One of the Misuratan Jews named Ḥai Ḥaddād had known Hai Khalifa through commercial contacts in Tripoli. Both the Gharian families and the Misuratans were eager to leave the camp and settle as soon as possible.[1]

Several Gharianites said that the main hardship they suffered in the camps was that they were unable to eat the European-style meals that they were served. They usually explained their decision to settle on a moshav, rather than in a town, in terms of their lack of occupational skills. They also claimed that they were comfortable with rural life, were accustomed to hard work (particularly the ex-artisans), and were familiar with one another. Several non-Gharianite families (from Misurata and Zanzur) emphasized the fact that they wished to settle on a 'religious moshav'. (There is a 'transplanted community' of Misuratan Jews on a moshav that is

---

[1] Life and attitudes in the immigration camps (*maḥanei 'olīm*) are discussed by Shuval (1963) (who calls them 'transit camps'). As she indicates (1963: 9–10), despite the differences between the 'immigration camps' and ma'abarot they had much in common. The Binyamina camp had originally been an immigration camp and was later converted to a ma'abara. The novel *Gesher* ('Bridge', M. Ohel 1955) depicts the life of a family from Benghazi in a ma'abara.

linked to a non-religious movement; this moshav is alluded to in Marmorstein 1969: 149.)

Hai Haddad said that he could 'bring' several Misuratan families with him to form a nucleus of settlers who would move to the new location. This initial group was joined by two families from Zanzur, who were related to a family from Ben'abbas. It also included a family from 'Amrus, the head of which served as a resident teacher on the new moshav.[1] Thus, out of the first approximately 25 families to move to the new moshav, eight were from towns outside of the Gharian.

The representatives of the moshav federation had taken Hai Haddad, Hai Khalifa, and other community leaders to several sites that had been made available to them in various parts of the country. They selected a site – to which I have given the fictitious name of Even Yosef – in the central part of the country, about 30 kilometers north of Tel Aviv. The village was planned for 91 farms and about 12 non-farming, resident families. In order to be eligible to obtain a farm, a person had to be married. Several marriages of very young men and women were arranged so that the young couples could get a farm. At the other end of the 'life cycle', a number of older men falsified their ages so as to receive farms. (Later, after many years, some of these men revised their ages so as to obtain retirement insurance payments earlier.) Of the seven Gharian men who married in the Binyamina camp, two (29%) married girls from outside the Gharian, representing a much higher proportion of community-exogamous marriages than characterized the group after settling in Even Yosef (Goldberg 1967a: 178). The breakdown of families settling the moshav during the first year was as tabled overleaf.[2]

Initially, the settlers were housed in temporary quarters somewhat to the east of the planned village. They lived in the buildings of an older moshav that had been abandoned during the fighting in

---

[1] In most moshavim there usually are some *residents* who live on plots much smaller that those of the members and whose source of income is not from agriculture (though they may cultivate vegetables or fruit trees in their yards). These residents may be employees of the moshav (e.g. an accountant), teachers or craftsmen. In Even Yosef most of the residents' houses were occupied by the parents of members. Residents are not members of the moshav and do not vote in the general assembly.

[2] The five families which I have called 'Misuratan' included three cases of a 'pure' Misuratan couple, one case of a Misuratan man married to a Gharianite woman and one case of a Tunisian man (from Gabes) married to a Misuratan woman. The latter two couples were married in the Binyamina camp.

Farm-holders (*members*):		90
from the Gharian	83	
Misurata	5	
Zanzur	2	
Non-farmers (*non-members*):		3
from the Gharian	2	
'Amrus	1	
Total		93

1948. Several months later they moved into tents located on the site of their new home. Rebbi Shemuel (pp. 31–2) recorded the sequence of moves that had taken the community from the Gharian to Even Yosef on the inside cover of a bible where he wrote:

We left the Gharian on the 16th of Tammuz [July 13, 1949] and, with all the families, we travelled to Tripoli. We stayed in Tripoli 6 months. On the 16th of Kislev [December 7, 1949] we sailed on the ship Gallila. We travelled 3 days till we reached Haifa. We remained in Salluks [the immigration reception camp] 8 days and we travelled to Binyamina. We remained there 9½ months. From there we went to A.B. and stayed 3½ months. After that on Sunday, the first day of Tevet, 5711 [December 10, 1950], we moved to our moshav. Good fortune. (*Siman tov*) Amen.

IX

The site selected for Even Yosef is situated in the Sharon plain in the Central District of Israel. It lies about 50 meters above sea level. The mean annual rainfall is about 600 millimeters, spread over 50–60 days a year during the months of October through April. The average temperature ranges from about 40 °F in February to about 90 °F in September. The arable lands of the village are mostly a brown-red soil. This mixture of clay and sand is excellent for citriculture. The topography is one of rolling hillocks, cut by shallow *arroyos*, and covered intermittently by grasses and weeds. Before settlement, the land had been levelled and drained so to be fit for intensive agriculture.

Prior to the settlement of Even Yosef the site was uninhabited. The land had been used primarily for the grazing of cattle by Arabs, who lived further east, in or near the Nablus mountains (A. Cohen 1965: 411). There was standing, however, a citrus grove owned by an Arab who had fled the country in the 1948–9 war. Also standing were two traditional stone buildings, one covering an old well and the other built to house the tools and implements used in cultivating the grove.

The closest neighbors of Even Yosef were two other moshavim, 1–2 kilometers to the east, that were also affiliated with the Po'el Mizrahi. One of them had been founded in 1932 by European settlers. This moshav, which had been abandoned during the fighting in 1948, was where the settlers lived for $3\frac{1}{2}$ months before moving to Even Yosef (pp. 55–6). It was resettled after the war by a small group of Europeans and a large group of Yemenite immigrants. The other moshav was a new village, founded somewhat later than Even Yosef, and also settled by Yemenites. Two kilometers to the southeast was a veteran European moshav founded in 1930. Two and a half kilometers to the north was yet another moshav founded originally by German Jews, but settled by Yemenites in 1945. Three kilometers to the northeast was an Arab village that had served as a base for Iraqi forces in 1948.

X

The area allotted to Even Yosef was 2,700 dunams (1 dunam = $\frac{1}{4}$ acre). While most of the pre-state moshavim were planned in a nucleated settlement pattern, many of the new moshavim placed the houses of the settlers on their individual plots, resulting in a 'line village' pattern. This pattern was supposed to have the effect of (1) increasing security by dispersing the settled area, and (2) encouraging the attachment of the new settler to 'his' land (Willner 1969: 150–1).

Figure 5 is a sketchmap of the village. The villagers themselves normally divide Even Yosef into three 'neighborhoods', named 'up village', 'the center', and 'the camp'.[1] The houses on the plots are located near the roads. Each of the farm-holder plots is approximately 12 dunams while the plots given to the non-members are approximately 3 dunams. Surrounding much of the inner area of houses and plots are roughly 1,500 dunams, which were not immediately divided; most of this outer area was eventually devoted to citriculture. Somewhat less than 200 dunams are made up of the roads and the area in the center of the village.

---

[1] 'The camp' is the neighborhood where the villagers lived in tents when they first moved to the site of Even Yosef.

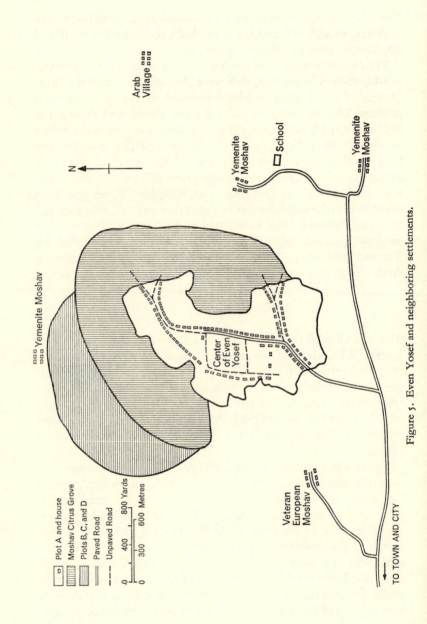

Figure 5. Even Yosef and neighboring settlements.

Three small synagogues were located in the village, one in each of the neighborhoods. A special synagogue building was constructed in 'the center' (and near this synagogue was built a *miqwa*), while part of the old Arab well building (p. 57) was converted to a synagogue in 'the camp'. In the 'up-village' neighborhood, one of the buildings originally planned for a non-member moshav resident was also made into a synagogue. There were many other 'public buildings' constructed, mostly in the center of the village, during the first few years. These are listed below:

Communal buildings	Farm-related buildings
Cooperative store.	Feed and fertilizer warehouse.
Village office.	Vegetable storehouse.
School building (for kindergarten and first grade).	Egg storehouse.
	Milk storehouse, refrigerated.
Infirmary.	A shed for cow insemination.
Club house.	Shed for the moshav truck.
Arsenal.	Shed for tractor and combine.

On the individual plots, along with the dwelling units, there also were built small barns, poultry runs, and so forth. Each settling family was given some agricultural implements and a milch cow. A horse (or donkey, or mule) was provided for every two farms. Each family also received some furniture such as beds, mattresses, a table and chairs. At the time of settlement there was no decision made about when, how, or if at all the Settlement Department would be repaid for their investment in the farms. One villager likened the Department's advance to the villagers to the arrangement between a Jewish herd owner and a Moslem herdsman (p. 17) in the Gharian.

XI

During the first year many of the men were employed in building the public structures and the houses that were to become their homes. Most of the houses consisted of two rooms, the larger of which was a general 'living-bedroom', and the smaller a kitchen. Ten homes in the center of the village were provided with an extra room and these were to be allotted to the families with the greatest number of children.

After the homes were built they were distributed on the basis of a lottery. Groups of families could decide to live next to one another and, if this were the case, one family would 'pull the straw' and the others in the group would be assigned adjacent plots. Almost half of the plots were allotted to groups of families, and more than half of these groups consisted of brothers, or father and son(s).

This manifestation of 'virilocality', of course, stemmed from cultural norms brought by the immigrants from Tripolitania. As had been the case in the Gharian, residing next to a father or brother did not mean that the two (or more) families were organized into an extended family. The relationship between fathers and sons in the immigration context may be briefly discussed while considering other aspects of the material culture of the immigrants.

As mentioned, most of the belongings of the villagers were left in the Gharian, where the first changes in material culture began to take place. The relief organizations in Tripoli sent shipments of clothing to the rural communities even before these communities migrated to Tripoli. This European-style clothing was quickly adopted by most of the younger men in the Gharian. Many men gave their traditional clothing to their parents who were not as quick to discard them. Many women were careful to keep their silver jewellery (normally acquired as part of the dowry), although some sold the silver when they were told 'it wasn't "modern" in Israel'. Other belongings which were sometimes saved included kitchen ware, such as brass bowls or mill-stones, and work implements, such as blacksmith's bellows or wool combs. In general, however, even if a family left the Gharian with a fair amount of their traditional belongings, they sold, lost, or abandoned many things as they moved from Tripoli to Haifa and Binyamina. Those few who said that they originally had taken certain documents, such as deeds of land ownership, usually claimed that they had been lost along the way.

The few items of material culture which eventually reached Even Yosef usually were given to a man's elderly parents. This was also the case with respect to any cash that the family might have succeeded in preserving. This transfer of 'surviving' capital to the parents was particularly significant in those instances when a son obtained a farm on the moshav, while his parents settled there as non-member residents. The elderly couples held on to these belongings as long as they could, selling them when they needed cash. The main buyers were representatives of museums and 'antique' dealers. The transfer of the remaining assets to the parents fit into a general pattern in which the elderly attempted to rely upon themselves as much as possible, and to avoid dependence on their economically-more-productive children (p. 105).

XII

The first dozen years in Even Yosef were years of 'development', in which various economic and organizational arrangements were 'tried out', as a relatively stable community organization took form. Some of these developments will be briefly discussed under the rubrics of the village farming base, labor, and village administration. It should be kept in mind that much of the economic development originated in the planned programs of the settling agencies, particularly the Joint Planning Center which was established in 1952 (Willner 1969: 172–3).

TABLE 3. *Farm activities in Even Yosef by year*

| Year | Area under irrigation (dunams) | Area under cultivation* (dunams) | | | Livestock | | |
		Field crops	Citrus trees	Vegetables	Mules, horses, donkeys	Milk herd	Poultry
1952	—	—	—	—	20	—	1,330
1953	450	2,034	—	480	57	56	1,430
1954	1,340	1,615	580	440	56	90	1,108
1955	2,101	1,051	1,080	580	41	112	2,061
1956	2,020	902	1,100	505	57	142	750
1957	2,020	810	1,100	913	58	168	1,150
1958	2,070	478	1,100	1,059	64	238	4,550
1959	2,070	870	1,100	430	65	265	7,150
1960	2,070	1,218	1,100	305	65	239	11,200
1961	2,081	1,531	1,260	380	69	229	23,615
1962	2,190	814	1,395	425	72	262	18,300
1963	2,519	776	1,495	500	70	159	23,450

* Land that is cultivated with more than one crop a year is counted for each crop cultivated.

Village farming – Tables 3 and 4 present data on the agricultural activities of the village from 1952 to 1963.[1] Some of the notable trends reflected in these tables are discussed below.

[1] Most of the quantitative data is taken from the annual 'balance' reports published by the Auditing Union for Agricultural Labor Cooperatives.

TABLE 4. *Income from various farm branches in Even Yosef by year (Israeli Lirot*)*

Year	Branch				
	Citrus	Vegetables	Poultry	Milk	Eggs
1954	—	31,788	—	1,817	—
1955	4,016	57,923	—	10,868	—
1956	16,380	75,368	—	28,530	—
1957	18,575	135,005	—	48,672	—
1958	91,130	216,878	4,704	76,426	4,292
1959	101,849	136,386	39,176	91,238	24,293
1960	—	111,656	141,719	95,589	35,737
1961	203,225	99,016	184,060	110,246	46,675
1962	255,792	116,419	260,426	119,750	82,619
1963	477,787	191,576	284,409	81,650	70,539

* The Israeli Lira has undergone successive devaluations from IL 1 = $2.80 at independence to IL 1 = $0.33 in 1963.

The number of dunams under cultivation increased from 450 in 1953 to 2,519 in 1963. Much of this area was devoted to a new cooperative citrus grove planted in 1953–5 (80 dunams of the abandoned citrus grove were given to the custody of the moshav). The increase in the area devoted to citriculture took place at the expense of the area devoted to field crops. The area devoted to vegetables remained relatively constant.

With regard to livestock there was a rapid increase in the poultry branch beginning in 1958. There had been a steady increase in the dairy branch through 1960, when this growth began to level off. At this time, considerations of national planning resulted in a policy in which only settlements with soils favorable to fodder crops were encouraged to maintain their dairy branch (the encouragement took the form of subsidies, easy credit and so forth). As Even Yosef was not such a settlement, dairy farming became less viable, with a resulting drop in the dairy herd in 1963.

From the point of view of income, there was a fairly steady growth of income from vegetables (reflecting, in part, the developing farm skills of the villagers) through 1963. A dramatic increase in income from the citrus grove took place in 1962 as the young trees matured. There was also a sharp rise in poultry-derived income in 1958. In 1963 the income from citriculture, vegetables and poultry constituted 85% of the agricultural-based income of the village.[1]

XIII

Labor – Table 5 presents data on the population growth of Even Yosef during the period under discussion. Between 1951 and 1963 the total population grew from 416 to 809 or by 194%. As only one additional family joined the moshav after 1951, the increase was due almost exclusively to new births. Weintraub and Lissak (1964a: 108–14) discuss the relationship between the manpower requirements of moshav farming, and the demographic characteristics of settling groups, and show that certain demographic configurations did not provide enough manpower in relation to the consumption demands of the group. In the case of Even Yosef, there was a steady growth in the number of non-productive, dependent family members, as indicated by the ratio of productive family members to non-productive members (Table 5). This growth in number of dependents was not great enough, however, to make the moshav economically unviable. This may have been due partly to the low age of many of the household heads at the time of settlement (the mean was approximately 30 years), which meant that most of these men were capable of agricultural labor. Moreover, there was a growing involvement in agriculture throughout the first dozen years of the moshav's existence.

As described, before the villagers were settled in their new homes, many were employed in building the houses and other structures in the village. Some of them were given work far from the moshav, such as in rock quarries, but were paid in coupons redeemable in the village cooperative store which was then being established. Even after all the families were settled in their homes on the plots, many 'man-hours' were spent in wage-labor outside the village. Most of this work was in neighboring, veteran

---

[1] These figures are based only on the produce that was marketed cooperatively. In many immigrant moshavim cooperative marketing broke down, to various degrees, because the immigrants wanted more 'cash in hand', or felt that too much of the profit was being 'eaten up' by the marketing agencies (cf. Weingrod 1966: 84–7). Individual marketing, however, was only a marginal phenomenon in Even Yosef so that these figures for the total moshav reflect fairly well the agricultural activities of the 'typical' farmer.

TABLE 5. *Population trends in Even Yosef*

Year	Total population	Percent increase	Ratio of workers* to dependents
1951	416	—	0.882
1952	487	17.1	0.703
1953	507	4.1	0.701
1954	522	3.0	0.662
1955	548	4.7	0.612
1956	598	9.1	0.612
1957	625	4.5	0.570
1958	651	4.2	0.550
1959	675	3.7	0.534
1960	710	5.2	0.527
1961	733	3.2	0.508
1962	774	5.6	0.548
1963	809	4.5	0.463

* *Dependents* are defined as the dependent parents (and relatives) of farm members and children under 18; all others are classified as *workers*.

moshavim in the district. Gradually, as technical know-how was acquired, and as the organization of credit, marketing and so forth became established and predictable, most of the villagers began to concentrate their efforts on working their own plots. By 1963 only about 10–12 family heads had their main source of income from outside the moshav. Many of these derived income from their plots of land, as well, by working partially themselves and/or by renting portions of it to others.

There were other sources of work within the moshav, such as in the cooperative grove or the cooperative field crops. At first there were more people looking for work than there was work available. The position of 'labor coordinator' was established to apportion work opportunities on a daily basis. In attempts to be equitable the coordinator would take into consideration such factors as the size of the family a man had to support. Needless to say this was a difficult role for a villager to assume (p. 126), and it was abolished in the mid 1950s when there was no longer any work shortage. By 1963 the situation had changed considerably. For example, when a truck arrived in the village with a delivery of fertilizer, poultry feed, or the like, it was sometimes difficult to find people willing to unload the heavy sacks, a task for which they could have earned about IL 10 in two hours. The unloading of the trucks, much to the annoyance of the drivers, had to be delayed till teenage boys interested in some pocket-money could be located. Adult villagers, who might just be 'hanging around' the village warehouse at these times often told me, 'five years ago we would have fought one another for the chance to unload that truck; now, nobody wants to work'.

An important source of employment, beginning in the late 1950s, was the annual citrus harvest lasting from November through April.[1] This opportunity for extra income was utilized extensively by the village male youth, and the men who were not engaged in farming their own plots on a full-time basis. Because the profits that could be realized from competent farming were greater than the income from daily wage-labor in the grove, many of the younger men devoted themselves primarily to vegetable farming. The manager of the citrus grove therefore had to recruit labor from outside the village, notably from the Arab village to the east.[2] In sum, during the first dozen years, there was an increasing labor commitment by the members of the moshav to agricultural work within their own village.

The growing productivity and the increased income were insufficient to keep apace with the rapid population growth described above. By 1963 there was considerable pressure on the land, particularly with respect to young families who were living with their parents. For a number of years the moshav federation and the Settlement Department had explored the possibility of settling these young families on other moshavim. One difficulty was that these families insisted on settling as a group; they would not agree to move, individually, to scattered, different moshavim.

---

[1] The cultivation and marketing of citrus fruit is handled in the following manner (which is common in moshavim throughout the country). The moshav contracts with outside firms for the cultivation and harvest of the fruit and its preparation for the export market. These firms employ a full-time manager for the grove of Even Yosef. The manager then hires workers from among the villagers, or from the outside, as they are required. These workers receive wages. At the end of the season, after the market value of the fruit is known, all the expenses of cultivation, including a percentage paid to the cultivating-exporting firms, are deducted and the remaining profits are divided equally among the member households. Each household thus enjoys its share of the season's profits and also has the option of earning wages in the grove.

[2] The gradual *de facto* and *de jure* relaxation of the Military Administration's restrictions on geographical mobility, made this labor supply available, at the time when the grove reached maturity.

A suitable moshav was finally found,[1] and in the winter of 1963 nineteen young families left Even Yosef to settle on another moshav located in a neighboring region.

XIV

Administration. In 1951, when Even Yosef was founded, a moshav committee consisting of 7 members was elected. Thereafter, elections took place on the average of once in fourteen months. The size of the committee varied from 7 to 9 members but has remained at the larger figure for the past several years. Formally, other committees were elected too, such as the comptrol committee, the farm committee, and the cultural committee but these did not function in actuality.

The moshav committee, as in other moshavim, periodically selected an external secretary (to be called 'the mazkir'), and other lesser administrators. The titles of these other administrative posts varied over the years (e.g. internal secretary, farm coordinator, treasurer) as did their incumbents and their functions. As will be described later, effective administrative control was initially placed in the hands of two men, Hai Khalifa from the Gharian and Hai Haddad from Misurata. After Haddad's death in 1956, Hai Khalifa became the single important decision-making administrator in the village. Most of the minor administrative duties then devolved on one individual, generally known as the mazkir pnīm (internal secretary).

One important administrative function that is handled by outsiders is that of bookkeeping, for which the moshav employs two full-time accountants. Even if some members of the community were to acquire the necessary skills (for example, one teenage boy took a short course in bookkeeping), it is unlikely that the other villagers would want them to serve in this capacity. The accountants are responsible for most of the financial records of the moshav, and of the individual families. It is they who 'determine' (based on the records given to them, of course), the profit (or loss) of each villager from his farming efforts. The accountants provide

---

[1] The decision to settle on the new moshav required the agreement of the Settlement Department of the Jewish Agency, the Moshav Federation of the Po'el Mizrahi, the extant settlers of the new moshav, as well as that of the young families from Even Yosef.

a financial statement to each villager together with his biweekly cash payment, and most villagers accept the accuracy of these statements with only partial rational evaluation. The non-involvement of the accountants in internal moshav affairs is undoubtedly one of the bases of the villagers' confidence in their performance.

The internal community leadership of the Gharian Jews (and the other families attached to them) was recognized by the settling authorities from the outset. This may be seen by considering the extension services provided for Even Yosef. The program developed by the Settlement Department called for a team of instructors to be appointed to each moshav, including an agricultural instructor, a communal instructor and a home-economics instructress. The agricultural instructor was to guide the settlers, teaching them the requisite skills and knowledge for modern moshav farming. The mandate of the communal instructor was much broader impinging upon practically all aspects of moshav economic and political organization. A communal instructor, however, was never appointed to Even Yosef as the authorities felt it wiser not to 'tamper' with the existing, and apparently viable, community structure.

I have little data on the first agricultural instructor(s) appointed to Even Yosef.[1] The instructor who was assigned in 1956 was still serving in 1965. When this latter individual first came to Even Yosef, a large proportion of the men still worked primarily outside the moshav. According to employees of the Settlement Department, this instructor was very influential in persuading villagers to commit themselves to agriculture. According to his own testimony, one of his main accomplishments was to persuade Hai Khalifa to extend credit to villagers who were yet to prove themselves in farming (pp. 93, 98–9).[2] My own observations suggest that he successfully influenced the villagers because he concentrated on teaching them farming, and did not pressure them to become 'more Israeli' in other areas of their lives.[3]

---

[1] The little that I heard about the previous instructor was negative. It was claimed that he decided on the materials to be brought into the village on the basis of possibilities of a kickback from the supplier. Willner states that it was common for new immigrants to complain that instructors stole (1969: 159–60), so it is difficult to evaluate reports about the previous instructor. (See also p. 92–3, n. 2.)

[2] Weingrod (1966: 168–70) sees the establishment of satisfactory credit arrangements as a crucial point in the development of a moshav that he studied.

[3] By 1968, this instructor was promoted to a higher position in the Settlement Department and no village instructor was appointed in his place. While the

Several instructresses served in Even Yosef and when the last one resigned, in 1964, she was not replaced. Overall, these women did not revolutionize traditional home-making in Even Yosef but did provide models for change when such change was congenial to the village wives and adolescent girls.

XV

A brief account of Even Yosef, written in 1960, contains the following description:

A view of the moshav gladdens the heart, as it is all wrapped in green. Near every house is a garden, in which are planted various flowers and trees which generously yield fruit each year.

Although there is some understandable exaggeration here, a new visitor to the moshav usually is impressed by the pleasant surroundings and comes away with the feeling that Even Yosef is an immigrant moshav 'that succeeded'.

In a comparative study of village development conducted by the Settlement Department in new moshavim, ten indicators of development[1] were utilized to assess the success of the communities in the study. Even Yosef has done well in terms of many of these indicators. For example, there is a low percentage of people drawing income from outside the village and most of the villagers have adapted to farm work. There is overall population stability as only two families who at one time owned farms have left the moshav. The marketing institutions operate effectively and the village works smoothly with the various outside agencies. In 1960 ownership of the cooperative store was transferred to the village and a year later one of the villagers was hired as its manager.

All of the villagers have learned modern farming techniques to

villagers continued to benefit from the advice of special regional instructors, the Department felt that they farmed quite well without close daily guidance of a village instructor.

[1] These indicators are (Weitz 1967: 137): (1) Percentage of settlers' income drawn from outside. (2) Acquisition of agro-technical know-how. (3) Adaptation to farm work. (4) Size of investments by the farmers in their farms. (5) Indebtedness of the village organizations. (6) Efficiency of village marketing institutions and their acceptance by the farmers. (7) General stability. (8) Stability of the village elected authorities. (9) State of village public institutions (cooperative store, consumer's and producer's cooperatives, cultural center, etc.). (10) Cooperation of the village and its elected institutions with the national authorities.

a certain extent, although there is a great deal of variation in this matter. For example, seeking the guidance of the agriculture instructor has become a matter of course. Most men below the age of 35 can drive a tractor and virtually all of the villagers have personally purchased power sprayers. There are a number of individuals who are keen to experiment with new agricultural techniques. Thus, in 1964, several men, for the first time, planted vegetables (e.g. cucumbers and squash) under a plastic covering so as to be able to harvest and market the crop early and realize a higher profit. Their success stimulated others to use this technique in succeeding seasons. In 1969 a few families experimented with the cultivation of strawberries to be airfreighted to European markets.

The growing personal investment in agriculture as the main source of income may also be seen in the villagers' concern that profits reflect the efforts of the individual. Initially, the marketing of vegetables was organized as follows. Each farmer would bring a number of crates to the village warehouse which he had graded according to the quality of the produce. The village produce was marketed as a unit and each farmer would share in the profits according to the number of crates of each grade that he contributed to the village shipment. Some families (women frequently helped grade the vegetables), however, were more diligent graders than others. These people complained that the negligent sorting of other villagers sometimes resulted in the downgrading of shipment when it reached the market and reduced profits for everybody. In 1962, at the suggestion of the instructor, marketing was then rearranged so that each family graded its own vegetables, which, although physically shipped to the market with the other families' produce, competed individually for a price.[1]

In 1963 the Settlement Department decided that village development in Even Yosef had proceeded to a point where the villagers were ready to farm new land. At this time an additional four dunams (called 'plot B') was assigned to each family at the edge of the village (Figure 5).

Several years earlier, several well-to-do families had planted citrus trees on their individual land. At that time only a few

[1] Weingrod (1966, see p. 67, n. 2) has argued that more individualized credit arrangements spurred agricultural activity in Moshav Oren. The shipping-marketing reform at Even Yosef, placing greater responsibility on individual families, also is reported to have had a generally constructive effect.

families could afford to let a portion of their land lie idle while waiting for the young trees to mature. With the receipt of the B plots, however, more than 30 additional families planted small groves on their own plots.

The development of citrus culture in Even Yosef, which lies in the rich citrus belt of Israel,[1] takes on the symbolic meaning that, economically, the villagers of Even Yosef 'have arrived'. It has become customary for a man, upon planting a private grove, to invite friends and relatives to help in the planting, and to conclude the planting-bee with fellowship and drink. Similarly, in 1963, the first year that a large portion of the profits of the cooperative grove was divided among the moshav families (rather than reinvested in the grove), the payment of the citrus profits (amounting to IL 5,250/family) was made the occasion of a celebration. This jump in income from the cooperative grove, and the growth in income from vegetables and poultry during the previous two years (Table 4), made their mark on domestic consumption habits in the village.

Up to that time the household appurtenances of most of the villagers were rather meager. In fact, four families who were not satisfied with their initial choice of house sites (primarily because of conflicts with neighbors), switched homes within the village during the 1950s. This was possible because few 'home improvements' had been made by the villagers, except that many families added a corrugated tin annex to serve as a kitchen. For the most part, all village homes were equal in their simplicity.

In 1961 this situation began to change. That year virtually all the village families installed gas stoves whereas previously they had cooked on kerosene burners. In 1962 stone tile floors were put in all the homes replacing the older concrete surfaces (p. 124). A year later, with loans from the Jewish Agency, indoor toilet facilities were built in all homes (previously outhouses had been provided), and at that time many villagers decided to purchase solar heaters to provide warm running water. Many people bought refrigerators, which are found in almost every home today and, in 1963 the first washing machine was purchased. Many families began to buy modern living room furniture. There is a radio in each home and, in 1964, one man purchased a television receiver.

---

[1] Up till the middle 1960s, citrus-culture constituted Israel's largest export industry, in terms of foreign currency revenue.

Concurrently, many villagers with large families began to add rooms to their home, financed by loans from the Jewish Agency or from private sources.

Also, at this time, the road into the village was paved, partially financed by a long term loan to the moshav to be repaid by the villagers. On the basis of various indicators, then, Even Yosef has developed into a productive and viable economic unit, and its members can already see the fruits of their labors.

XVI

A casual visitor to Even Yosef is not only struck by the village's economic well-being but comes away with another equally strong and seemingly contradictory impression: that of the moshav's *traditionality*. Among the more visible manifestations of this are the persistence of traditional cultural traits. Many old men dress in a Tripolitanian-style shirt (*qmīja*) and trousers (*surwāl*) and during the winter, cover themselves with a cloak (*'abā*). Women of all ages, when it is cold, may wrap themselves in a *χdād* (a long sari-like cloth that is wrapped around the body several times), while they wear a European-type dress underneath. It is also quite common for younger men to cover themselves in an *'abā* at night, while during the day they wear European clothes.

A somewhat longer visit to the village reveals that men and women never speak to one another in public and neither do adolescent boys and girls. Within the home, most husbands and wives address one another by a vocative term (e.g. *ēi* or *esm'i*) rather than by personal name. If invited inside, a visitor frequently will be given a seat at a table, with the man of the house, while tea is prepared by his wife who sits on the floor with the children.

The celebration of festivals and *rites de passage* is predominantly traditional. While Tripolitanian cuisine is maintained throughout the year, it takes on a special significance during holidays. For example, the women normally purchase packaged flour at the village store but some may grind their own flour in preparing a holiday meal. Similarly unleavened bread (*ftīra*) for Passover, is baked in barrel-shaped mud ovens that stand outside most homes.

In preparation for a circumcision a male baby is elaborately beautified with a spice necklace, kohl around the eyes, black lines on the forehead and wears charms to ward off the evil eye. Before a wedding, a bride undergoes several days of cosmetic treatment with henna and the customary week of partying is maintained (Goldberg n.d.). This list of traditional traits could be easily expanded to other areas such as synagogue customs, funerals and faith healing.

XVII

All this, however, in itself is not surprising. Anthropologists can easily cite instances of the coexistence of ancient customs with modern innovations, particularly those which are technologically advantageous. This coexistence also is common in Middle Eastern moshavim in Israel,[1] although, by comparison, Even Yosef would rate high on a scale of preservation of traditional forms.[2] The main point, however, is not to stress the quaintness and unpredictability of the way immigrants behave, or change their behavior, but to suggest that there is an intrinsic link between the rapid technoeconomic adaptation of the community to its new environment and the pronounced preservation of other aspects of its traditional culture. This link, less easily observable than economic change and specific cultural practices, consists of the social structure of the community and its fate in the Israeli milieu.

We have seen that the Gharian Jews maintained both a sense of community, and concrete social ties, during the period of migration and settlement. In particular, community leadership continued to function in Tripoli, in the Binyamina camp, and throughout the initial and later stages of settlement in Even Yosef. The traditional socio-political arrangements, featuring a single strong leader supported by a lesser elite group, proved to be adaptable to the social environment of the rural settlement program in Israel. The structural principles that the immigrants imported from their Tripolitanian past, in the course of relatively few years, provided workable solutions to the problems of community organization posed by moshav life. The problems of internal political and economic organization being met, the majority of

[1] One young man (age 29) in Even Yosef, asked one of the local amulet writers (p. 80) to provide him with an amulet on the eve of his test for a tractor-driver's license.

[2] Some comparative examples, in the realm of social life, are presented in Chapter 6 (pp. 154–6).

the members of the community were free to commit their energies to individual economic matters, namely the development of their farms. Their success in agriculture, in turn, relieved external pressures to modify their communal arrangements and allowed them to preserve cultural traditions insofar as they wished to do so. The chapters that follow contain a detailed exposition of this thesis. Before discussing this in greater detail, the 'success story' of Even Yosef will be considered in a comparative context.

XVIII

Chance (1960), in his discussion of the Eskimo community of Kaktovik, summarizes a number of factors cited by various authors[1] which seem to encourage rapid and successful cultural change. Weingrod (1966: 194–203) finds this analysis applicable to the study of a Moroccan moshav in Israel, and Even Yosef appears to belong in the same tradition. Several of these factors will be reviewed here, and I will suggest, by reference to the Gharian Jews, some ways in which they may be logically and functionally interrelated.

One matter stressed by Chance (1960: 1036–7) is that there was a certain degree of 'flexibility' and 'openness' built into the socio-cultural system of the Eskimo of Kaktovik. A similar factor, that of the *predisposition to change*, has been cited in many of the studies of immigrant absorption in Israel (cf. Eisenstadt 1954: 112–24).[2] We have already stressed that the Gharian Jews had continually experienced change, both with regard to economic and political matters. In the following chapters we shall develop the theme that inherent within the political organization of the community was an institutionalized mechanism for coping with change, a mechanism that proved equal to the task of guiding the community during and after settlement in Israel.

A second matter, which is similarly difficult to deal with in a rigorous manner, is the factor of *choice*. While Chance (1960: 1035), and others (Nash 1958: 113; Mead 1956: 442 f.; Adams 1959: 211), emphasize the importance of choice, Weingrod (1966:

[1] See Redfield (1950), Mead (1956), Nash (1958) and Adams (1959).
[2] The notion of 'predisposition to change' has been used with reference to individual (psychological) openness to social change, but here we are referring primarily to structural arrangements which appear able to comprehend changing external conditions.

197–8) argues that choice was absent from many aspects of the settlement process of the Moroccan community at Oren. He states (1966: 197) '…the immigrants never chose to settle at Oren, never wished to become farmers, and certainly did not desire to live within a cooperative system'. Weingrod points out (1966: 199 f.), however, that once settlement had taken place, the settling authorities proved responsive to pressures from the immigrants, and the Moroccan settlers began to feel that they could influence the bureaucratic agencies that had such an overriding impact on their lives. It should also be kept in mind that the settlers were not 'relocated' on the immigrant villages[1] with the threat of physical coercion, but rather, economic incentives were heavily weighted so as to make rural settlement the only 'sensible' option.

The comparative study of choice, or freedom, has received little systematic sociological treatment (Hillery 1971). One point is obvious, however, that the attempt to assess the degree of choice in a given situation should pay attention to the subjective view of the participants, as well as to the objective conditions. One only has to think of nomadic Middle Eastern pastoralists, who are 'forced' to move their flocks and homes in search of pasture and water, but who view their nomadic migrations as the high point in the round of their activities, and the essence of their freedom.

The Jews of the Gharian, too, were placed under great economic and political pressure to leave their native village, but this very same flight was viewed by them, also, as a long-yearned-after religious fulfillment. This sense of commitment, and the fact that in Israel they did enjoy greater political freedom than before, may have dwarfed the salience of the constraints of the moshav settlement within their overall view.

The question of coercion versus freedom is reflected in a third factor mentioned by Chance (1960: 1034)[2] that successful change is related to the ability of the *members of the community to conduct their own affairs*. Thus, the bureaucratic structure of the settlement

---

[1] On the other hand, Kushner (1971), finds it illuminating to compare the moshav situation to American Indian reservations and relocation centers of Japanese Americans during World War II. In this context it should also be noted that, for the most part, the integrity of the family was not threatened by immigration and settlement in Israel.

[2] See also Nash (1958: 115).

process did not attempt to control all aspects of community life, and was even reluctant to meddle with the traditional political arrangements, insofar as these meshed with the settlement program. While political continuity may have been greater in Even Yosef, than in many other moshavim, Weingrod too (1966: 199–201) indicates how the settling authorities gradually encouraged the Moroccan immigrants to take over the leadership of their own village.

Given limited interference with internal community affairs, it appears that the Gharian Jews had the opportunity to exhibit the *able leadership* they had in their midst, a factor that is mentioned in other studies as well.[1] Various aspects of communal leadership will be discussed in the two chapters that follow, while Chapter 6 will present a social-psychological interpretation of how the community insures that it has an adequate supply of leadership in each generation.

The presence of able leadership, and the consensus accorded that leadership imply a fifth factor,[2] that of *total community participation in change*. While some members of the community (the elite, as will be shown) were more receptive to change than others, the community cannot be said to exhibit traditional as opposed to acculturative factions. Similarly Even Yosef was not split along generational lines, despite the fact that the youth participated in many specific items of Israeli culture not shared by the parents.[3] Taken as a whole, all the members of the community moved in the direction of integration into Israeli society, albeit at different rates.

This overall commitment to change was due partially to the fact that change was 'total', a matter that has been highlighted by Mead (1956: 445–7), Chance (1960: 1035 f.), and Weingrod (1966: 194–7). Thus, because change at Even Yosef took place in the context of migration, there was a radical alteration in the community's material surroundings which dramatized the irreversibility of change, and the need to adapt to new conditions. With

---

[1] See Redfield (1950: 168–9), Mead (1956: 188 ff.), Adams (1959: 216–17), Chance (1960: 1034), and Weingrod (1966: 202).

[2] See Mead (1956: 452), Nash (1958: 115), Adams (1959: 215–16), and Chance (1960: 1035). A discussion of the link between able leadership and the lack of factionalism is found on pp. 132–3.

[3] The lack of factionalism in general is discussed in Chapter 5, while relations between the generations are considered in Chapter 6. See, also, pp. 146–53.

regard to the Gharian Jews (and, perhaps, in the other cases as well), it would be more precise to say that *the awareness of, and potentiality for, change were total*, but, because of the aforementioned reasons, the villagers could change drastically in one sphere of behavior, and change slowly, or not at all in other areas.

Lastly, the benign bureaucratic setting (cf. Weingrod 1966: 199–201), and the various internal factors already cited, meant that the community was able to *realize the newly defined goals*[1] of economic development (as outlined in this chapter). Economic success (in farming) met both the aspirations of the villagers and the demands of the land settlement administration. This success, in turn, forestalled (administrative) environmental pressure toward changes in the community's structure and traditions.

To summarize, the Jews of the Gharian traditionally enjoyed a fair amount of social and cultural autonomy within the context of a dependent political status. This was made possible by the leadership of the sheikh and other elites who were skilled in guiding the community through an unpredictable political environment. The individual community members, as well, were quite accustomed to change in external economic conditions.

Events in Libya and in Israel in the 1940s forced this community to leave their home and migrate to a new country. While the coercive aspects of this migration are apparent, it was viewed as the fulfillment of a deep religious commitment by the participants. The rigors and deprivations of migration and settlement were therefore felt to be an outgrowth of the value-choice that individuals and the community had made.

Despite the dislocations and strains of immigration and subsequent settlement, the community never disintegrated as a sociocultural unit. The traditional leaders, and form of leadership, were able to guide the Gharian Jews through this most recent crisis. This ability was recognized by the settling authorities who did not violate community autonomy more than was required by the implementation of the settlement program.

The factors already cited, and the irreversibility of the migratory change, encouraged the settlers to adopt the new technoeconomic arrangements, and, to a lesser degree new communal and political forms. On the whole, however, the traditional political structures proved viable in the new setting. While the elite provided leader-

[1] See Redfield (1950: 167), Mead (1956: 444–5) and Chance (1960: 1033).

ship in accepting change, the willingness to learn new ways was demonstrated by all villagers. Thus, a feedback mechanism was set into motion in which the 'inherited' political structure successfully coped with moshav life, bringing economic rewards to the village and its members, and this success mitigated the pressure for cultural change. The chapters that follow contain a detailed exposition of this thesis.

4. Leadership in Even Yosef

The migration from the Gharian to Even Yosef involved a dramatic change in the economic and sociocultural environment of the community. From a certain point of view, however, the relationship of the community to the world about remained the same. Economically, Even Yosef was linked to the Israeli economy, and its citrus fruit was sold on a world market. Politically, the Gharianites became part of Israel's Jewish majority, whereas previously they had been a small confessional minority. In other ways, however, the community remained isolated from the 'world outside'.

THE ENVIRONMENT OF EVEN YOSEF

Economics

The gradual disengagement from wage labor outside the village, and involvement in agriculture in the moshav, has already been described (pp. 63–4). This shift meant that most of the men spent their working day inside Even Yosef, limiting their contact with other segments of the Israeli population. This social disengagement went on at the same time that the village agricultural produce increasingly reached the general market.

The main crops grown have been indicated in the preceding chapter (Table 3). Included in the category of vegetables (and listed roughly in the order of economic importance) are tomatoes, cucumbers, squash, potatoes, peanuts, carrots, radishes, beans, and peppers. Almost all families have fruit trees and mint bushes in their yards. In addition to hens, some people keep geese and turkeys. Many families keep several sheep and a few keep a goat. While some of these items are primarily for home consumption (e.g. peppers, fruit, turkeys, and goats which are slaughtered for religious festivals), the majority of the produce is marketed. Similarly, the villagers depend on the cooperative store for many domestic supplies, as domestic production meets only a small proportion of their consumption demands.

The cooperative marketing of the produce means that few of the villagers have to come into direct contact with purchasers. The weighing and loading of the vegetables takes place near the vegetable warehouse and, after that, only the internal secretary and the moshav driver are personally involved in bringing the produce to market.

There are a variety of special sources of income available to certain villagers. These vary from the full salaries paid to the secretaries and the Rabbi,[1] to the small, part-time salary paid to a man who distributes mail after it has been brought by the rural delivery truck, or the small profit realized by the village bread vendor. These 'specialties' are listed below and are classified as economic, administrative and religious.

Economic
Full-time employment in the citrus gove (6 individuals).
Guard of the citrus grove.
Employees of the village cooperative store (5 individuals).
Milk-collector.
Egg-collector.
Moshav truck driver (full-time).
Moshav tractor driver (seasonal).
Bread vendor.
Newspaper vendor.
Kerosene vendor.
School Janitor (in neighboring Yemenite village, 2 individuals).

Administrative
External secretary.
Internal secretary.
Local commander (in charge of organizing nightly guard duty).
Mailman.

[1] Till 1955 the children of Even Yosef were taught by a resident of the moshav who had originated from 'Amrus (p. 55), and who conducted classes in a one-room schoolhouse fashion. In 1956 the children began to attend a newly completed State Religious School (Eisenstadt 1967: 247–51), in a neighboring Yemenite village (Figure 5). Only the first grade, kindergarten and nursery still met in Even Yosef. At that time the 'Amrusi teacher left the village (the first grade, kindergarten and nursery teachers came from outside), and a Rabbi, who had recently arrived from Ben Gardane in southern Tunisia (see Deshen 1965: 69), was appointed to the village. It had been quite common in the past for Jerban Rabbis (Ben Gardane was a 'colony' of the Jerban Jewish community) to serve in rural Tripolitanian communities (Slouschz 1927: 43, 262).

Religious
> Ritual slaughterers (4 individuals).
> Ritual circumcisor.
> Rabbi.
> Amulet writer[1] (2 individuals).
> Synagogue sextons (3 individuals).
> Miqwa attendant.

With the exception of the two secretaries, the manager of the co-operative store, the local commander, and the truck driver, these specialties do not bring their practitioners into anything more than circumscribed interaction with the wider society. Most of these jobs are held by older individuals, including several resident non-members, who have limited capacities for agricultural labor. There are, however, a few individuals who have more extensive contacts with the outside world as a result of their own economic initiative.

Two villagers own heavy trucks and are members of a trucking cooperative (located in the nearby town); one man has an irrigation plumbing business, and another has a butcher shop in one of the rooms of his house. The son of Hai Haddad (the leader from Misurata), has the position of 'youth coordinator' for the three moshavim affiliated with the Po'el Mizrahi. Two men are employed in a tractor station (run by the Settlement Department) in the vicinity, and five men still work as wage laborers in the citrus groves of neighboring villages. The land of these individuals who work outside the village does not lay idle, but is usually cultivated by a teenage or adult son, or rented to another villager.[2]

A few individuals derive occasional income from services they provide for other villagers. For example, one former shoemaker continues to make shoes for his family and sometimes makes them for neighbors. A former blacksmith occasionally shoes the horses owned by villagers, or by neighboring Arabs from time to time. Some people hire out their labor to other villagers for the construction of a new poultry run or storage shed. Several women

---

[1] These two individuals had a reputation for their skill and effectiveness far outside the village, among both Middle Eastern and European Jews.

[2] Renting land is officially prohibited by moshav rules but is widely practiced in the village. Similarly many villagers illegally hire workers (mostly Arab women) for the vegetable harvests. Both of these practices are recent developments in Even Yosef, linked to the villagers' commitment to agriculture as their most important source of income.

who have learned the rudiments of dressmaking, sew dresses for other women and girls.

Israeli law provides for a small subsidy to be paid to every family with four or more children, which includes over sixty percent of the families in Even Yosef. Social welfare payments constitute a very small fraction of the total moshav income, though they are important to the few families, mostly consisting of dependent parents, who receive them.

Organization and administration

The cooperative organization of moshav agriculture and the ramified ties with the Israeli economy mean that complex links must be maintained between the village and outside organizations. Some of the more important of these outside organizations are the Joint Planning Center (p. 61), the Jewish National Fund, the Moshav Federation of the Po'el Mizrahi, the marketing co-operatives, the marketing councils, suppliers, the utility companies, the Ministry of the Treasury, social service agencies, and banks and other sources of credit.[1] Despite the importance of the moshav's connections to these organizations, few of the villagers have clear ideas, nor care to have a clear idea, of their various functions and rights and obligations vis-à-vis the moshav. For example, few people realize that they are share-holders in the

---

[1] Examples of these types of organizations are as follows:

Marketing cooperatives – *Tnuva*, The Purchasing Organization of the Po'el Mizrahi;

Marketing authorities – The Citrus Marketing Board, The Vegetable Marketing Board;

Suppliers – *Hamashbir Hamerkazi*, The Organization of Poultry Breeders;

Utility Companies – The Electric Company, *Mqorot* (water company);

Social Welfare Agencies – The Sick Fund of the *Histadrut*, National Insurance.

Below are listed various sources of credit and the amount owed them as of the 1963 Balance statement:

Source of Credit	Amount (Thousands IL)
Contracts and Securities Division of the Jewish Agency	1,443.2
The AB Regional Council	21.9
Hapo'alim Bank	6.7
Nir Shitufi (see Weintraub et al. 1969: 260–2; Willner 1969: 64–5)	3.8
The Moshav Fund of the Po'el Mizrahi	2.6
Yaniv	2.5
The Agriculture Bank	2.3
The Mizrahi Bank	1.6
The Soldier's Treasure (bank)	1.0

marketing cooperatives. Most of the villagers label many of these agencies the *sokhnut* (literally 'the agency', namely the Jewish Agency), which is *the* organization most closely involved in the agricultural development of the village. Thus, the agricultural extension worker is 'from the sokhnut' (which he is); an inspector from the Ministry of Health who made a spot check on the village milk was 'from the sokhnut' (which he was not), and the anthropologist entering the village was 'from the sokhnut' (which I was not).

Within the Israeli administrative framework, Even Yosef is a member of a *regional council*, along with eight other settlements, and sends a member to council meetings (see Samuel 1960: 222–4). The position of representative to the council meetings is held by the mazkir, though legally there is no connection between the two positions. In terms of partisan politics, the mazkir also functions as the main link between the moshav and the Po'el Mizrahi, although these roles are formally distinct as well. Thus, in the political realm, the majority of the villagers have little involvement in the world outside the village.

Neighboring settlements

With regard to the 'social' environment there is limited exchange between the people of Even Yosef and their neighbors. No links of friendship developed between the Gharian Jews and their employers in the neighboring villages in the early years. (Neither, however, did hostile relations develop.) Most of these employers were European Jews, but the Gharianites seem to be almost equally insulated from their Middle Eastern neighbors in the Yemenite moshavim.

There are four young couples, originally from Even Yosef, who have farms in one of the neighboring Yemenite moshavim. These Gharianites have good relations with their neighbors, but are still strongly oriented to their home village. They attend the central synagogue in Even Yosef on the Sabbath and Festivals, stating that they cannot follow the traditional Yemenite rendition of the Hebrew prayers.[1] Two or three girls from Even Yosef have

[1] Morag (1963: 265 ff.) discusses the unique development of the Yemenite pronunciation of liturgical Hebrew in comparison to the traditions of Hebrew pronunciation among other groups. I am sure, however, that if it had been socially necessary, the Gharianites would have learned to follow the Yemenite pronunciation.

married Yemenite men and gone to live in the Yemenite moshavim, but no Yemenite girls have married Gharianites. Of the 52 men who have been married since settling in Even Yosef, 94% have married moshav girls. About a dozen girls have married outside the moshav, more than half of them to Tripolitanian men in nearby communities.

There are relatively few Gharian Jews living outside of Even Yosef (the major exception is the group of 19 young families that moved away in 1963, p. 66) and visits to other communities are limited by that factor. This is in contrast to the dispersion of relatives throughout Israel which is characteristic of other immigrant groups (Shuval 1963: 12; Weingrod 1965: 33). Several old women have been outside of Even Yosef only once or twice since settling in the village. Trips outside the community are usually made either on religious occasions or for the purpose of shopping.

Every year the villagers hire a truck or bus to take trips to Meron in Galilee at the occasion of the *hillūla* (the 18th day of the month of Iyyar),[1] or to take guided tours to various parts of Israel during the intermediate days of Passover or Tabernacles.[2] These trips are thus taken as a group. One year they hired a truck together with one of the Yemenite moshavim, but after that trip decided 'it was better to do things with your own people'.

The villagers are more individualistic with regard to shopping. They travel to the nearest town (five to six kilometers away – 20 minutes by bus), or city (20 kilometers – one hour by bus) for larger purchases, such as clothing, furniture or appliances. Buses come to and leave the village about six times daily which means that a trip outside consumes a fair portion of a working day. There are usually no more than a handful of people on any one trip out. In recent years an increasing number of travelling salesmen, having learned of the purchasing power of Even Yosef, visit the village to sell all sorts of merchandise, including some of the larger items

---

[1] This day is known as *Lag Ba-'Omer* in other Jewish traditions (see *The Jewish Encyclopedia*, Vol. 9, p. 399). It commemorates the death of *Rabbi Shim'on Bar Yoḥāy*, a Talmudic sage who is the putative author of the Zohar, the central text of Jewish mysticism. In Tripolitania it was customary to make pilgrimages to local shrines on that day (Benjamin 1859; Guweta' 1960b), but in Israel devotees can visit the tomb of Rabbi Shim'on near Meron in Galilee (see Zenner 1965: 209–11).

[2] If economically possible the villagers refrain from work on the 'intermediate days' of these week-long festivals, but travel is permitted.

mentioned. This, too, serves to limit the contacts of the villagers with the outside. Most of the older generation do not travel outside the village for purposes of entertainment, but many of the men under 30–35 years do go into the neighboring town to see a film on Saturday nights.

Even Yosef is situated about 6–7 kilometers southeast of a former ma'abara which had been the home of many Tripolitanian immigrants. In the first years after settlement there had been some black-market ties between members of the moshav and immigrants in the ma'abara, but these did not develop into permanent social ties. More than 500 Tripolitanian families who formerly lived in the ma'abara now reside in the nearby city (p. 83). Still, there are few links between these Tripolitanians and the Gharianites. As mentioned, several Tripolitanian men have married girls from Even Yosef. In all cases, these were 'older' men (over thirty), several of whom had been married previously. Their contact with Even Yosef girls was established through intermediaries. When boys from Even Yosef visit the city they sometimes eat at restaurants owned by Tripolitanians but, overall, relationships between the villagers and the city dwellers are limited.

Cultural surroundings

In terms of cultural interchange with the wider society, Even Yosef remains somewhat of an isolate. While most of the men can easily converse in Hebrew with outsiders, Arabic is universally used by the villagers among themselves. Children are first exposed to Hebrew in nursery school. Most villagers listen to Arabic language radio programs, from Israel and from the Arab countries, though not to the exclusion of Hebrew language programs. About 30 of the moshav families receive a daily Hebrew newspaper *Hatzofeh*, reflecting the views of the National Religious Party, though in a few instances it is only the teenage children (sons) who read the papers. Modern Hebrew books are very rare in the village homes, except in conjunction with the formal schooling of the children.

There is, without doubt, an overall attachment on the part of the villagers to symbols of Israeli statehood and society, such as the flag and the military. Many homes contain pictures of the Israeli Presidents and Prime Ministers alongside such traditional figures as Moses, King David and *Rebbi Shim'ūn Bar Yuhāy*.[1] Parents very clearly assign Hebrew names to their new-born children in preference to the Arabic names which were current in their own childhood in the Gharian (see Slouschz 1927: 202). If one could quantify the rate of cultural infiltration from the wider society to Even Yosef, however, and compare it to other moshavim it would be found to be rather low.

In some ways the wider society has shown a greater interest in the Gharian Jews than the latter have in Israeli society. The story of the 'cave-dwellers of Tripolitania' was quite popular among Israeli journalists during the first post-immigration years, and the village is still visited by reporters from the popular dailies from time to time. A government-backed handicrafts business has attempted to perpetuate the rug-weaving tradition of the women and bring the rugs to the tourist market. As part of this effort, when Israel once participated in an international folk-handicraft exhibition, two women from Even Yosef were flown to the United States where they presented carpets to Mrs Eisenhower. For a variety of reasons, rug weaving has declined among the women,[2] and, in any event, the sale of village rugs did not require any change in the structure of the community's relation to its environment (p. 28).

One interesting indication of the cultural insulation of Even Yosef is the relative ignorance, on the part of the villagers, of the widespread negative stereotypes concerning Middle Eastern Jews in Israel. Ethnic strain is manifest in Israeli life in various ways (Weingrod 1965). Several years ago one European Israeli wrote a book advocating an extreme position of Ashkenazic (European) supremacy.[3] This book caused so great a furor that the question of the 'fusion of the communities' was debated by

[1] See note 1, p. 83. *Rebbi Shim'ūn* is a central figure in Jewish mysticism but also has a special importance to the Jews of Tripolitania because of a song composed in his honor by Rabbi Shim'on Lavi. The latter is generally credited with stimulating the revival of Judaism in the city of Tripoli in the sixteenth century and is thus considered the spiritual founder of modern Tripolitanian Jewry (see Hirschberg 1965a: 174–5). Of even further local relevance is the fact that Lavi's hymn recalls the legend that Bar Yoḥāy hid from the Roman government, in a cave, for 13 years. The mention of the *cave*, during the singing of the hymn, frequently evokes a giggle from the pre-adolescent boys of Even Yosef.

[2] A general discussion of 'cottage industries' in moshavim is found in Willner (1956).

[3] K. Katznelson, *Hamahapekha Ha-ashkenazit* (The Ashkenazic Revolution), Tel Aviv, 1963. For a contextual discussion of the book see Rejwan (1964).

the parliament, with the Prime Minister giving the opening statement (and condemning the book). This public debate, covered widely in the mass media, was going on at the time of my field work. As part of my interview schedule, I asked 24 adults whether or not they thought there was discrimination in Israel. Three replied that there is none, two replied that there is discrimination, and nineteen (79%) said that they do not get out of the village often enough to be able to answer the question (Goldberg 1965).

One of the widespread stereotypes concerning Middle Eastern Jews is that they are 'primitive' (Hebrew: *primitivi*, cf. Zenner 1963: 220). To an outsider, the fact that the Gharian Jews 'had lived in caves' easily validates this stereotype. Most of the adult villagers, however, have not heard the term 'primitive', or if they have heard it, are unaware of its meaning (or have a vague understanding of its negative connotation). In contrast, the concept was well-known to the mazkir, who several times used it, in reference to the villagers, in his conversations with me (p. 93).

More importantly, however, the basic categories within which the Gharianites view the ethnic structure of Israel differs from those of the wider society (which are quite varied, see E. Cohen 1968). A high-school educated Israeli would label the villagers of Even Yosef as 'Tripolitanians', seen as a sub-category of 'North Africans' (see Shuval 1962), and, in turn, as a sub-category of 'Middle Easterners' (*'edot hamizrah*). To most of the villagers, however, the Hebrew term 'Tripolitanian' (*tripolitani*) takes on the same meaning as the Arabic *trabūlsi*, namely a person from the *city* of Tripoli. They themselves, according to this scheme, are not Tripolitanians, but *Ghaina* and *'Abbāsīya*. Broader categories such as 'North African' or 'Sefaradi' (from the Spanish-Jewish tradition, i.e. 'Middle Eastern'), are peripheral to their ethnic group typology, and the popular stereotypes attached to these terms do not, for the most part, affect them (Goldberg 1965).

The community of Even Yosef has thus remained relatively insulated from Israeli social and cultural life, except for the market ties and the ramified organizational links associated with the formal moshav structure. For the most part, these ties to the outside have been channelled through the office of the mazkir, just as, in the Gharian, the sheikh was the outstanding political 'broker' between the community and its social environment. In many other respects as well, the status of the Israeli mazkir embodies the same structural principles as that of the former Gharian Jewish sheikh.

THE MAZKIR OF EVEN YOSEF

From the founding of the moshav through 1956, leadership of the village was shared by Hai Khalifa Hajjaj, who had briefly been sheikh in the Gharian, and Hai Haddad, formerly of Misurata. Formally, Haddad was the external secretary (mazkir ḥutz), and Hai Khalifa the internal secretary (mazkir pnīm), and they both had to sign official moshav papers. The annual moshav Balance Statements indicate that Hajjaj received a higher salary than Haddad, suggesting that he was the more influential leader. After Haddad died in 1956, Hai Khalifa Hajjaj became the single leader, with no close rivals. Haddad seems to have been structurally 'forgotten' by many people in Even Yosef, as they usually do not mention him except after intensive quizzing about the moshav's history. When the villagers use the term 'mazkir' they refer to the status of external secretary, occupied by Hai Khalifa since 1956. The singular importance of Hai's position will now be described.

The mazkir's control of communication channels to the outside is illustrated by an incident involving the village telephone. The only telephone in Even Yosef is located in the moshav office. There are usually a number of villagers gathered around the office who can easily listen to any telephone conversation. Any important information communicated by telephone is eventually passed on to the mazkir. Once a member of the moshav, driving a newly purchased tractor, collided with the horse of another villager, and the owner of the horse immediately went to the moshav office to telephone the police. The mazkir, who happened to be in the office at the time, dissuaded the fellow from notifying the police, promising that everything would be settled satisfactorily within the moshav. If the police were involved, the tractor driver would most probably lose his license, he argued, and thereby be cut off from an important source of income. The owner of the horse complied with the mazkir's request. Had the tractor driver lost his license, he would not have been able to repay the moshav the money he had borrowed to purchase the tractor. By virtue of his access to the telephone, the mazkir not only aided the driver but protected the moshav's interest in him and his tractor.

Most of the financial affairs of Even Yosef are left in the hands of the mazkir.[1] He also has considerable control over the financial affairs of the individual families. For example, a villager may ask the mazkir to purchase a power sprayer for him on his next trip to town, and leave the details of the transaction, and the terms of payment to the decision of the mazkir. Another example concerns the citrus grove, where the amount given to members and the installments in which it is paid, are decided by the mazkir. In 1964 the share promised to the villagers was paid four months behind schedule, and no one could offer any explanation except that the mazkir decided that the payment had to be delayed.

The mazkir limits control over his financial decisions by circulating misinformation or by allowing misinformation to be circulated by others. During the field investigation Even Yosef expanded its holdings by occupying neighboring uncultivated land. Before this land could be of any use it had to be leveled by bulldozers, divided into plots by a surveyor, and supplied with irrigation lines. The mazkir arranged for these preparations, and no one else in the village knew exactly what expenses were involved. The mazkir asked that IL 100 per season be paid to the moshav for renting the land. The villagers provided the ethnographer with varying explanations of the high rent.[2] Although most of them were erroneous, the mazkir made no attempt to clear up the misconceptions.

The decision-making power of the mazkir is further augmented by his domination of the moshav committee. According to moshav law, the mazkir is bound by the decisions of the committee, but in Even Yosef the committee is frequently only a 'rubber stamp' for the decisions of the mazkir. The law requires that a quorum of at least half of the committee members be present at a meeting (in Even Yosef this means five out of nine

---

[1] The mazkir, of course, makes decisions with the guidance of the land settlement administrations.

[2] For example one villager said that the moshav had to rent the land from the regional council which was not the case. The land belongs to the Jewish National Fund. Another villager believed that the rent would have been even higher, had not Hai Khalifa done the surveying work himself, saving the cost of a professional surveyor. This villager was mistakingly crediting Hai with a skill that he did not possess.

men); minutes must be kept at each meeting, and the committee members in attendance must affix their signatures to the minutes. In Even Yosef, the committee meetings are run by the mazkir. While the positions of 'external secretary' and 'committee head' are legally quite distinct, these two roles are not differentiated in the eyes of most of the villagers, and are both associated with the status of mazkir. Moreover, the mazkir also serves as the 'recording secretary' at the committee meetings, compiling the minutes as the meeting progresses. At the end of each meeting the minutes are signed and validated by the other members of the committee in a perfunctory manner without attempting to examine their contents. And if a quorum is lacking at any meeting, the necessary signatures are added by the absent members at some convenient future time.

Hai's control over the flow of information and resources into the village is one of the major bases of his 'power'. This power is not completely 'naked' however, but is legitimized to the villagers in a number of different ways.

Most of the villagers state that Hai, the mazkir, has the ability and knowledge to fulfill his role, a set of skills not possessed by the majority of the community. He is one of the two people who completed the Italian elementary school in the Gharian. His house boasts a wall covered with books, both religious and secular, which contrasts to the small collection of prayer books to be found in other homes.

The possession of the required intellectual skills is a necessary but not sufficient condition for fulfilling the role of mazkir. The mazkir must be *trustworthy*, an attribute that is stressed when the villagers discuss how Hai Khalifa has managed the village during the past decade and a half. The more the villagers rely on the mazkir to manage their communal and individual affairs, the more the attribute of trustworthiness becomes crucial to an incumbent of that role. Hai communicates his trustworthiness to the villagers in a number of different ways.

Hai exemplifies the religious values of the community. Not only does he observe traditional law and ritual as do other members of the community, but these observances hold a central place in his life. He is frequently accorded the privilege of leading communal readings in the synagogue on festivals. He is a *tūqi'a*, or one who sounds the ritual ram's horn on the *Rūshshana* (Hebrew: *Rosh*

Hashanah, The Solemn New Year). His reputation for knowledge extends to the religious realm as he is respected for his religious learning by other members of the community.

Hai is a 'quiet' person. He is distant from the other villagers with regard to recreation, visiting and so forth. He rarely appears at the village kiosk (which is appended to the cooperative store) in the evening where men gather to drink, chatter and play cards. Also, he rarely attends the celebration of a wedding, of *tfillīn* (religious majority), or a circumcision. Because it is not apparent that he has close friends, it is difficult to charge him with favoritism. 'If there is favoritism', some people say, 'at least he does not show it.' Showing favoritism publicly would be an affront to the social values of the community (p. 127).

A similar stand is taken by the villagers with regard to any personal benefit accruing to Hai from his handling large sums of money going in and out of the moshav. For example, many people feel that Hai takes 'commissions' for himself from the money paid for materials that he brings into the village. Once, when this was discussed by the villagers, Hai posted a notice in the village store that he was deeply hurt by the current rumors and, that so far as he was concerned, the villagers could be responsible for acquiring their own materials in the future. The rumors quickly subsided, as the villagers preferred to leave this task in Hai's hands rather than assume the responsibility themselves. Their attitude was that it is 'natural' for someone to take a small commission, so long as the amount is reasonable. Others in Hai's position, they believed, would take a great deal more.

Hai is financially well off. Aside from the salary he receives as mazkir he enjoys a share of the profits of the citrus grove. He has also planted an additional grove on his own plot, and grows vegetables and raises poultry as well. Because of his wealth he is not as tempted, as would be a poorer man, to tamper with public funds. Also, his own financial security frees him from potential pressure from other wealthy individuals and groups.

Lastly, the mazkir of Even Yosef occupies an interesting kinship position. His father was a Hajjaj, his mother a Hassan, and his wife is from Ben'abbas (the village of origin of the Guweta'). He has no brothers nor did his father have any. He thus occupies a 'balanced' position with regard to the patronymic and village-of-origin groups. To the extent that some villagers are prone to see patronymy and village-of-origin as important principles that might influence Hai's decisions, his balanced position helps structure their perception of the mazkir as being equally 'close' to all.

In a number of immigrant moshavim, where factionalism has hindered the emergence of consensus-based leadership, the villagers and settling authorities have decided to appoint a mazkir from outside the community, who works for a salary, and is accepted by a majority of the villagers (Weintraub and Lissak 1964b: 135). Hai Khalifa, while having lived his life among the Gharian Jews, performs the role of secretary very much like an 'outsider'.[1] I was somewhat startled the first time I observed his behavior in the moshav office when bi-weekly cash payments were made to the members. The villagers came to the main room in the office where Hai sat, and he gave out numbered tickets establishing the order in which the villagers would receive payment. The villagers then went to the next room where, each in turn, the actual payment was made to them by the mazkir pnim. This room was noisy and crowded with people trying to push their way in close to the mazkir pnim, despite the fact that they had received numbers establishing their turns. The beleaguered internal mazkir had to continually extricate himself from a nexus of personalized 'multiplex' relationships, while Hai, in the first room, continued to give out tickets in a quiet and orderly manner, a textbook picture of bureaucratic universalism.

Another incident illustrates the same point. There is a fund in the village which pays premiums on insurance to cover the accidental death of young chicks. The mazkir must affix his signature to any claim made by a villager for the loss of chicks. The mazkir, for his part, must be satisfied that the death of the chicks was accidental and not due to the negligence of the farmer. As the mazkir is not usually on the spot to make this judgement, he relies on the judgement of the agricultural instructor to determine

---

[1] Once, one of the villagers, upon entering the moshav office found me chatting there with several other people. He jokingly said: 'Who is that fellow? Let's make him the mazkir!' He then told me: 'Once an "outsider" came to us in ḥutz laaretz (literally: "outside the land", i.e. in their country of origin), and we made him mazkir (sic!) for twenty years.' He was referring to Sheikh Berkhani (pp. 25–7), about whom he proceeded to give me further information. Shlomo Deshen (personal communication) has suggested that the position of the mazkir in Even Yosef might be illuminated by applying Frankenberg's (1957) concept of 'the stranger'.

whether the claim is legitimate or not. The villager first has to approach the instructor with his claim; if the instructor is satisfied, he signs a note which the villager brings to the mazkir. While the task of the instructor has been characterized as representing 'the village and its affairs... to the outside world' (Willner 1969: 248), in this instance he acts as the mediating link between the villagers and their own mazkir. The procedure of asking the instructor to intervene with the mazkir also is adopted by some villagers who seek loans from moshav funds when they are unsure of getting the mazkir's assent.

There are set hours during which the mazkir is available at the moshav office, and when he walks about the village to see what is going on, because most of his work week is spent away from the moshav in contact with the various bureaus of the land settlement program. In his relationship with the workers in these bureaus, Hai is as much a 'stranger' as he is to the villagers of Even Yosef. He does not have any close friends among the employees of the bureaus, with whom he maintains restrained, albeit cordial, relations.

Just as he attempts to control the flow of information from the outside to the village, Hai also attempts to manage the reverse flow of messages. For example, he will attempt to cover up violations on the part of the settlers, such as the sale of a cow provided to a villager by the Settlement Department. He attempts to maintain an image of Even Yosef as being a quiet and stable community, contrary to a widespread stereotype of Middle-Eastern moshavim, as fraught with kin-based political rivalries.[1] A few of the more sophisticated villagers understand his relationship to the authorities and say that he is 'shy' with respect to them. He only passes on community demands which he considers reasonable and necessary for the moshav's overall development.[2]

[1] This is a popular stereotype about Middle Eastern moshavim which, for example, appears in the newspapers from time to time (cf. Marmorstein 1969: 141–2), and is held by many of the land settlement administrators. This view is also found in sociological analysis, where the label of '*ḥamūla* organization' has been applied. See the extended discussion in the next chapter (pp. 108–11, 118–23).

[2] The following incident is instructive, though I must admit to not having explored the matter thoroughly. Some time about 1955–6 there was insufficient water pressure to irrigate the crops. Despite many complaints by the villagers nothing was done to rectify the situation. The previous agricultural instructor (p. 67) organized some villagers to stage a demonstration at the regional office of the water company (see Weingrod 1966: 94 and Willner, 1969: 372 for accounts of

For their part, the employees of the bureaus are aware that Hai selectively transmits information about village affairs. They believe that so long as the moshav continues to do well in terms of the overall goals of village development, they should not meddle in internal moshav matters. From the very beginning the settling authorities recognized the internal leadership of the community and a 'social instructor' (as opposed to an agricultural instructor, see above, p. 67) was never appointed to Even Yosef. When the current instructor first came to the moshav in 1956, he complained to the authorities of the Settlement Department that Hai Khalifa was somewhat arbitrary in his decisions to extend credit. (Hai was probably over-reluctant to make loans to 'poor-risk' villagers for fear of criticism by the settling authorities.) The workers at the Department's district office said that they knew everything was not perfect in Even Yosef, but that it was best for the instructor 'to play along with Hai'.

Hai Khalifa's 'distant' interpersonal style, with the villagers and with the workers of the bureaus, seems to have psychological, as well as structural, bases. His father died when Hai was very young, and this may be related to his 'acceptance of isolation' (Roe 1953: 48; it will be remembered that Sheikh Berkhani also was an orphan). His cousins report that he would frequently run away from (his mother's) home to their (i.e. his mother's brothers') homes and back again, playing one set of adults off against another.

On the ideational level Hai sees himself as a 'man above the crowd', and his political values are that of a philosopher-king. He claims that democracy is the ideal political arrangement but that 'primitive', uneducated people need a dictatorship until such time as they gradually attain the knowledge necessary for democratic rule. At the present, Hai feels he knows better than the villagers what their own interests are. In discussing leadership with me, Hai once mentioned Winston Churchill, several of whose works, in Hebrew translation, stand on a bookshelf in his home.

In summary, there are many similarities between the status of the Gharian Jewish sheikh and the mazkir of Even Yosef, despite

similar incidents). Hai absented himself from the demonstration saying that he had an appointment in Tel Aviv on that day. Shortly after the demonstration a second well was dug to supply the village with more water.

the vast difference in the concrete role played by each (p. 28). The mazkir is the main link between Even Yosef and the 'outside', and the position has been held by Hai since immigration to the present. The mazkir is by far the most knowledgeable villager about the outside secular world, but he also exemplifies the religious values of the community. He has no close personal or kin ties within the community. The mazkir, like the sheikh, is wealthy. He no longer is expected to help the needy with his personal funds, but does allocate moshav funds for this purpose (p. 99). Similarly he does not entertain outsiders with his own money, but arranges for receptions which are paid for by the moshav.[1] Thus, despite the organizational changes in the role of the community leader, the mazkir is clearly the structural 'descendent' of the sheikh,[2] a status (with a changed name) that has 'survived' in a new social environment.

THE ELITE OF EVEN YOSEF

The mazkir is counted, of course, among the community elite. In terms of knowledge of the world about him, he is head and shoulders above the other members of the community, including most of the elite. This, however, in some measure is due to the nature of his task, which involves the successive learning of inter-action skills demanded by the outside world. These skills, supposedly, could be learned by other individuals with a pre-disposition to do so. The selection of one individual for this unique role (over a long period of time), should not obscure the fact that many of the characteristics of the mazkir are shared by the community elite, in quality, if not in quantity. The present section will consider the elite of Even Yosef in terms of its composition, functions, and continuity with the past.

[1] For example, during my acquaintance with the village, two prominent guests were entertained there. One was a British Jew (well known for his philanthropy and investments in Israel) who had contributed money for the building of a synagogue, and Even Yosef had been selected as the recipient of this donation. He visited Even Yosef when the new synagogue was consecrated. The second was the Head of General Staff who visited Even Yosef during a tour of 'outlying settlements' in which special educational programs were run by the General Staff for village youth (p. 141).

[2] Hai Haddad (from Misurata) also met the traditional requirements of sheikh. Most saliently he (1) had been a wealthy merchant in Tripolitania, (2) apparently was knowledgeable about Israeli society, (3) had a reputation for above-average religious learning, and (4) was an *outsider* with regard to the Gharianites.

Rigorously speaking, it would be desirable to be able to define and operationalize elite status independently of such sources of that status, as wealth and political power. As described below (pp. 100–1), however, the ethnographic reality of Even Yosef provides few public markers of status differentiation, making it convenient to define elite status by using an index of political and administrative participation. I will thus define as 'elite' all those who have been elected to the moshav committee and/or have held important administrative positions[1] in the moshav since its founding to the present.

Twenty-six different members of the community were elected to the moshav committee at least one time in the 13 elections that took place from 1951 to 1965. There is a great deal of overlap between this indicator of elite status and being selected for an administrative position; if we add the individuals who have only served as administrators, it brings the total number of elite individuals to 28. By electing these people, and assigning them responsible jobs, the villagers of Even Yosef give formal recognition of their elite position within the community. The criteria by which the elite are selected are similar to the criteria employed in the less formal selection of the elite in the Gharian, namely wealth, knowledge of the outside world, and religious and social propriety.

In the first instance, there is a clear association between elite status and wealth. Table 6 which is based on a sample of 23 families,[2] and uses an indicator of wealth derived from the ownership of a private citrus grove,[3] shows that in Even Yosef, the elite families tend to be wealthier than the non-elite.

---

[1] These include the following: external secretary, internal secretary, manager of the village store, and local commander.

[2] Data was collected from the households in the village that included male youth (Appendix A). This is not a random sample of the moshav's households, but I see no reason why this sample would be biased with respect to the variables presented in Tables 6 and 7.

[3] The citrus-wealth index is based on the area of citrus grove privately planted by each household, multiplied by the length of time the household owned the grove. As described above (p. 70), many villagers recently have begun to plant citrus trees on their own land. These trees do not bring any income for four years, but after that time the grove yields a fairly secure annual return. The ability to relinquish income from seasonal vegetables while waiting for a grove to mature is thus a good indicator of a family's financial position. Similarly, Weintraub and Bernstein (1966: 510) found that the area cultivated by a moshav farmer to be a 'good measure of development and innovation'.

TABLE 6. *Relationship of elite status and wealth*

Family status	Family wealth		Totals
	Wealthy	Not wealthy	
Elite	6	4	10
Non-elite	3	10	13
Totals	9	14	23

$\phi = 0.375$; P (exact) = 0.073.

As was the case in the Gharian, wealth, in Even Yosef, is associated with 'knowledge of the outside world'. Farming is the most important source of wealth in the community. As moshav farming takes place in a modern technological and economic context, to be a successful farmer involves more than hard work and the mastery of certain technical skills. Weintraub and Lissak (1964*a*: 115–20) discuss the commercial and managerial skills required by the moshav-farmer role. With respect to Even Yosef, I devised an index of 'orientation to the wider society' composed of the following, intercorrelated items:[1] farming ability, receiving a daily newspaper, occupational aspirations for sons, and criticism of the education of the children in the local elementary school. Table 7 shows that the elite tend to be more strongly oriented toward the outside world than the non-elite.

Wealth alone (and greater knowledge of the wider society), is insufficient to earn elite status. A man must demonstrate that any power entrusted to him will be used toward the good of the community, and not solely for his own benefit. Only a man who lives up to the social and religious norms of the community can be so entrusted. Thus there are several entrepreneuring individuals in

[1] The intercorrelation of the items is presented in Appendix B. The relevance of these items to a general variable of 'orientation to the wider society' needs little explanation. Smith and Inkeles (1966) have devised a scale of 'individual modernity', consisting of 119 items, based on research in six developing countries (including Israel). A highly distilled 'short form' of their scale, consisting of 10 items, includes questions dealing with the areas of (*a*) innovation in farming, (*b*) interest in 'news' of the wider society, and (*c*) the importance of education. Questions dealing with occupational aspirations are included in the longer forms of their scale. Later (p. 148), I explain why 'criticism' of the local school is diagnostic of an overall stronger orientation to the wider society.

TABLE. *Status and orientation to the wider society*

Status	Orientation to the wider society		
	High	Low	Totals
Elite	7	3	10
Non-elite	2	11	13
Totals	9	14	23

$\phi = 0.555$; P (exact) $= 0.012$.

the village who have met with economic success but who have not been entrusted with a position of leadership.[1]

The members of the community elite, therefore, also tend to be members of the religious elite. Religious elite status is defined by the practice of a specialty such as shoḥeṭ, mohel, member of the burial society, sounding the ram's horn on rūshshana, or having been a synagogue school teacher in Tripolitania (an indicator of general learnedness). Families[2] that include a member of the political elite, usually include a member of the religious elite, as shown in Table 8. This strongly suggests that political elite status must be backed by religious legitimation.

TABLE 8. *Relationship of elite status and religious status*

Family status	Family includes a religious specialist		
	Yes	No	Totals
Elite	13	3	16
Non-elite	8	20	28
Totals	21	23	44

$\phi = 0.507$; $P < 0.02$.

[1] Two examples are Khlafu the butcher and Bachu the farmer who are discussed in the next chapter.
[2] Here I refer to the 'expanded family', discussed later on (pp. 106–7). Operationally the members of a man's expanded family are his father, his father's father, his brother(s) and his father's brother(s) (and the reciprocals of these). These are the people who are likely to have lived in the same household as Ego at some time in his life.

4

Further evidence of the traditional nature of the elite may perhaps be seen in the fact that the average age of the committee members is generally close to that of the male moshav members (Figure 6, p. 130). In contrast to some other moshavim (e.g. Weingrod 1966: 63–4; Weintraub and Bernstein 1966: 511–12), leadership has not been placed in the hands of the younger members. This will be discussed more fully below (pp. 128–31).

The villagers of Even Yosef utilize traditional criteria in assigning status ranks to members of their community, and also retain traditional expectations with regard to the activities of the elite. The formal moshav framework assigns certain functions to the moshav committee; these might be summed up by saying that the committee should be the executive arm of the political structure of the moshav (Weintraub 1964: 4). However, just as the office of mazkir has been reinterpreted in terms of the traditional sheikh, so the moshav committee is expected to act very much like the traditional elite. Because of this, two of the 'informal', but communally important functions of the moshav committee are the provision of welfare and the settling of disputes.

As described earlier, the moshav committee often 'rubber stamps' the mazkir's decisions. One technique employed by Hai in running the committee is to select, beforehand, how issues will be brought before the committee for decision. This happens, in particular, with regard to making loans to individuals from moshav funds. Villagers often approach Hai personally, requesting to secure a loan from moshav funds. If Hai thinks he should, and can, give the loan, he tells the person to appear at the (approximately bi-weekly) committee meeting and present his request. The fact that the individual concerned appears at this meeting, in a face-to-face encounter with his fellow villagers, is a good indication that he will be granted the loan. If Hai doesn't want to give the loan, he will tell the person that there is no money available, and the petitioner will never appear at a meeting. Villagers who are unsure of Hai's response frequently ask the instructor, or a member of the committee, to intercede with Hai on their behalf.

When Hai makes a decision to grant, or not to grant, a loan, he seems to be concerned, primarily, with the economic sense of the decision. A main consideration is the past performance of the person in agricultural production. This means, to a certain extent, that he extends credit to those who have already demonstrated initiative and achieved economic success. As an antidote to this 'vicious' circle, however, he allows the moshav committee to grant modest loans to poorer villagers, for whom the money represents welfare rather than funds for investment. In financially helping the poorer villagers the moshav committee is fulfilling the same function as the traditional elite (p. 33).

Rather than making executive decisions to implement moshav policy, the moshav committee spends a great deal of time resolving disputes brought before it by members of the community. These disputes are similar to those of villagers everywhere: damage by stray animals, the non-fulfillment of agreements by partners, fist-fights, husband and wife quarrels and so forth. In this realm the committee members feel that they are qualified to express opinions and reach decisions. Hai generally does not attempt to dominate the discussion when the committee deliberates cases that are brought to it. The internal mazkir (who has served on every committee since 1956) and the manager of the cooperative store (who has served on every committee except one – and is probably the most knowledgeable villager next to the mazkir) both complain that the committee wastes too much time deliberating these cases, and not enough time discussing village affairs. However, in playing the roles of mediator and arbitrator, the community elite is again perpetuating its traditional functions.

In addition to the continuity already discussed there is also continuity in the personnel that make up the moshav committee. In terms of the history of the community in Israel, the elite has remained relatively stable, though not rigidly so. In any given election there are usually one or two people elected to the moshav committee who had not been chosen the previous time. Of the 26 different members of the community who had served on the committee through 1966, seven men have served on the committee only once, while six men have been elected to the moshav committee nine or more times.

Next, we may compare the composition of the elite in present-day Even Yosef with the community elite in Tripolitania. While an informal elite existed in the Gharian, there was no official structure parallel to moshav committee (p. 30). Nevertheless, when I asked informants about the composition of the community elite in the past, there appeared a high degree of consensus with regard to the individuals named.

There are seven individuals who were named by all informants as being members of the community elite during the period of the British Military Occupation. We will consider these seven to be 'the elite' and all others to be 'non-elite'. Next, we may ask whether the present-day elite in Even Yosef tend to come from the same expanded families as did the elite under the British. Table 9 shows the cross-tabulation of those families that were members of the elite and non-elite in Tripolitania and in Israel. As may be seen from the table, there is a relatively high degree of continuity of membership in both the elite and non-elite categories.

Table 9 shows seven families who were not members of the elite in Tripolitania, but who have 'risen' to elite status in Israel. This figure is, in part, an artifact of the operational definition of elite status. It might have been more valid to consider, as elite, only those families that have 'sent' members to the moshav committee in several elections. On the other hand, it should be recognized that a certain amount of social mobility has taken place after the community's move to Israel.

TABLE 9. *Elite families in Tripolitania and Israel*

| | Israel | | |
Tripolitania	Elite	Non-elite	Totals
Elite	6	1	7
Non-elite	7	15	22
Totals	13	16	29

P (exact) = 0.019.

While there is a definite tendency for elite status to adhere to the same families, over time, Even Yosef is not a rigidly stratified community. Elite status is more acheived than ascribed and there is an egalitarian ethos that pervades much of daily life in the village (pp.111–17).

There are no clear markers that publicly distinguish the elite from the non-elite. For example the elite and non-elite do not dress differently. It is true, however, that those elite who have salaried (economic or administrative) positions wear 'clean' clothes in their daily work while the farmers necessarily wear 'dirty' clothes. However, the most industrious (and hence very 'dirty') farmers are often wealthier than many of those villagers earning salaries. In the Gharian, the quality of the clothing that one wore on the Sabbath (or other festive occasion) was usually a good indicator of wealth, but, in Israel, the finer distinctions of contemporary clothing have not filtered into the village culture.

With regard to housing, all villagers were given equivalent housing at the outset, except for 10 families given an extra room because of family size. By 1965 many families had added an extra room (or two), sometimes with the loans from the Jewish Agency and sometimes with private capital. Despite this, the exteriors of most houses were still very similar to one another. During my brief visits to the village in 1968–9, however, I was startled by the extent of change in house exteriors. Not only had more people added rooms, but the outsides of many houses had been adorned with porches and colorful decorative stucco. House beautification, while obviously related to wealth, still would not be an infallible index of elite status. A number of people who could afford to decorate their homes have not done so while others who (according to local gossip) 'could not afford to', have spent money on home decoration.

More importantly, however, the people who are in the elite category, ranked by whatever criteria one chooses, are not seen by others, nor do they see themselves as constituting a self-conscious interacting *group*. Thus, there is no clear-cut social-elite category whose boundaries definitely include some people and exclude all others. I offended the egalitarian ethos of the community when I asked 'Who are the "big" or "important" people here?' Replies to this question were: 'Everyone is the same here', or 'You've been around long enough to know who's who'.

The view that, within the community, 'everyone is equal', is contradicted by the economic facts, but does have some basis in institutional arrangements. In addition to the equality in economic opportunities and political rights inherent in the moshav framework, marriage links within the community act as an equalizing factor. As shown in Table 10, while there is some tendency toward 'class endogamy', elite men and women take spouses from the non-elite somewhat more often than they do from families of their own status. This 'free circulation' of women, of course, contributes to the homogeneity in life style among families who differ widely in their economic position.

TABLE 10. *Marriage between elite and non-elite*

Males	Females		
	Elite	Non-elite	Totals
Elite	8	13	21
Non-elite	9	26	35
Totals	17	39	56

Our discussion of leadership in Even Yosef has shown that the community has remained, to a very great extent, autonomous. The traditional forms of leadership, involving the sheikh and the elite have persisted and succeeded, while there has been a direct continuation of personnel, as well. This discussion has been couched in 'structural–functional' terms, and one may legitimately ask whether this portrayal exhaustively describes the political life of the community. In particular, anthropologists have been interested in the way 'kinship' factors influence the political and social life of local communities. The following chapter will consider kinship in the politics of Even Yosef, a matter that has been studied in other moshavim as well.[1] In the course of our discussion we hope to reveal some of the 'dynamics' of village life, that is, sources of potential conflict within the community, and some of the informal ways in which consensual support for leadership, and communal harmony are achieved.

[1] See the next chapter, p. 108.

5. Daily life and politics

FAMILIES IN EVEN YOSEF: NUCLEAR, EXTENDED, AND
EXPANDED

The nuclear family is by far the most frequent form of household
composition in Even Yosef. This is in part due to the formal
structure of the moshav which assigns a plot and house appropriate
to a nuclear family (of 'Western' size) to each settling couple.
I have already discussed (pp. 60–1) how some fathers and sons
divided their remaining goods (such as clothing and utensils)
during immigration and settlement. This should not be taken to
mean that the patrilineal extended family was universal (where
demographically possible) in the Gharian (pp. 35–7). Traditionally,
a certain proportion of sons would hive off from the father's
household, before the father's death. It is likely that the rate of
household fission increased somewhat with the economic opportunities brought by the Italian occupation. The almost complete
disappearance of the extended family form in Even Yosef thus
continued a trend that had started earlier, and which was related
to traditional structural tensions within the family.

The extended family, on the other hand, is not completely a
thing of the past in the moshav. The family of Rebbi Shmuel
(pp. 31–2) is a case in point. Upon arriving in Israel, each of Rebbi
Shmuel's two sons was assigned a house and plot. Rebbi Shmuel,
who was close to 65 years old, lived with his younger son Mūshe,
while the older son set up a separate household. Mushe's eldest
son, Bikhūr, married in the Binyamina camp, but lived in the same
house as his father upon reaching Even Yosef. After several years
the family purchased a plot[1] from an old villager who was not
strong enough to run a farm, but who, by falsifying his age, had

---

[1] Such a purchase can only take place with the agreement of the moshav members,
the Settlement Department and the Jewish National Fund.

been assigned a plot, which he sold, and then moved in with his son. Bikhur moved into his new house which was several hundred meters from his father's home. Later, Mushe's second oldest son married but lived in a section of the house that was added to the original structure. To this day, the nuclear families of Rebbi Shmuel, Mushe and the latter's two married sons constitute a single domestic unit.

Rebbi Shmuel, now close to eighty years old, cuts weeds and grass for fodder, mends bridles, and runs various errands. Mushe, who assisted his father in the Mizda post exchange, works primarily in agriculture, farming his own land and that of Bikhur. The latter is employed full-time in the village store while his younger brother works on a tractor owned by the family. The sons' wives also work as a unit. The household numbers 20 souls. They eat meals together despite the fact that Bikhur lives some distance from his father. Similarly, Bikhur's house has not been provided with hot water and an indoor shower, so his family uses facilities at his father's house. Bikhur and his wife may be seen nightly, returning to the house where they sleep, with four sleepy or slumbering children, after having eaten the evening meal with the other members of the household.

In another case, two brothers, living on adjacent lots, organized themselves as one household. One brother worked full-time as a farmer, cultivating the land of both brothers. The second brother was employed outside the village. After a while, the brothers were able to invest in a second-hand tractor and then in a truck. The first brother continued to work as the farmer, while the second brother brought in an income from working as a tractor operator and hauler. Today these brothers, still unseparated, constitute one of the wealthiest households in the community.[1]

There were two other cases of brothers living on separate plots, but maintaining joint households, but both of these households fissioned during the time I was in the field. The first two cases cited may be contrasted with other families which, from a demographic point of view, have an equal potential to organize themselves into large cooperative domestic units. These other families, however, stand at the opposite end of a continuum of domestic solidarity. There is the instance of a father who has not spoken to

---

[1] The elder of these brothers has been elected to the moshav committee 9 times. Bikhur, the son of Rebbi Shmuel has been chosen in 4 different elections.

his son for over two and a half years. And there are several cases of brothers who are involved in an endless cycle of dispute, reconciliation and dispute.

In addition to the two cases described there are 25 other cases of married fathers who have married sons living in the village. The distribution of residence and domestic arrangements of these 'families' is as follows:

Father and son(s) residing on separate plots and organized into separate families – 9 cases.

Father and son(s) residing on the same plot but organized into separate families – 6 cases.

Father and son(s) residing on the same plot and organized into an extended family – 10 cases.

In six of the last ten cases the farm is 'owned' by the son and the married parents are economically dependent.[1] In two cases the father is the official owner of the farm, but the son is the effective breadwinner and heir apparent to legal household headship. In another two cases the son is the major breadwinner, but is dependent on the housekeeping services of the mother because of separation from his wife.[2] In almost all cases where an elder father has more than one married son living in the village, he lives with the youngest son, who generally has less children than his elder brothers, so the father is less of an economic burden. Thus, the economic separation and independence of fathers and sons appears to be preferred whenever it is possible.

If fathers and sons prefer economic separation, this preference is even stronger with regard to brothers. While there is a marked tendency for brothers to live next to one another in the village (p. 59), this, in most instances, does not imply positive economic cooperation. Rather, the attitude tends to be that living near one's

[1] In most instances the elderly parents contribute as much as possible, in the form of help around the house and light farm work, to the domestic productive effort (p. 104).

[2] In one of these cases the wife continues to live in the house owned by the separated couple while the husband lives in the house (on the plot) next door, with his mother and father. In the second case the wife is institutionalized in a mental hospital. In this latter instance the man's mother died in October 1964 and, as all his daughters were married and living away, there was no woman in the household to carry out the domestic chores. With the help of the mazkir, this man was able to get permission from the Sephardic Rabbinate to enter into a second marriage (with a Moroccan woman), without divorcing his sick wife, as the prognosis indicated that the latter would never recover to lead a normal life.

brother helps *prevent* conflicts that might arise between non-related neighbors. Thus, if children fight, or if a cow strays and destroys crops, it is easier to iron out these matters among brothers than among non-related families.

I have collected 58 cases of economic cooperation in the village, ranging from one-day 'partnerships' for tasks such as seeding a field, through setting up tomato vine posts, to larger enterprises such as the joint ownership of a tractor. The majority of these cases involve a season-long partnership to grow a certain crop on a certain piece of land.[1] Out of these 58 cases, 12.0% involved patrilateral kin, 1.7% involved matrilateral kin, 18.9% involved affines, and 67.3% involved unrelated persons.

For the most part the 'jural' aspect of the relationship between brothers is more in evidence than any sense of fellowship. The primary attitude that a man should adopt toward his father or brothers is that of respect; the relationship between patrikin may frequently be described as mild avoidance. One man explained to me his preference for non-related economic partners in the following terms. 'If I get mad at X (his partner) and "curse him out", the next day we'll forget it. How could I do that with my brother?'

Affinal ties seem to offer better possibilities for economic connections than do patrilineal ties. Perhaps this is because affinal ties have both 'familial' and 'contractual' aspects. A man's 'affines' are those whom he may call *nsībi*, which applies to the following kin-types: wife's father, wife's brother, wife's brother's son, daughter's husband's father, daughter's husband's brother and their reciprocals.

Daily economic cooperation among brothers is infrequent and the same may be said with regard to political cooperation. This does not mean, however, that the brother–brother tie does not have the *potential* of becoming politically significant. A useful concept for discussing this is that of the 'expanded family' (see p. 96, n. 2).

The term 'expanded family' is used by Fortes (1949: 69–70) to denote a group of people who formerly belonged to a single joint family but have since segmented into separate domestic units.

---

[1] For example, a villager may rent a portion of his land to another villager for a season and get a percentage of the profits (usually around 12%), or get a flat sum.

There may exist, among the members of an expanded family, certain types of cooperation, mutual aid, political support, and other forms of solidarity. However, there is a great deal of choice involved in determining the degree to which former members of a single domestic unit will coalesce into a cohesive group.

The expanded family may receive its importance as a social unit because of the way it is perceived by *other* members of the community. For example, the expanded family is the unit that is ranked on a prestige scale by the members of an Arab village community (A. Cohen 1965: 55–9). In other words, members of a community may treat the expanded family as a unit, in disregard of the actual degree of solidarity existing within that group.

In the case of Even Yosef the expanded family is perceived as the significant unit of potential political support. People who at one time lived within the same household expect political support from one another. Though daily interaction between brothers may be casual, there is the expectation among the brothers that when support is needed, a man's brother will stand at his side. Similarly, if X and Y are brothers, then all the members of the community likewise would expect that X will stand by Y's side whenever necessary. They may be perceived as separate units with respect to economic affairs, but politically they both represent the same expanded family. Thus, when a person is elected to the moshav committee, he is seen by his expanded family as their representative, when their interests are involved, and it is assumed by others, also, that a person elected to the moshav committee will act in accordance with his family's interests.

For this reason, it would not make sense to elect two members to the committee from any one family, and thus give that expanded family an unduly strong voice in moshav affairs. Though several members of one expanded family may be elected to the moshav committee in *different* years, they are almost never elected to the moshav committee simultaneously.[1] The rotation of elected committee members within an expanded family reflects changes of a person's status within the family and within the community.

Looked at from this perspective, the 99 individual families of

[1] There is one exception to this generalization. In 1953 two brothers were elected to the committee. Each of these brothers, however, represented different interests, in that the younger was a leader in a movement to place control of the committee in the hands of younger men, and his elder brother represented the traditional elite. This issue is discussed later on in the chapter (pp. 128–9).

Even Yosef may be grouped into 44 expanded families, (some of) which, under certain conditions, may coalesce into politically significant units. The solidarity of the expanded family may be given ritual expression by eating together on festivals such as Passover. There is little evidence, however, of the existence of socially important patri-groups larger than the expanded family. For example, there is no patronymic group endogamy. Neither is there a tendency for patri-relatives to predominate in family celebrations, such as at circumcisions or weddings. In other 'traditional' Middle Eastern moshavim, however, various observers have seen patriliny as an important component of the community's political structure.[1] For this reason the muted patriliny of Even Yosef requires further description and discussion.

THE WEAKNESS OF POLITICAL PATRILINY

Studies of other immigrant moshavim have shown some communities segmented into groups based on kin ties (e.g. Weintraub and Lissak 1964*b*: 135–6), and this phenomenon has been interpreted in terms of the political importance of patrilineal descent in Middle Eastern society. In the case of Even Yosef, as in the Gharian, there is little evidence of the political importance of the patronymic groups (see pp. 35–7). The term *ḥamūla*, which has often been used by the land settlement administrators to refer to Middle Eastern kin factions, is not known to most of the villagers[2] in Even Yosef. Rather than being based on the balanced (or unbalanced) opposition of descent groups, the political structure of Even Yosef features the central position of the mazkir vis-à-vis the other families of the moshav.

Virtually all observers of village life concur on this view. Workers of the Settlement Department call Hai the 'king' of the village, and a few villagers (in partial humor) refer to him as 'our dictator' or 'prime minister'. Being confronted with this mono-

---

[1] There is a popular stereotype of Middle Eastern moshavim as suffering from incessant kin-based feuding. This view appears in the press from time to time (see p. 92, n. 1), and is held by many of the administrators of the settlement program. Social analysts have applied the label of 'ḥamūla organization' to this phenomenon (Weintraub and Lissak 1964*b*: 135–6).

[2] Both Shokeid (1968) and Willner (1969: 199–202), who criticize the 'ḥamūla' model of Middle Eastern moshavim, state that the term 'ḥamūla' often was learned by the settlers from the administrators.

lithic portrait of the impressive power of the mazkir, in relation to everyone else in the moshav, naturally led me to see if I could find anything that was hiding behind it.

One of the most disturbing experiences of my investigative activities in Even Yosef was that, despite my daily visits to the village, I almost never chanced upon overt situations of 'trouble' or dispute. While not wishing to develop the reputation for conflict-mongering, I cautiously proceeded to ask the villagers to tell me about disputes that took place in the village's past. In discussing this matter all informants agreed that there had been more conflicts in the 'history' of Even Yosef than at the time of my field research.

There were two common explanations given for the decline in conflicts in the community over the years. One may be called the *anomie* explanation which stressed the fact that 12 years earlier everyone had been 'new immigrants' who did not know what was expected of them in their new setting. This situation led to many frustrations and conflicts. The second explanation cited economic competition for work opportunities (pp. 64–5) as the main cause of conflict in previous years. A third reason was given by only one man, from Gabes in Tunisia (pp. 55–6, n. 2), and is somewhat more complicated, but worthy of careful consideration.

This individual stated that the first years, after the founding of the moshav, saw the initiation of competition for power among the families of the village. This competition was relatively open, in the new-old community of Even Yosef, and often led to physical confrontation. Gradually, however, a power hierarchy began to emerge with the top position held by an expanded family consisting of ten brothers. Over the years, the man from Gabes claimed, the other Gharianites had become accustomed to this hierarchy even to the point where they take its existence for granted. Consequently the position of the ten brothers is never challenged, resulting in the observable decline in community conflict.

There were several other villagers who, in response to my excessive queries about kin ties in the community, expressed the opinion that kinship was politically important. These people invariably cited the same expanded family, with the patronym Hajjaj, that consisted of ten brothers. The three eldest brothers were sons of one mother, and the seven youngest were sons of another. Nine of these brothers were married, and they ranged in age from 57 to 23 years. Their father was reputed to be 100 years old.

The few individuals who talked about the political activities of the ten brothers complained that 'they control everything'. One man stated that 'they run the moshav and the mazkir is in their hands'. These people pointed to the fact that one of the brothers had been given the job of operating the moshav tractor during the citrus harvest, and that several other brothers had received sizable loans from moshav funds. These sources of income and credit, of course, enhanced the economic position of the brothers.

Most of the villagers, however, denied that the mazkir granted favors on the basis of kinship, and did not admit the existence of kin-based cliques. Faced with conflicting interpretations of moshav political organization, I attempted to collect data on cases in which the ten brothers acted as a political unit.

During the one and a half years of my research in the moshav, I observed (as opposed to heard about) only one instance of concerted action on the part of patrilineally related relatives. This took place at a meeting of about half of the moshav members. The village had acquired temporary rights to a new tract of land. This land was to be divided, by lottery, among those families that wanted additional land. Before the meeting, the villagers had informally decided that new plots would be given only to those families who would personally farm the land. Land would not be allotted to anyone who intended to rent out his plot. One individual, Khlafu the butcher, had registered his intention of securing a new plot, but there was a certain amount of suspicion that he did not plan to engage in the manual labor necessary to cultivate the land. Among those suspicious of Khlafu's intentions were several of the ten brothers.

About 40 individuals had gathered in the moshav office to participate in the lottery and determine which plots would be assigned to which families. When it was Khlafu's turn to receive a plot, one of the ten brothers shouted that he should get no land because he had no intention of farming it himself. Khlafu retorted saying: 'Who do you think you are? You and your brothers grabbing all the jobs! You are not worth a fraction of me.' A second brother joined in and said that Khlafu should be fined several thousand pounds for speaking in that manner and making a scene in the village office. Khlafu again retorted, and a third brother chimed in. This brother, who was a member of the committee, said, however, that everyone should calm down and that Khlafu would get what was due to him as a member of the moshav.

Later, when Khlafu discussed this incident with me, he said that 'they all supported one another because they are brothers'. This case, I repeat, was the only overt manifestation of the political solidarity of brothers that I observed. In order to interpret the activity of the brothers it is necessary to understand their resentment of Khlafu. This leads us to a consideration of the egalitarian aspects of life in Even Yosef.

EGALITARIANISM IN EVEN YOSEF

There is a pronounced egalitarian tradition in the community with reference to the ability of families to provide for their own needs. This is manifest in a number of social contexts. I have already mentioned how charity was given with great discretion (p. 33) so as not to embarrass the needy. The fact that 'gleanings' left in the field were collected mainly by Moslems (p. 17) and not by the Jews, may be an indication of the 'shame' associated with economic dependency.[1] Similarly, after each burial, money is collected from members of the community and this is used to provide the 'meal of recovery' for the bereaved family (cf. Addadi 1865: 126a). The family, no matter how wealthy, cannot refuse this prestation, a practice which is locally interpreted as disallowing the public display of wealth differentials. Thus, in discussing the egalitarian ethos (or ethic), I will refer to three things: the belief that the needy should be helped; the notion that it is shameful to be dependent on others (and a religious duty to provide for oneself and one's family);[2] and the rivalry among

---

[1] I base this interpretation on a parallel case among the Jews of the Jebel Nefusa. The Book of Esther (9: 22) prescribes that on the holiday of Purim the Jews 'send portions' to one another and give 'gifts to the poor'. This customary exchange is not practiced among the Jews of the Nefusa (Hacohen ms: 218b), but rather gifts are given to the children and to Moslems. Hacohen (*ibid.*) explains this in terms of the shame of receiving gifts, and this may also be the reason why Moslems rather than Jews gathered the gleanings in the Gharian.

[2] In terms of the great tradition, the prayer to be said at the conclusion of each regular meal contains the following passage: 'And make us not depend...on the gifts of men, nor from them lend; but let us depend on your abundant, open,

families for economic and social status. Egalitarianism, it will be seen, informs much of the daily life in the moshav.

Egalitarianism and economic innovation

During the initial years of the moshav's existence the villagers purchased meat, to the extent they could afford it, in the neighboring town. During this period Khlafu took the initiative of establishing contacts at the local slaughterhouse. After several years he purchased a second-hand meat-refrigerator from a butcher he had met. He installed this refrigerator in his home, converting one room into a butcher shop. This meant that his family of ten souls (himself, his wife, his father, and seven children) had to confine themselves to three rooms of living space. He became the primary supplier of meat to the village.

On his weekly trips to the slaughterhouse Khlafu met many cattle merchants. He brought these dealers into contact with villagers who had cattle for sale, and for each deal he received a commission from both the villager and the merchant. These activities were one of the sources of resentment which many villagers bore him. Khlafu had a monopoly of the meat business. While the villagers had the option of buying their meat in town, in spite of him, this would have increased the cost to them, because Khlafu undersold the town butcher, and the trip to town involved some expense and a good deal of time.

Khlafu had begun his economic venture at his family's expense. He was one of the last in the village to add new items of comfort to his home, such as modern furniture, indoor toilet facilities, and a washing machine. At a time when other people were adding extra rooms to their homes to accommodate expanding families, Khlafu forced his family into cramped quarters to make room for the butcher shop. He profited on the cattle deals by 'just talking' while everyone else was 'breaking their back' in the fields.

More importantly, however, Khlafu did not hesitate to inform any villager of his opinion of him, and antagonized people who 'had to work with their hands while he worked with his brains'. Some people said that half the village were not on speaking terms

holy and extended hand that we shall never be embarrassed nor ashamed.' Marmorstein (1969: 27) provides a succinct description of egalitarian components in traditional Jewish communal organization (cf. Joffe 1953).

with him. A number of men would never enter his shop but, instead, would send their children or wives on meat purchasing errands.

One individual who was not on speaking terms with Khlafu was a man named *Dīsi*, who was 30 years old and the father of only one son. The average number of children for men in his age category was four to five. Disi, while not an unpopular man, also experienced the criticism of his peers when attempting to 'get ahead'. One of the consequences of large families in Even Yosef is that the women spend many hours washing clothes. Disi was the first individual in the village to purchase a washing machine (in 1963). Neighbors and relatives quickly came to inspect this new item of technology, and their first reaction was critical. The women said to Disi's wife that it did not clean clothes as thoroughly as manual washing. The men said to Disi: 'Why does your wife need a machine? You have only one child.'[1]

These expressions of disapproval were not without ambivalence. By the end of 1964, close to 60% of the village families owned washing machines, and I conjecture that the figure today is in the vicinity of 90%. The cases of Khlafu and Disi exemplify how economic innovators, in production and consumption, respectively, are subjected to the leveling criticism of their peers. The initial criticism, however, is often followed by attempts to imitate the innovator.

Equality, shame, and interpersonal relations

Gossiping, backbiting, and ridicule are common mechanisms of egalitarian social control in small communities. In Even Yosef, face-to-face confrontations (as between Khlafu and the brothers at the meeting) are relatively rare. Although there is much criticism of others, particularly anyone who attempts to raise his position in the economic or prestige pecking order, this criticism is usually indirect rather than forthright.

The villagers of Even Yosef openly recognize this feature of their interpersonal relationships. They say that shame and embarrassment (*ḥāshim*) govern much daily interaction. A person will not directly criticize his neighbor, even though he feels the latter

---

[1] Given the Middle Eastern emphasis on progeny, this is a fine example of how 'a person can...cut another member to the quick by a seemingly innocent statement' (Gluckman 1963: 314).

has wronged him. Rather he will discuss the matter with other members of the community and avoid face-to-face 'embarrassment'. Another common shame-saving technique is to send children on errands which potentially involve a 'loss of face', as Disi and other villagers do when they send children to buy meat from Khlafu. Sometimes villagers sent their children to me, asking a special favor, such as to take them on a long trip. I might easily refuse the children and later both the father and I could pretend that 'nothing happened between us'.

The avoidance of face-to-face confrontation also occurs with regard to economic conflicts. As noted above, the village obtained temporary rights to a new tract of land. This was divided among approximately 40 families and a temporary irrigation network was set up to bring water to the new fields. The new plots, however, strained the water supply available to the village. If everyone tried to irrigate their plots at the same time, very little pressure was available for any one plot. The water reached the new plots through a main pipe line which then branched into two lesser mains, one servicing the upper plots and the other bringing water to the lower plots. When one of the main branches was turned off, there was adequate pressure for the other set of plots. No schedule, however, was established for alternating the water supply between the upper and lower plots.

Initially the villagers handled this dilemma in the following manner. One group would come to the juncture point and shut off one of the main branches, thereby directing water to their own fields. Later still, the first group would return to direct the water in their own favor, and so forth. Oddly enough, despite this hydraulic tug of war, the two groups never appeared at the juncture at the same time and no group switched on the water in the presence of the opposing group.

When I asked the villagers to explain the situation, several people were quite explicit about 'the rules of the game'. Each group was well aware that the other group was turning off the water, but, so long as they did not meet at the juncture point, they could all claim that 'someone was fooling around with the water'. The villagers rerouted the water 'behind one another's backs', in order to avoid a conflict-producing situation, and not because they believed they had successfully concealed the facts about who was tampering with the irrigation system. After about a week of maneuvering, the villagers asked the mazkir to establish a definite irrigation schedule for the new fields.

The villagers are quite cognizant of the nature of their interpersonal relationships. They claim that everyone in the village is 'ashamed' of everyone else. 'Shame' is one of the major reasons they offer to explain the political inactivity of the majority of the community. Everybody is 'embarrassed' to speak up publicly. If a family wishes to refuse a marriage offer made for their daughter, they say 'she is too young to get married' in order to avoid giving an embarrassing rebuff. The term 'embarrassment' or 'ashamed' constantly is used to reprimand children, and to interpret social interaction in the community.

Some villagers see the pervasiveness of embarrassment in community interaction as a function of the kinship network. 'Everyone here is related to everyone else', they say, referring to both consanguineal and affinal links. Several people utilized the image of a *net* in depicting the interrelationships of the village families. Relatives, of course, should not involve one another in embarrassing situations.

Egalitarianism and prestige

That the villagers attempt to avoid situations which will publicly embarrass people, or show one person to be the inferior of another, does not mean that the community of Even Yosef is not concerned with social ranking. On the contrary, the egalitarian emphasis is the obverse of a persistent concern with rank and prestige.

As stated, one of the primary factors in determining social rank is wealth. Village norms do not tolerate an ostentatious display of wealth, but individuals may hint at their growing affluence in subtle ways which do not invite leveling attacks. For example, Ma'atūq Hajjaj, who works as an irrigation plumber, sometimes drives to the village store in the evening to purchase a pack of cigarettes. He may not need the cigarettes at the particular time, but he does not miss the opportunity to let others know that he owns a pick-up truck.

Ownership of a tractor is also a significant indicator of wealth. More than a dozen families own tractors, either singly or in partnership. In some instances, when tractors are utilized during most of the work week, they represent economically sensible investments (e.g. as in the cases of extended families cited earlier). The average moshav farmer, however, does not need a tractor regularly. It is economically wiser for him to hire a tractor from time to time when needed. Nevertheless, a number of villagers, hesitant to invest in productive enterprises outside the village, have purchased tractors for their farms. These tractors, which sit idle most of the time, are an economic liability, but they serve to bring prestige to their owners.

Washing machines have also become significant status symbols in the village. Most families own locally produced machines while the mazkir and one other villager named *Bachu* own Italian-made automatic machines, which cost nearly twice as much as the Israeli models, and thus clearly indicate the wealth of the owner. In short, the egalitarian ethos of Even Yosef does not grow out of an absence of concern with prestige, but refers to the lively and continual participation in the village ranking system.

Egalitarianism and politics

The villagers of Even Yosef, though they seek wealth and prestige, are quite cautious with respect to political power. They do not want power because it means responsibility and vulnerability. Those who are elected to the moshav committee are glad to accept the prestige which accrues to that position but they do not, by virtue of their election, become important participants in the decision-making processes of the community. In addition to the prestige involved, the villagers are glad to be elected to the committee for two further reasons. First, membership in the committee sometimes provides an avenue to economic gain, and, second, such membership may lead to the institutionalization of rules that actualize the egalitarian ethos of the community.

Elections for the moshav committee were held once during my stay in Even Yosef. Two individuals were elected who had not served on the previous committee. They were Ma'atuq Hajjaj (the irrigation plumber) and *Eli* Hassan. Ma'atuq, at an earlier date, had purchased a movie projector. At one of the first meetings of the new committee he proposed that the moshav provide entertainment for the youth and show films once a week. This program was adopted and Ma'atuq got the contract to show the films. At the same meeting, the committee had to select an individual to work on the moshav tractor during the coming citrus harvest. This job had been held the previous year by one of the ten brothers. The new committee did not, however, select the Hajjaj brother again, but chose, instead, another person who was the economic partner of Eli Hassan.

Later, when I asked the Hajjaj brother in question what he thought of the new committee, he replied that 'they were no good and they were only out for themselves'. He asserted that Ma'atuq Hajjaj and Eli Hassan colluded, each voting for the other's economic advantage. I did not attend this committee meeting, but my guess is that there was no conscious 'deal' between Ma'atuq and Eli. Rather, Eli was probably 'embarrassed' to vote against Ma'atuq's movie proposal, and Ma'atuq was, in turn, 'embarrassed' to vote for a tractor-operator other than Eli's partner. In any event, it is clear that the moshav committee is perceived as instrumental in furthering one's personal economic position. The villagers do not campaign actively to be elected to the committee, but they do not hesitate to exploit this position if they are elected.

The committee is also used to establish rules aimed at egalitarian leveling. One such rule was mentioned above, namely, that new land be allotted only to families who would farm the land themselves. Another instance had to do with Bachu, the wealthy villager with the Italian washing machine. During the 1963–4 citrus harvest a new method of shipping oranges from the groves was initiated. This involved the use of large crates which could not be lifted manually. In order to move them, a hand-operated hydraulic fork-lift had been developed which could be harnessed to a horse. These lifts cost several thousand lirot apiece, and the moshav purchased four of them. Bachu got the idea that if he personally purchased a lift he could rent it to the moshav, as well as use it on his own land. Other villagers were resentful, and they suggested to the committee a rule that the moshav should use only its own lifts, and should not rent any from private individuals. As Bachu was the only person who owned such a lift, it is clear that he was the target of this rule.

EGALITARIANISM AND THE PATRONYMIC GROUP MODEL: THE TEN BROTHERS INTERPRETED

The preceding section, I believe, provides some of the clues to understanding the case of the ten brothers. Villagers often participate in the political process with nonpublic goals in mind. Similarly, the political activities of others are frequently interpreted primarily as instrumental to their private economic advancement. The egalitarian ethos stresses help to, and non-embarrassment of, the poor, but it provides no justification of direct criticism of another's economic success. Rather, leveling attacks against economic advancement are transformed into other types of criticism, notably, complaints about political machinations. The statement that the ten brothers 'run the village' should be interpreted as 'some of the ten brothers are rising too rapidly on the ladder of economic and social success'.

The father of the ten brothers, who is the oldest man in the village, began his career as a humble blacksmith in the Gharian. Over a period of about 50 years he significantly improved his economic position. He became one of the large-scale merchants, and he built an olive press on the main street of the village. After the beginning of the Italian colonization, he was one of three villagers to import diesel engines to power his olive press. Initially, his older sons were partners in his business enterprises.

Along with its accruing wealth, his family also grew in prestige. His eldest son was appointed 'assistant sheikh'[1] under the British

---

[1] The assistant sheikh was a status that was introduced by the British. As far as I can ascertain, it came about in the following manner. At first the British Military administration approached the urbanized Jews of Gharian-town to seek their advice and aid in administering the local Jewish community (p. 27, n. 1). As a result of this, a separate sheikh was appointed for each of the three settlements. The man who was appointed sheikh of Gharian-town was a lawyer who originated from Tripoli. He suggested that an assistant sheikh be appointed in Tighrinna to forestall quarrels between the Hajjaj and the Hassan. This, of course, challenges the claim that the patronymic groups were politically unimportant. It is my interpretation, however, that the lawyer's suggestion was not based on an accurate knowledge of social organization in Tighrinna, but on a common stereotype of the various 'mountain' Jewish communities as being 'just like the Arabs' (cf. Goldberg 1965), implying the importance of lineage organization. Thus, the contemporary Israeli view of Middle Eastern moshavim as being organized into *ḥamūla*s, has precedents in the urban-rural stereotypes of North Africa. With regard to the assistant sheikh, the evidence I have indicates that he did not share in the power of the sheikh, and that leadership was linked to one status as in the past,

Military Occupation. However, the family was still considered *nouveau riche*, partly owing to the recentness of their wealth, but also because they had not consolidated and legitimized their social position by assuming roles of religious leadership, or learning specialized religious skills.[1]

As previously discussed, the migration to Israel brought about a general economic leveling of the community (cf. Weingrod 1962: 125–6). For many of the families, their new economic position was as poor as it always had been, but some of the older elite families, who experienced this sudden economic decline, nevertheless retained some of the prestige of their former social standing.[2] In the case of the family of the ten brothers, the economic leveling attendant upon migration seemed most appropriate to the egalitarian ethos of the community. The ten brothers, in the eyes of many of the villagers, returned to the economic position 'in which they belonged'.

Despite the setback, a number of the brothers, in Israel, in effect recapitulated the successful career of their father. They learned the techniques of modern agriculture and devoted themselves to the labor necessary for successful farming. They were receptive, also, to the economic and managerial skills called for by moshav organization. Some of them also exploited non-agricultural sources of income, such as truck driving, operating a tractor, guarding the citrus grove, and assisting with administrative details in the moshav office. The brothers, along with other enterprising villagers, pressed the mazkir for loans, and the latter tended to give extensive credit to those who demonstrated economic initiative and success. In short, many of the ten brothers 'made good' in relatively few years, and consequently earned the envy of the other villagers.

On the other hand, it would be incorrect to maintain that the economically successful brothers were simply clean-cut, thrifty entrepreneurs, unjustly maligned by the less fortunate villagers. An explanation of their political and economic position, that was given to me by Bachu (the man with the Italian washing machine and the hydraulic fork-lift), seems to be close to the 'truth':

[1] The family did, however, take steps in that direction. One of the sons served as an assistant to the rebbi-teacher in the Gharian, and another was initiated into the communal burial society in Israel.

[2] See Willner (1962: 227–8), Deshen (1965: 76–81), and Minkovitz (1967) for examples of intra-community prestige relationships surviving the migration to Israel.

Bachu told me that he has more land that anyone else in the village. I asked how that came to be. He said he just took some land (small plots on the edge of roads or public places not belonging to anyone). He said that once the members of the committee decided that he was grabbing too much land, and said that they would fine him IL 200 if he were to plant on a certain public parcel again. He said that he took one of the committee members aside, he didn't want to say who, and threatened to kill him if the fellow didn't defend him (Bachu) at the next meeting. Bachu listened to the next committee meeting through the window and the fellow did speak up. Hai (the mazkir) asked the fellow why he changed his mind on the matter, but he still defended Bachu. I asked him if there were other villagers who used these sorts of tactics, but he didn't want to mention names at first. Later he mentioned X, Y, and Z (the latter two are among the younger ten brothers)...He said that recently Y got a loan from Hai (that is, from the moshav funds with Hai's authorization) of IL 5,000. Bachu wanted a loan of IL 3,000 and went to Hai, who told him that he didn't have the money. Bachu asked him 'How did you get the money for Y?' Hai said that he gave the money 'for the sake of peace'. Bachu said, 'Well give it to me too for the sake of peace'. He eventually got the loan. Bachu said that the people who threaten like that really don't intend to do anything, they just want to see how far they can get with threatening. They know that if they were to carry out their threats they would be taken to court...He said about the people who threaten in order to get their way that 'a barking dog is less dangerous than one which is quiet', indicating that this is an Arab proverb...He said that when people like Y or Z threaten others, a villager is not afraid that all ten brothers will gang up on him, but is afraid of them individually (extracted from field notes).

Another villager who claimed that the mazkir gave in to pressure of this sort from some of the ten brothers cited a different Arab proverb about *c. familiaris*, namely, 'when a dog barks, throw him some meat'. In any event, it seems that the social advance of several of the brothers may be a function of both economic and interpersonal 'aggressiveness'. Threats of violence to other villagers, or threats about 'causing trouble for the mazkir', might be made as individuals, but the individual brothers may capitalize on the tendency of other villagers to perceive greater family solidarity than actually exists among the ten brothers. It is clear that the unity of the aggressive brothers does not extend to all ten of them, and the aggressive tactics used by two of the brothers is not exclusive with them, but may be resorted to by other individuals. Any mutual support that might exist among the brothers in this matter is no greater than one might expect from any 'expanded family', and does not indicate the importance of lineage organization in village politics. The opinions of other villagers about this matter will now be considered.

A survey of models of community political structure

My interpretation, then, of statements such as 'the ten brothers run the village', is that they do not portray accurately the village political structure, but rather reflect the resentment of certain villagers toward the economically 'aggressive' brothers. To test this interpretation, I decided to survey which villagers held which political opinions, and I extracted from my field notes all the statements that had been made to me about village politics. I found that I had sampled the opinions of 33 moshav members, two resident non-members, and two ex-residents of the village. These individuals do not constitute a systematic sample; they were selected in an ethnographic fashion, namely, by seeking individuals who, it seemed, would further my understanding of moshav political organization. The sample is undoubtedly biased in that it contains a relatively large number of individuals who are active in village politics, and it is probably biased in containing a relatively high proportion of people who have come into conflict with one or more of the ten brothers. It is, therefore, interesting to compare some attributes of this sample to the attributes of the universe of (male) moshav members. Table 11 presents the distribution of patronymic groups in my 'political opinion sample' and does not differ widely from the distribution of these groups within the village as a whole (see p. 35). The average age of the villagers in the sample is 38 years, whereas the average age of all village members is 44 years. Within the total village, 28% of the members have served on the committee at one time or another, whereas 38% of the sample have served as committee members. The social significance of these latter two differences is that the sample overrepresents politically active villagers, and probably also people who are 'trying to get ahead'.

In order to add an extra measure of objectivity to the evaluation of the political opinion data, I asked a graduate assistant to rate the individual opinions on the question of whether the ten brothers controlled the village. After completing his initial judgements,

TABLE 11. *Patronymic groups in the political opinion survey*

Patronymic group	Number of families	Percentage
Hajjaj	15	41
Hassan	9	24
Guweta'	6	16
Others	7	19
Totals	37	100

I suggested that he re-evaluate the ratings and take into consideration data not included in the extracted field notes. The second set of judgements resulted in the following ratings:

Rating	Number
Ten brothers do not control village	17
Ten brothers do control village	7
Insufficient information	9
Opinions expressed by ten brothers themselves (not rated)	4
Total	37

In four out of the 'insufficient information' cases I confidently assigned the rating of 'do not control'. The set of combined ratings yields 21 out of 28 people, for whom ratings were made, who do not think the ten brothers run the village. Table 12 lists the seven individuals rated as believing the ten brothers do control the village, and some data concerning each of them.

A perusal of Table 12 suggests that many of the individuals so listed, either aspire to social rank that they have not yet achieved (D Guweta', I Hajjaj), or aspire to regain a rank which they once occupied (AB, C Hajjaj, E Guweta', GH?). From a social psychological perspective they may be characterized as experiencing 'status inconsistency'. Thus Bachu Hassan is highly respected for his agricultural skills but does not have the overall prestige that his wealth would suggest. Similarly, AB and E Guweta' are held in regard for their knowledge of the outside world, as indicated by their election to the moshav committee, but neither of them feels that his economic position is commensurate with his prestige rank. Research has suggested that 'status inconsistency' is related to a preference for change in the distribution of power (Goffman

TABLE 12. *Social characteristics of villagers who believe that 'the ten brothers control the village'*

AB The man from Gabes	Elected to the moshav committee twice, in 1952–3, but not re-elected since. Works primarily as a small-scale construction contractor outside village.
C Hajjaj	His wife is the sister of former sheikh Khalifa (1942–9). Relatively prosperous in the Gharian, as a merchant, and relatively poor in Israel.
D Guweta'	A non-Gharianite but raised by his sister in Even Yosef. No longer lives in Even Yosef. He is one of the most achievement-oriented villagers whom I met.
E Guweta'	Former farm-work coordinator of the village (about 1954–5). Often elected to the moshav committee but rarely attends meetings.
Bachu Hassan	The wealthiest farmer in the village, his income coming solely from agriculture (see pp. 120–1).
GH	From Misurata. His family suffered many medical misfortunes, and he is dissatisfied with the welfare and insurance payments. He is subject to the severe criticism of the other villagers because of his unwillingness to work in agriculture (he was an itinerant peddler in Tripolitania). He eventually left the moshav.
I Hajjaj	Son of the mazkir. Lives in a neighboring Yemenite moshav. He is not highly regarded by the villagers, particularly in comparison to his father.

1957), or influences an individual's perception of the structure of his society (Landecker 1963). In the case of Even Yosef, it thus seems, status inconsistency is related to the political opinion that the village is controlled by the ten brothers.

EGALITARIANISM AND ECONOMIC DEVELOPMENT

Foster (1965), in his formulation of the 'Image of Limited Good', has shown that egalitarian leveling is common to peasant communities in many areas of the world. It is difficult for me to judge to what extent the leveling behavior in Even Yosef is governed by a Limited Good cognitive orientation, though it is interesting to note the presence of symptomatic traits, such as 'tales' about finding hidden treasures (Foster 1965: 306). The Gharian Jews, however, have long been familiar with buying and selling as a source of profit, and their own economic development in Israel would, it seems, belie the validity of any zero-sum world view that they might have had. Moreover, in certain ways, the egalitarian ethos seems also to work for positive economic development, and not only toward leveling.

It was noted above that innovations are often imitated quickly by the villagers. The agricultural extension worker successfully exploits this 'keeping-up-with-the-Hajjaj's' motivation, for the purpose of diffusing new agricultural techniques within the community. Sometimes slavish imitation leads to waste, as in some cases of tractor buying cited above. Another instance occurred when two wealthy farmers attempted to compete with Khlafu's butcher business and built a shop to contain a new refrigerator and meat counter that they purchased. As the result of a personal insult their partnership dissolved after a week, and the new butcher shop remained unused. In other cases, however, egalitarian-motivated imitation has led to the acquisition of improved techniques of farming and marketing.

Similarly, egalitarianism serves to raise the consumption standards of the villagers. Villagers are 'shamed' into providing their families with the same new comforts that neighbors and relatives have acquired. In one case the advance in living standards was channeled through the political structure. A number of people wished to replace the original concrete floors of their homes with stone tiles, the standard flooring material in Israeli homes. After some discussion, it was decided that every home in Even Yosef ought to have tiled floors. The village's reputation would be stigmatized if a few families, who could not afford a new floor, retained the cement floor indicative of the status of new and poor immigrants. The task of tiling the village homes was delegated to the mazkir so that the issue would not depend upon individual initiative. The mazkir implemented this program, and today every building in Even Yosef boasts a tile floor.

In sum, egalitarian leveling may curb the economic advance of some villagers, but just as often it promotes the economic development of others. In the political sphere, too, egalitarian-oriented activity may serve both to support the autocratic community structure and to provide checks on excessive inequality.

EGALITARIANISM AND POLITICAL LEADERSHIP

In the 'political opinion survey' described above, ten individuals spontaneously explained the political inactivity of the majority of the villagers in terms of 'shame and embarrassment'. People do not question the decisions of the mazkir because they 'are embarrassed in front of him'. Issues are not discussed openly at public meetings because opposition to a point of view is interpreted as a brazen attack on some other person's interests. For example, many young farmers point to the fact that a good proportion of the committee members also earn salaries (pp. 95, 128), and claim that their own economic interests are not adequately represented on the moshav committee. At the same time, they bemoan the fact that they lack leadership because 'everyone is ashamed to speak up'.

Anyone who does attempt to assume leadership risks the embarrassment of being shouted down or ridiculed. On the other hand, a person who will not assume leadership, after much quiet complaining about decisions and policies, is also criticized for lack of 'blood'. A certain villager, who was elected to the committee a number of different times, was frequently criticized for not voicing his privately expressed opinions at public meetings. This individual, and others, do not 'speak up' at public gatherings because they lack confidence in the strength of their support. A person who is wealthy, or who, according to some, has many relatives, may be somewhat more willing to challenge public opinion, or the mazkir. Those who lack such supports fear that, were they to voice their opinions publicly, their supporters would silently 'back down' and leave them exposed in embarrassing solitude. Moreover, by openly challenging the opinion or decisions of the mazkir, a person presumes to be of equal status to him. Few villagers are willing to risk the exposure to shame implied in that sort of challenge.

The egalitarian ethos, then, serves to encourage prestige competition among the members of the community while inhibiting challenges to the position of mazkir. Leveling competition among many individuals and families also emphasizes the importance of a status which stands above personal and particularistic loyalties. In short, egalitarian activity serves to maintain the position, and facilitate the effectiveness, of the community leader.

On the other hand, because the mazkir is assured of his position, he is expected to refrain from wantonly shaming those below him. This may be illustrated by briefly considering the status of the internal secretary of Even Yosef (pp. 52, 66). This position involves a great deal of responsibility, and relatively little authority, in comparison with that of the mazkir. The latter makes the major decisions regarding the allocation of resources within the community, whereas it is the task of the internal secretary to assure that these resources are in the right place at the right time; that the irrigation system is working, that there are crates available for the harvests, that poultry is delivered to the market, and the like. The internal secretary is in daily contact with the villagers, while the mazkir spends much of his work week away from the village. The former, therefore, bears the brunt of much of the daily bickering and leveling challenges of moshav life.

The position of internal secretary has been held, for about nine years, by an individual named Nissim, who is five years younger than the mazkir, and is the age-mate of some of the active farmers. Though he is respected, he is considered fair game for egalitarian challenges, and people do not hesitate to insult, curse at, and argue with him over minor inconveniences. Nissim believes that the villagers are not angry with him personally, but that 'they just act that way when they are annoyed'. He explains that it is necessary to 'treat them as your children', that is, gradually coax them out of their 'temper tantrums'. He claims that both he and the mazkir are able to keep aloof from this sort of bickering, but it is his opinion that few other villagers have that ability.

Many villagers agree that Nissim's willingness not to reciprocate in egalitarian exchanges is an essential ingredient to his maintaining the position of internal secretary. Three individuals held similar jobs before him, but neither of them lasted more than a few years. These individuals took the egalitarian challenges and insults 'to heart', and so were not able to withstand the pressures. One informant explained that Nissim, whose family was one of the wealthiest in the Gharian, was thus able to shrug off these challenges. The preceding petty administrators, less sure of their social positions, could not confidently remove themselves from the area of competition. Therefore, he explained, they had to eliminate themselves from their positions of minor leadership.

Another implication of the egalitarian ethos is that the mazkir, whom everybody acknowledges to be 'superior', ought not ostentatiously to display reminders of his status. Rather, he should be 'quiet' and modestly conduct himself with dignity. Were he to communicate 'loudly' the fact of his high position, e.g. by excessively beautifying the outside of his home, or by purchasing an automobile for leisure and display, this would immediately bring forth leveling criticism. The interior of Hai's house is, in fact, quite nice, as behooves a man in his position. His house, and the front yard of his plot, however, are hidden by a tall hedge which makes his home invisible to the passerby. The only other villager who has such an impervious hedge is the man who manages the village store. While the interior of his house is quite modest, he may be fencing-off curious and potentially envious eyes, because he earns a good salary for work that in process and product is not very visible.

VILLAGE OF ORIGIN, AGE, AND OCCUPATION

In discussing the place of kinship in village politics, I have concluded that patriliny beyond the limits of the expanded family is politically unimportant. Nevertheless, as seemed to be the case with patronymic groups in the Gharian (pp. 41–3), the villagers do retain the *awareness* that patrilineal links may become the basis of political loyalty. Another potential line of cleavage (which is somewhat related to patriliny) is along the lines of village-of-origin in the Gharian.[1] There are several reasons why this has not become significant. In the first instance the Ghaina greatly outnumber the 'Abbasiya (p. 12), so that the latter in no way could constitute an effective political rival to the former. Secondly, the 'Abbasiya feel 'close' to the mazkir, as his wife is from Ben'abbas. She has two married brothers and two married sisters which gives Hai four 'brothers-in-law' (nsībāt) among the 'Abbasiya, three of whom have served on the moshav committee.[2] The Ghaina and the 'Abbasiya have been elected to the committee in numbers roughly proportionate to their strength in the village. While I never specifically asked villagers for whom they voted in elections, I feel

---

[1] Deshen (1965) analyzes an immigrant moshav characterized by conflict between two groups originating from neighboring, but distinct, communities in Jerba.

[2] As noted in Chapter 2, several sheikhs were nsībāt with the sheikhs they succeeded by virtue of marriage to the daughter of the sheikh (pp. 24, 26–7).

safe in asserting that voting does not strictly follow village-of-origin lines (though this factor probably plays some part), and that in many instances people cast votes for individuals from the other village of origin.

There are two other factors which are potential (but not actual) symbols of serious political cleavage: age and occupation. These are interrelated and now will be briefly discussed.

As indicated above (p. 95), the villagers who are given responsible administrative jobs are also likely to be elected to the moshav committee because of their greater knowledge of the wider society. This means that a fair number of the committee members have an important source of income other than agriculture. The non-farmer character of the committee is further emphasized by the fact that it includes several people who have shown individual economic initiative. This is illustrated in Table 13 which lists the most recent committee members (elected in 1967), and their 'occupations' (aside from farming).

TABLE 13. *Committee members* (1967) *and their special occupations*

Committee member	Special occupation
Hai Khalifa Hajjaj	Mazkir
Nissim Hassan	Internal mazkir
MN Hassan	Night watchman
OP Hajjaj (one of the ten brothers)	Watchman of the citrus grove
Eli Hassan	Part owner of a tractor
QR Ba'dash	Part owner of a tractor
ST Hassan	Manager of the village store
UV Haddad	Youth activities coordinator for the three Po'el Mizrahi moshavim
Ma'atuq Hajjaj	Irrigation plumber

A few of the younger and active farmers have complained that the committee does not represent their interests. Their contentions seem to place equal stress on the notions of 'young' and 'farmer', and it is difficult to know which is uppermost in their thinking. There have been, in the past, some attempts among the young to organize their voting, and to place their age-mates in the committee. This happened as early as 1952, when two of the ten brothers were elected to the committee, one 'representing' the younger leadership, and the other identified with the traditional elite. There were similar attempts in 1963, and, perhaps in the succeeding elections. While there has been greater representation of the young in recent years, the shift has been gradual, rather than dramatic, and there does not seem to be any drastic change in the criteria people employ in selecting committee members. Thus, the members of the above listed committee tend to be wealthy, to come from expanded families that include a religious specialist, and to be relatively knowledgeable about the wider society. In spite of the desire to have 'farmers' on the committee, it seems that the election of younger members has not changed the traditional 'non-farmer' nature of the elite.[1]

The gradual change in age composition of the committee is shown in Figure 6. The straight (dotted) line shows the average age of the adult male members of the village (extrapolated from 1965), while the zig-zag line shows the average age of the committee members (from 1951–67). As may be seen, the two lines do not differ widely, but in the earlier years the committee members tended to be slightly older than the average villager, while in recent years they have been slightly younger. Thus the gradual change in the age of the committee personnel does not seem to stem from a dramatic change in structural principles.

If this is so, then one would expect the younger members of the committee slowly to come to resemble the older elite. The nightly male gathering near the village kiosk may provide one example of this process. Each weekday night many of the adult and adolescent males gather outside the kiosk[2] to drink, play cards and discuss village affairs. While many different men might play cards from time to time, there are a handful of individuals who gamble almost nightly. Playing cards for money is not viewed as a moral violation,

---

[1] In Deshen's analysis of the conflicts in a Jerban moshav (1965: 85), he found that the claim of some villagers that only farmers should serve on the moshav committee did not reflect an ideological commitment but a political maneuver, disguising community-of-origin based loyalties.

[2] Thwaite (1969: 93), in describing his visit to Gharian-town notes that it is rare 'for an urban Libyan to invite one into his home...cafes are the places for social meetings'. This seems similar to the main pattern of informal male gatherings in Even Yosef, namely, meeting at the kiosk in the evening. There are no chairs and tables at the kiosk, but people 'stand around' or sit on the ground. In the neighboring Yemenite moshav, homevisiting seems to predominate over outside 'socializing'.

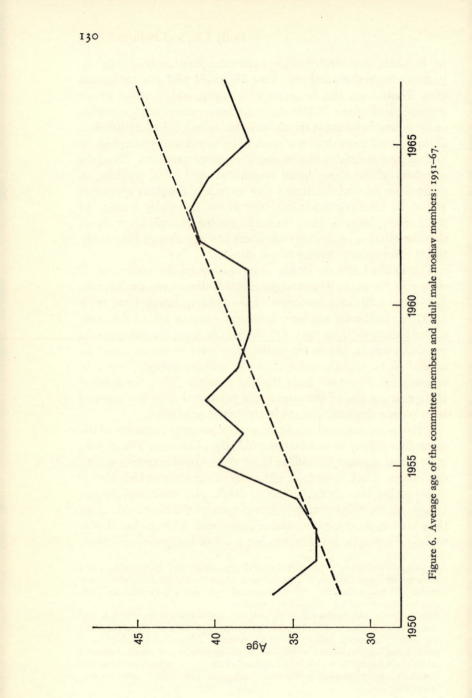

Figure 6. Average age of the committee members and adult male moshav members: 1951–67.

but it is acknowledged that there is more merit in abstention than indulgence. Among this handful of regular players are three men who challenged the mazkir, in the name of the 'young', during the early years of the moshav's existence (Hai Khalifa was only 37 in 1951 but these men are 10–15 years younger). Their nightly game probably shows, indirectly, the players' ability to lose money, thus qualifying them for leadership on the criterion of wealth.[1] On the other hand, their more casual morality puts them in structural opposition to the mazkir, who never socializes at the kiosk. One of these men was elected to the committee in 1964 and 1965. If my thesis about the stability of criteria for elite status is correct, one would predict that this man's card playing will gradually diminish. I do not have the data, however, to confirm, or infirm, this prediction.

It would be an overstatement, however, to claim that the present elite is an exact replica of earlier elites. The younger members of the committee have a greater understanding of Israeli society than their elders. They also have a greater knowledge of, but a varying commitment to, the democratic principles that ideally should govern moshav life. Thus the gradual change in committee personnel is perhaps bringing with it subtle changes in the committee's *organization*, which, over time, could result in significant *structural* change (Firth 1954: 17).

A similar position might be taken with regard to the criteria for selection to elite status. While wealth and socio-religious propriety were important criteria in the Gharian, and continue to be important in Even Yosef, their *relative* importance may have changed, the former gaining at the expense of the latter. Thus, one villager said to me: 'Then (in the Gharian), we would compete as to whose children studied or chanted better; now we compete as to who has the most money.' Again, my data does not enable a refined comparison of the criteria of social rank in the Gharian and in Israel, which might illuminate some of the mechanisms of gradual change.[2]

[1] Gambling is also a special feature of the holiday of Purim in the village. Each year there are some individuals who lose (and, of course, who win) large sums of money (up to IL 1,000). Those people who lose money can afford to do so, and the fame of their economic losses is immediately credited to their prestige account.

[2] The notion that detailed organizational change can, over time, result in structural change may be likened to the biological process whereby individual mutations and intraspecific variation account, in the long run, for evolution into new structural

We have examined family life in Even Yosef, from the point of view of its relevance to village politics, and have concluded that patrilineal kinship ties are not politically important outside of the expanded family. Thus, Even Yosef, viewed as a community which has coped and is coping with a changing environment, is not internally divided into opposing factions (cf. Shokeid 1968). Rather, the individual families are the main units competing for economic rewards, prestige, and to a lesser extent political power. While there is some dissatisfaction with existing leadership arrangements, the 'opposition' is not great enough to bring about structural change, and is 'handled' adequately by the existing social mechanisms. In particular, the rank-and-file members of the community, while they lag behind the elite in realizing the newly defined material goals of the Israeli setting, have not dropped out of the 'egalitarian' race, and both aspire to and successfully attain some of these newly desired rewards.[1]

There is, it seems, a rather close connection between the continuity of leadership and the lack of factionalism, which becomes clearer on the basis of a comparison with North African immigrants to Israel from the countries of former French domination. While the immigration of Jews from Libya to Israel was almost total, the direction of immigration from French North Africa was divided almost equally between Israel and France (Bensimon 1969). This differential migration was (self-) selective as well, for the migrants who moved to France were, on the whole, more urbanized and westernized in terms of education, occupation and income than those who moved to Israel (*ibid.*). If we assume that these attributes (more modern education, a Western type profession, and so forth) were associated with leadership in the former Jewish communities of North Africa, then the selective migration

forms (species). Parsons' (1953) model of social stratification, and Kluckhohn's (1961) theory of value orientations emphasize that societies differ in the *relative emphasis* given to different values. Kluckhohn and Strodtbeck (1961: 46–8) suggest that value-orientation changes in which the relative emphasis placed on different values is only slightly altered, may be less disruptive than those changes in which there is a total shift of emphasis. In a comparative study of four moshavim, Weintraub and Parness (1968) find 'modernization' associated with a shift of emphasis, in assigning social rank, from 'reward-consumption' criteria to 'means-production' criteria.

[1] As will be described in the next chapter, there is no great intergenerational cleavage in Even Yosef with respect to the attachment to and acceptance of Israeli culture, further sharpening the picture of 'smooth' cultural change.

of North African Jews (excluding Libya) resulted in the 'decapitation' of many of the original communities.

With regard to settlement on the moshavim this means that many of the North African communities[1] confronted the settlement crisis without the benefit of traditional leadership which proved so important in the case of Even Yosef. In short, the 'decapitation', or, if I may, 'decephalation' of these communities, may partially account for the widespread phenomenon of 'acephalous' (Evans-Pritchard 1940: 296) organization in the new North African moshavim, reflected in factionalism dressed in the garb of 'patrilineages'. To document this hypothesis would require a set of comparative studies of new moshavim which pay detailed attention to each village's particular history.

In the case of Even Yosef, by contrast, there is clear continuity with the past in leadership forms and personnel.[2] The chapter that follows will attempt to account for this continuity on a social-psychological level, by looking more closely at certain aspects of the social life of the youth in Even Yosef, and at domestic organization.

[1] According to the Zionist Organization (1960) there were about 65 moshavim of 'pure' North African origin and about half that number consisting of (French) North African Jews living with other groups.

[2] One evening, after the conclusion of a moshav committee meeting, I was standing outside the moshav office, chatting with Nissim (the internal secretary, pp. 66, 126). Nissim, in a seemingly reflective mood, commented to me: 'You know, here (in Even Yosef), everything is just as it was in ḥutz laaretz (i.e. in Tripolitania); you won't find that in other moshavim.' While I did not quiz Nissim on this point, it is clear that he was not referring to technoeconomic matters, and I doubt that he had in mind the preservation of specific customs or beliefs. Rather, judging from the situation in which the remark was made, I believe that he was reflecting on the 'intangible', but real, continuity in forms of social relationships.

6. The youth of Even Yosef: mechanisms of continuity and change

In the past two chapters we have seen that the elite of Even Yosef are simultaneously the most traditional members of the community and the most 'acculturated'. They uphold the old social and religious norms at the same time that they are oriented toward the wider society. This association of a structural position (elite status) and an attitudinal orientation ('cosmopolitanism'), I suggest, constitutes an *institutionalized mechanism for coping with change*. When change occurs in the sociocultural environment the elite are the first to come into contact with the sources of change. Because they have a greater knowledge of extra-community affairs, they are better equipped to handle change than non-elite. To the extent that they successfully adapt to these changes, they maintain their elite position. This is particularly true in the technological-economic realm; i.e. as the elite quickly learn to exploit a changing technoeconomic environment, they also succeed in maintaining the wealth differential between themselves and non-elite.

The traditional elite (and pre-eminently the mazkir), play the role of 'cultural brokers', mediating change between the outside and the villagers. This arrangement has several implications. First of all, various 'innovations' are *reinterpreted* by the elite and transmitted to the non-elite in forms that are congruent with traditional patterns. Thus formal moshav organization has been 'translated' into terms compatible with the traditional forms of leadership and prestige. Secondly, the non-elite do not have to come into direct contact with the outside world in order to learn new modes of adaptation. Innovation in the village follows the pattern on a 'two-step-flow of communication',[1] so that the

[1] See Katz (1957) for a discussion of this model of communication. Examples of the two-step sequence may be seen in the introduction of washing machines (p. 113),

isolation of the majority of the community from the outside world is preserved as a structural feature. Last of all, the rapidity with which the elite adopt and transmit new patterns in the technoeconomic realm significantly relieves acculturative pressures in other spheres such as family organization, customs, and religious practices. Quick adjustment in economic affairs *retroacts* on these other spheres to slacken their pace of change.[1]

The association of elite status and a stronger orientation to the outside world thus has the *latent function* of coping with change. This felicitous association, of course, is not inevitable. It has frequently been noted that low status individuals are the first to accept changes (Barnett 1953: 401). Often, too, elite groups are perceived as having a vested interest in retarding change. In some instances, acculturated individuals who are suited to leadership roles are reluctant to assume those roles (Watson and Samora 1954). It has sometimes been asserted that 'historical accident' is the best explanation for the emergence of capable leadership in instances of 'successful' sociocultural change (e.g. Mead 1956: 213; Redfield 1950).

If indeed this 'traditional' community has a built-in mechanism for 'producing' leaders and 'handling' change, it may be asked: How is the hypothesized association of cosmopolitan orientations and elite status maintained over the generations? The answer, I suggest, involves two phases: first, the families with the 'elite–cosmopolitan' fathers tend to socialize children who are more oriented toward extravillage affairs than the children of the 'non-elite locals'; and secondly the 'cosmopolitan' children of the elite are selected for leadership upon attaining adulthood. This latter pattern is prefigured in the organization of the (male) 'adolescent society' of Even Yosef which *replicates*[2] the main structural features of the total community. Each of these mechanisms will be discussed in turn after describing some features of adolescent life in Even Yosef.

tractors (pp. 115–16), and the use of plastic covers for the early sowing of vegetables (p. 69). Two-step cultural communication among the youth will be discussed later in t he chapter (pp. 157–8).
[1] The notion of retroactive change has been put forth by Moore and Feldman (1960: 365–6), and utilized by Weintraub and Shapiro (1968: 297) in analyzing traditional family forms in a changing Kurdish moshav.
[2] For a discussion of the concept of 'replication' see Vogt (1965).

My description of the youth of Even Yosef, which follows, draws upon data collected by participant observation, but also relies on the responses to systematic interviews. The necessity for interviewing, and its execution, are detailed in Appendix A (which also discusses the interviews with the parents). The data thus collected lends itself to quantitative treatment which will be used extensively in this chapter. The main advantage of quantification is that it permits detailed study of intra-communal variation which is crucial in understanding both stability and change.

I define my universe of male youth as all the village boys born in the years 1940–9. This is a demographic rather than a cultural definition. To the people of Even Yosef, some of the individuals in the sample would be considered 'children' and a few others would be considered 'young men'. A cultural indication of membership in the category of 'youth' is the non-wearing of a beret. A beret is standard attire among the village adults, particularly if they are 'dressed up' for a special occasion (p. 101). Also, many of the male children are dressed in berets and wear them as part of their school attire. A male adolescent, however, never wears a beret. If he should wish to adhere to the religious norm of always keeping his head covered, he would then wear a skullcap, rather than a beret. Employment of the 'beret definition' of adolescence would slightly lower the number of adolescents in the village, but on the whole, the demographic and cultural definitions coincide.

TABLE 14. *Social characteristics of the*
male youth of Even Yosef

Number	Year born	Completed 8 grades of school	Average number years in school	Served in army	Married
20	1940–4	6 (30%)	5.6	9	12
21	1945–9	14 (67%)	8.2	6	1

Table 14 presents some of the social characteristics of the universe of male youth in Even Yosef. Within the total universe, those youths who were born from 1940–4 were twenty to twenty-four years old at the time of the study. Of these 20 youths, six

(30%) have completed eight years of schooling, and their average educational attainment is 5.6 years. Nine of them have served in the army. Eight of the 20 youths are married and living in the 'new moshav' (p. 66). Three are married and living in Even Yosef, one is married and living in a neighboring village, and eight are single.

The 21 youths who were born from 1945–9 constitute the younger segment of the sample interviewees studied. Fourteen (66.7%)[1] of them have finished the eighth grade, and their average schooling is 8.2 years. Six of them have served in the army, and others are still to serve. However, about one-third of this group probably will not serve in the army.[2] One member of this group is married, and a second is engaged to be married. Gradually, then, the youth of the village are becoming more involved with the national institutions of the school and the army. Still, these youth, like their parents, are relatively isolated from the rest of Israeli society.

Contacts outside the community

The children of Even Yosef attend a State Religious School[3] along with the children of two neighboring Yemenite moshavim. All of their schoolmates, therefore, are other children of a Middle Eastern cultural background. This school is located in one of the neighboring Yemenite villages. The grades of the school are subdivided into classes by scholastic level. This usually results in a *de facto* situation in which the Yemenite children are in the higher class within a grade, and the Tripolitanian children are in the lower class. Casual observation in the school yard during school 'recesses' indicates that until about 6th–7th grades the Even Yosef children and Yemenite children each keep very much to themselves. Even though the older Even Yosef boys and

---

[1] In a survey of moshavim carried out in 1961, Weingrod and Minkovitz (1963: 367) found the 58.4% of the youth (*n* = 310), ages 14 to 17, had finished 8 grades of schooling.

[2] Weingrod and Minkovitz (*loc. cit.*) also found that many youths on moshavim did not serve in the army, in comparison to the country as a whole.

[3] A State Religious School is a state educational institution, established under the 1953 State Education Bill. It differs from a (secular) state school in that it is 'religious in its way of life, curriculum, teachers and inspectors' (Avidor 1960: 58–60). On the whole the curriculum of these schools is the same as that of other state schools, except that various materials are taught with a religious interpretation. See, also, the discussion in Marmorstein (1969: 144–7).

Yemenite boys are friendly while at school, I know of no instance when youths of one village visited youths of another village, nor of boys from these groups arranging a meeting 'in town'.

Twelve of the youths, in the sample studied, report having 'none' or 'one' friend outside the village, while 24 youths report having two or three friends outside the community. In all cases, however, they report seeing these 'friends' either 'sometimes' or 'rarely', but never 'frequently'. None of the boys has continued friendships that developed in the army, after being discharged.

Thirty-one youths report having relatives outside the village, but they visit these relatives rarely. The number of 'relatives' and 'visits' is even smaller than the figures immediately suggest because some of the relatives are related to a number of youths in the village, and the few Gharianites not living in Even Yosef usually live in neighborhood clusters in several towns in Israel. With regard to contact with outside individuals and groups, then, it may be seen that the youths of Even Yosef, as the adults, are relatively isolated from the environing society.

Work patterns

An Even Yosef male, from the time he reaches pre-adolescence, begins to be involved in the productive effort of the family. He is able to perform many simple chores, and this releases the older males of the household for more productive work. By the time he is in the eighth grade (age 14–15) he is an important contributor to the family labor force and, as likely as not, spends many days out of school helping on the farm.[1] Frequently, the motivation to work on the farm rather than remain in school comes from the youth himself, who will stay out of school in opposition to his parent's wishes. In other cases, the parents pressure the youth to contribute as much labor as possible, and do not give him a chance to study beyond the eighth grade, even though he may have the opportunity to do so. Even the boys who continue into high school spend much of their time, during vacations, helping on the farm.

A boy who has finished elementary school is presented with opportunities for earning money outside of his contribution to the

---

[1] On one day during the writer's field trip, 20 men of the village were served summonses by the police because their children were truant from school. Most of these men had children in the seventh or eighth grades.

household unit. He may be employed in the citrus grove during the harvest (November–April), or may work at unloading trucks which deliver agricultural materials to the village. He may be hired by another villager who needs an extra hand. Nightly guard duty in the village is another source of income, and sometimes work is available in neighboring settlements.

A few youths have taken steps to learn skills outside of agriculture. Eighteen have never made such an attempt, while 20 have made some attempts, such as learning the trades of mechanic, carpentry, construction, and so forth. In general, these attempts have not been carried to completion. Moreover, most of the youth who seriously have considered the possibility of learning a trade assess their real future to be in agriculture in the village. Some of the youth, though not formally owning land, work as full-time farmers by renting plots, on other farms, whose owners do not fully exploit their land. Thus, at a fairly young age, many of these youth assume full responsibility for growing a crop, and executing the technical and economic tasks that this involves.

Most of the youths are glad to be somewhat financially independent of their parents, though there is a wide range of attitudes in this regard. On the whole, the boys contribute some of their earnings to the household purse. Thirty-four out of thirty-six youths report that they give some of their earnings to their parents, while only two report that they keep their earnings entirely to themselves. Thirty-one out of thirty-six report contributing labor to the household labor force, while five do not contribute labor. Twenty-three also take money from the household purse, while 13 do not take money from their parents. Twelve of the latter 23 take money from their parents 'only when necessary' while eleven of the 23 claim that they share 'one purse' with their parents. These various items, concerning the economic arrangements obtaining between the youths and their families, fit the pattern of a Guttman scale as shown in Table 15. Later, I shall utilize this data to devise an index of parent–youth 'solidarity' (p. 150).

Consumption and recreation

Most of the youth take the responsibility for acquiring the consumer goods and services they desire, such as clothes, bicycles, watches, and transistor radios. They are particularly

reluctant to ask their parents for money to spend on non-tradi-
tional forms of recreation.

The recreational activities of the youths center in the village,
but this is an unsatisfactory arrangement as far as most of them
are concerned. The male youths frequent the village kiosk in the

TABLE 15. *Patterns of youth/parent economic arrangements*

Step	Number of youths	Patterns of economic arrangements			
		Takes freely from household purse	Takes from household purse 'only when necessary'	Contributes labor to household work force	Contributes money to household purse
1	11	X	X	X	X
2	12	O	X	X	X
3	8	O	O	X	X
4	3	O	O	O	X
5	2	O	O	O	O
	Total 36				

X = Yes; O = No.

evenings, but normally do not drink liquor and do not gamble.
They all speak of how 'boring' life is in the moshav, and contrast
it to the 'good time' one may have in the city. On two nights a
week there is public transportation available to the neighboring
town, and on one of these nights (Saturday night), all the boys
travel into town to see a film. When in town they keep mostly to
themselves, and have relatively little contact with other youths,
even with the Yemenite boys they know from school.

The youths show little interest in the traditional forms of
'recreation' which take place in the village in a religious context.
For example, few of them come to the celebrations of circumcision during which the adults sit around, sing songs, eat, drink,
and gossip.[1]

Both the Po'el Mizrahi and the army have made attempts to
provide youth leaders and sports instructors for the village, but

---

[1] The youth do participate, however, in wedding celebrations during which there
are a series of 'bachelor parties' and rituals for several days before the nuptial
night (Goldberg n.d.).

these attempts have met with only moderate success. Partially as a result of these programs some of the youths have learned modern social dancing; sixteen out of 36 youth report that they know how to dance to some extent.

Eight of the 41 youth own motorscooters, and others plan to purchase them in the future. They all claim that once everyone has a scooter, no youth will be in the village at night, because 'they'll all be in town having a good time'. However, those who already own a scooter use them only occasionally for going out at night, and still seem to remain in the village. Most of the boys say that they feel somewhat uncomfortable about going into the cafe (which has a juke box) in the neighboring town because they hardly know anyone there.

Heterosexual relationships

With regard to heterosexual relationships, village life is also un-satisfactory to the boys. Community social pressures prevent the adolescent boys and girls from interacting in public. 'If you speak to a girl in public', the youths say, 'the village will begin to have you "married off" to her'. If a group of girls should walk past a group of boys in the village there is not even an exchange of glances, to say nothing of an exchange of comments.

In 1963 the army sent a female youth leader to teach Israeli folk dancing to the youth of the village. The girls attended the first few sessions along with the boys. The Rabbi (from Jerba), in his synagogue talks, began to speak against social dancing. He claimed that it was shameful and that dancing could lead to 'other things'. He exhorted the fathers to prohibit the girls from attending these sessions. The fathers followed the Rabbi's teaching and the girls stopped coming (see Goldberg n.d.).

Many of the girls also go to the movies in town on Saturday nights but stay to themselves in groups. Just as in the village, there is no public interaction between the boys and the girls while they are in town. Rumors would quickly transmit the happenings of the town to the adults in the village.

There are some clandestine sexual liaisons between the male and female adolescents, but as far as can be judged from reports, these are relatively rare. Most of the boys who report that they have had some pre-marital sexual experience report that it took place with girls outside the village. When it comes to selecting a marriage partner, however, most of the boys marry village girls (pp. 55, 83). For the most part, communication between male and female youth is carried on by 'intermediaries', who usually are females and/or relatives. A typical example is given by Luma, an adolescent informant who explained how he 'chose' his fiancee. As will be seen, Luma's choice of a mate was influenced by the fact that his father is one of the residents of the moshav, and not a farm-holding member.

At first I 'loved' Dīna, who lives across the road, and she loved me (Luma had never spoken directly to Dīna about love, but Dīna's father's sister was married to Luma's elder brother, and via the female relative they have in common, Luma knew that Dīna loved him). But her cousin (her father's father's brother's son) began to say – 'Why marry Luma? – He doesn't have a farm'. Her cousin turned her head and we broke up. Then I began to think about whom else I might marry. I thought of Tamar though I had never thought of her before. Before I asked her father I had to find out if she agreed, so I asked her. My friend Ṣion (who is actually Luma's older brother's son, but the same age as Luma) was then going with Raḥel who is a good friend of Tamar. I asked Ṣion to ask Raḥel, to ask Tamar, and Tamar consented to the marriage. Once I heard this I went to her parents to ask if they agreed to the marriage. They asked Tamar if she agreed to the marriage and she did.

In this way Luma and Tamar decided to marry without exchanging a word. Most of the other cases of courtship on which I have data contain similar 'traditional' elements.

The sociometric structure of adolescent male society

Just as the male youth, like their parents, are relatively insulated from the wider society (though undoubtedly more knowledgeable than their elders), so in other ways the structure of 'adolescent society' in Even Yosef seems to replicate some of the structural features of the adult community. Thus, as the community is not divided into factions, and concentrates power into one political status, so the male youth are not divided into cliques, and show considerable consensus in bestowing leadership on individuals.

As part of the interviews the youths were asked to name their 'three best friends'. Seventeen out of 37 youths at first replied 'I have no special friends, I'm friends with everybody'. Seven of these 17, with prodding, went on to name three friends. Ten of the 17 refused to answer the question but were willing to name the boys with whom they 'went out most frequently'. The boys, thus named, will be called sociometric choices. If we then look at the first sociometric choice made by each of 37 youths, we find that only three youths are involved in reciprocal choices. If we consider all the sociometric choices (up to three) made by each youth, then 15 of the 37 youths are involved in reciprocal choices. Even when considering up to three choices made by each boy, 6 out of 37 youth appear as sociometric isolates who received no choices at all. Thus there is a clear absence of sociometric cliques among the male youth. (The sociometric choices are presented in Appendix C.)

Although there is very little sociometric reciprocity, there is a clear tendency for the appearance of sociometric 'stars'. Thus, five individuals received 32 (41 %) of the 78 choices made. As I will presently explain, I think that in responding to the interview question, the youths named others whom they *respected* most, more so than they named their friends (though the two are by no means mutually exclusive). In other words, the pattern of sociometric choices reflects leadership more than it does friendship. For the most part, my observations of adolescent life corroborate the results of the sociometric questioning.

During their leisure hours, 'socializing' among the youths is very informal. For example, if several boys are 'standing around', they may (or may not) be joined by others who happen to be in the vicinity. While certain individuals are close friends with one another, and others rarely spend time with their peers, there are no recruitment norms that encourage the formation of tightly bounded cliques.

The social atmosphere among the youth is egalitarian. When several boys go to a Saturday night film together, one pays for the bus rides of all, another for the tickets, a third for refreshments, and so forth. This egalitarianism, as among the adults, is a two-edged sword. For example, one boy was criticized for 'bragging' about a butcher shop that his father was about to open. Another boy (a grandson of Rebbi Shmuel), who with his father's financial help had set up a little welding and tire shop, was showing his peers a rubber stamp with his name on it, that he had made for his 'business'. His friends promptly took the newly acquired stamp and imprinted his name all over his white shirt.

Another way in which adolescent egalitarianism resembles adult behavior is in the reluctance to assume leadership. The village had built a soccer field and a small 'club house' for the children and youth. Although these are not kept in very good condition, they are nevertheless usable. There are, however, few successful attempts to utilize these facilities though the boys often talk about wishing to do so. They succeed only under the leadership of an 'outsider' such as youth leaders from the party or the army.

In analyzing leadership among the male adolescents, the case of one of the mazkir's sons is instructive. Hai's second son had completed two years of high school. Afterwards he went into the army where he met with some success. He eventually received a commission and planned to remain in the army an additional five years after his mandatory service. He thus was outside of Even Yosef, more than he was at home, in contrast to what is typical for the other male youths.

During one of his visits home, while spending time with his age-mates, he suggested they get together and play pingpong in the club house. The suggestion was quickly taken up and carried out. I had never seen these youth play pingpong in this spontaneous manner before (that is, with no 'outside' leaders present), though there was nothing to prevent them from doing so. What they had lacked, apparently, was the leadership.

Several aspects of Hai's son's leadership are noteworthy. First, he won all the pingpong games he played. One can only speculate as to whether he was a leader among the youth because he was a good pingpong player, or whether he won pingpong games because he was a leader. Secondly, he received the second highest number (7) of sociometric choices despite the fact that he was very rarely present in the village. I thus tend to believe that the sociometric choices reflect leadership rather than friendship. Thirdly, the basis of his leadership, and the prestige given to the other sociometric 'stars', resembles leadership among the adults, namely a better knowledge of, and competence in dealing with, the wider society.

One other feature of the structure of adolescent society in Even Yosef should be mentioned, and that is the relative unimportance of the adolescent age-group as a structural entity within the total community. There are few occasions at which the male adolescents are publicly set apart from other groups in the community, except during certain phases of wedding celebrations. Neither is there

1   Village youth outside the cooperative store. The store manager is center right; the anthropologist is center left

2   Villager with a hand-operated hydraulic fork-lift in the citrus grove

3   Former blacksmith bending a piece of metal

4   A villager in his seventies. The black turban was worn by many Jews in the Gharian, particularly the old men

5   Family of one of the petty administrators in the village

6   Woman in traditional garb (zdād), with her grandchildren

7   Even Yosef – general view

8   Small synagogue near the centre of Even Yosef. In the right foreground, tomatoes; left background, eucalyptus

any formal ceremony marking the transition into or out of adolescence.[1] On the level of individual attitudes this implies a relative *lack of age-group consciousness*, particularly with reference to acculturation. I, several times, asked the youths if they ever discussed the problem of 'modernity' among themselves and compare the 'modernity' of their respective parents. They replied that this is rarely discussed, and when the subject is aired, one person is usually surprised to find that his friends encounter the same sort of intergenerational tensions in the family as he does.

In summary, the structure of adolescent society in Even Yosef replicates certain structural features of the total community such as: the relative isolation of the group from the environing society, the weakness of factions or cliques within the total group, and the importance of a small number of leaders who are more knowledgeable about the wider society than the 'rank-and-file'. This, in turn, implies that, on the attitudinal level, there is significant variation among the youth in their orientations toward the wider society.

Variation in orientations to the wider society

As in the case of the adult males, I devised an index of Orientation to the Wider Society (hereafter: OWS) for the village youth. This index, which differentiates the stronger OWS from the weaker OWS youths is based mainly on the interview schedule. There are four items which serve to distinguish these two sets of youths. Two of these characteristics are 'attitudinal' – the attitude toward village endogamy and occupational aspirations. The other two are behavioral items – the use of Hebrew in daily speech and the attempt to learn a non-agricultural trade. Those youths who have aspirations toward non-agricultural occupations prefer to marry a girl 'from the outside', or at least state that it is not important that one marry a girl from the village. They are also the boys who tend to use Hebrew more (as rated by themselves and their peers),[2]

---

[1] Unmarried boys (*bḥurīm*), and married young men are grouped together during wedding celebrations (see n. 1, p. 140). There is often mild teasing directed toward pre-adolescents' who begin to assume adolescent forms of behavior, such as experimenting with cigarette smoking.

[2] As far as the writer was able to observe, Hebrew is almost never spoken in the village, even among the youth. The only exceptions to this are several boys who have studied in high school. The other youths, at most, use Hebrew perhaps 25% of the time in conversations among themselves. This is probably a high estimate. Nevertheless, most of the youth, during the interview, reported that they and

and usually have taken concrete steps toward acquiring non-agricultural occupational skills. Those youths who have no aspirations toward non-agricultural occupations are the ones who tend to prefer village endogamy. They also tend to use Hebrew less, and have made no serious attempts at learning non-agricultural skills (Appendix D).

Two sets of questions concerning this variation will now be considered. The first concerns the *antecedents* of the observed attitudinal variation – what are the factors that tend to make some youth more oriented toward the wider society than others? The second concerns the *consequences* of this variation, or how it is related to the ways in which the community retains its structure while adapting to a changing environment.

SOURCES OF ATTITUDINAL VARIATION AMONG THE YOUTH

In situations of culture contact, and particularly in studies of youth, it is common to look for outside acculturative influences and pressures to explain variation in attitudes and the formation of factions. In Even Yosef, however, the variation in acculturative tendencies among the youth is primarily related to the pre-existing variation in the degree of orientation to the wider society. I will first attempt to demonstrate this internal continuity and then argue against alternate explanations.

The data in Table 16 show the relationship between OWS among the adults and acculturative orientations on the part of the youth.[1] It is strikingly clear from Table 16 that families with fathers who are more orientated to the wider society have sons who are more acculturated. In fact, the label 'acculturation' may be considered inappropriate because this type of attitudinal variation is entirely traditional. In a word, orientations toward the wider society are, in the first instance, learned within the family.

There are several other variables which theoretically might be related to degree of acculturation such as age at the time of immi-

their friends in the village used Hebrew 'most of the time'. At first the writer tended to discount these reports but later became convinced that, subjectively, the youths saw themselves as speaking mainly Hebrew (see Appendix D).

[1] Where more than one boy in a family are included in the sample, I have utilized the mean acculturation score of all the boys in the family.

gration, service in the army, and amount of education. In the first case, with regard to age, there is no tendency for those boys who were younger at the time of immigration to be more acculturated than those who were older. Secondly, it is generally believed that, in Israel, service in the army has been an important factor in the acculturation of immigrants (Eisenstadt 1967: 197). The data on Even Yosef, however, show no relation between army service and the degree of acculturation. The relationship between length of education and acculturation, however, is more complex.

TABLE 16. *Orientation to the wider society*
among the fathers and the youths

	OWS of the youth*		
OWS of fathers	Strong	Weak	Totals
Weak	9	0	9
Strong	1	10	11
Totals	10	10	20

* The average OWS is used when there is more than one boy in a family.
$\phi = 0.905$; $P < (\text{exact}) = 0.005$.

Table 17 shows that there is a strong association between education and acculturation among the youth of Even Yosef. Those youths who have finished eight grades of school, or more, tend to have stronger OWS than those who have finished seven grades of school, or less. This data, by itself, of course, does not permit an inference as to the direction of causality. Do eight years of grade school 'cause' certain boys to be more acculturated than those who have finished less than eight grades? Or do those youths who are more oriented toward the wider society more often tend to complete grade school than those who are less oriented toward the outside? Although both processes are undoubtedly at work, I prefer to emphasize the latter interpretation.

Rather than interpreting education as a 'cause' of acculturation, I believe that the completion of eight grades of school is better understood as another indicator of a strong OWS, an orientation that is derived, in the first instance, from the strong OWS of the fathers. This may be seen from the fact that when Table 17 is divided into partial tables for 'strong' and 'weak'

OWS of the fathers, the covariation between 'education' and OWS of the youth disappears.[1] The high OWS youths' propensity for finishing (and continuing) their elementary education stems initially from their fathers' positive attitude toward the school. Thus, in devising the index of 'orientation to the outside world', as it applies to the fathers (p. 96), I utilized 'criticism of the local school' as an indicator of acculturation. The strong OWS parents criticize the school not because it changes the traditional behavior patterns of the community's youth, but because it fails to realize the goals of a 'good education', as that is conceived of by these parents and by members of wider Israeli society (see Eisenstadt 1954: 152).

TABLE 17. *Education of the youth and their orientation to the wider society*

Education	OWS		
	Strong	Weak	Totals
High (8 years or more)	13	5	18
Low (7 years or less)	3	12	15
Totals	16	17	33

$\phi = 0.520;$ $P < 0.01.$

In Israel there is compulsory universal elementary education from the ages of 5 through 14 (i.e. 8 grades). In the case of Even Yosef, however, if a boy wishes to be a truant during his 7th and 8th years of school, he may do so with relative impunity from the authorities. The fines imposed on the parents of the truant school children are not commensurate with the economic advantages accruing to the parents by the children's entrance into the family labor force. For this reason, a boy in the seventh or eighth grade, who is personally motivated, or pressured by his parents, to work rather than to complete school, may do so without concern for severe sanctions. Those boys who complete eight grades of school do so, in a real sense, out of choice.

[1] The partial tables are presented in Appendix E. This procedure for examining the interrelationship of the three variables is discussed in Anderson and Zelditch (1968: 163–83).

It appears, therefore, that those youths who chose to complete their elementary education take cognizance of the relevance of wider Israeli society to their own personal future. Though most of them do not continue in high school, nor become permanently involved in work outside the village, they still *consider the possibility* of these courses of action. The youths who do not complete grade school have never given any realistic thought to a future outside of the village of Even Yosef. Although the completion of grade school undoubtedly reinforces a pre-existing orientation toward the wider society, it does not, in itself, account for the variation in OWS among the youth. Rather, internal community factors, in particular, the traditional variation among families in their OWS, are initially responsible for the differential orientations among the youth.

One further aspect of this internal continuity should be noted. If strong OWS were primarily the result of contact with the wider society, then one would expect, as in many situations of culture contact, that those youth who are most acculturated would exhibit the greatest degree of intergenerational conflict. Table 18 shows that the association between OWS on the part of the youth and intergenerational conflict (see Appendix A), while in the predicted direction, is weak and hardly statistically significant. Moreover, when the variable of 'fathers' OWS' is controlled, by partialling Table 18, it appears that there is no association between intergenerational conflict and strong OWS-youth for the parents with a more positive orientation to the wider society, while the 'classical' relationship between acculturation and conflict holds for the weak OWS families.[1]

Family dynamics of continuity

If the male adolescent's orientation toward the wider society is socialized initially within the family, it may be asked whether there is any difference in internal organization, among the village families, that parallels the variation in their OWS. The responses to the interviews suggest that there is an important difference, and that those families with a stronger OWS display greater solidarity than those who are more locally oriented.

[1] The partial tables are presented in Appendix E. Parent–youth conflict also was found to be relatively weak in a Kurdish moshav studied by Weintraub and Shapiro (1968).

TABLE 18. *Orientation to the wider society among the youth and intergenerational conflict*

| | Conflict | | |
OWS	High	Low	Totals
Strong	8	6	14
Weak	8	9	17
Totals	16	15	31

$\phi = 0.100$; $P > 0.50$.

My main indicator of family solidarity is the data on parent–youth economic arrangements presented above (Table 15, p. 140). Those families in which the boys are more integrated into the household economy are deemed more solidary, and those families in which the youths are more economically independent are considered less solidary. Based on this data, a solidarity rank was assigned to each household,[1] and the relationship between the OWS of the father of the household and its solidarity rank was tabulated. As may be seen from Table 19, high domestic solidarity occurs in all the strong OWS families, save one, while it appears in less than half of the weak OWS cases.

TABLE 19. *Orientation to the wider society of the father and family solidarity*

| | Solidarity rating | | |
OWS	High	Low	Totals
Strong	8	1	9
Weak	7	8	15
Totals	15	9	24

$\phi = 0.422$; P (exact) < 0.10.

[1] Households with sons appearing in steps 1–2, in Table 15 (p. 140), are classified as exhibiting 'high solidarity', while households whose sons appeared in steps 3–5 appear under 'low solidarity'. In the three cases (out of eight) where brothers had disparate solidarity ranks, the family was considered as showing 'low solidarity'.

The interview data also show that mutual consultation between the youths and parents, in matters such as farming decisions, purchasing a motorscooter, and serving in the army (if deferment is a possibility), is more common in the solidary (and strong OWS) families than in the less solidary families.

Family solidarity, particularly in economic matters, influences the intergenerational transmission of OWS in several ways. As discussed earlier, those youths whose parents have strong OWS are thereby influenced to complete grade school (and possibly go on to high school). The completion of grade school is further encouraged in that these boys do not feel the pressure of earning their own money, which would necessitate stopping their formal education. They are comfortable in accepting their parents' economic support, and, to the extent that their greater education results in greater earning power, they feel that they will 'repay' the family's 'investment'. Their greater exposure to education, and in some cases the learning of a new skill, then reinforces the originally strong OWS.

The youths from the less solidary families, on the other hand, do not readily accept their parents' economic support. They are quick to leave school so as to be able to earn 'their own' money. Because of the lack of formal education or vocational training most of their economic effort is concentrated in village agriculture. There is little opportunity for them to become engaged in economic activities which would widen their sociocultural worlds.

Psychologically speaking, economic solidarity within the domestic unit is paralleled by the relative lack of internalized intergenerational conflict, while economic 'independence' is linked to psychological tensions between parents and youth. This is shown in Table 20 which presents the association between parent-youth economic arrangements and intergenerational tensions.

As may be seen, there is a strong association of high economic solidarity and low parent-youth tensions. The relative absence of intergenerational tensions also may make the youths from the solidary families more receptive to their parents attitudes than the boys from the less solidary families, and, in this way also influences the transmission of OWS from parents to children. One further possibility is that the strong OWS fathers are the more effective 'parental mediators' of social change in the community, that is they are quick to alter their 'inherited' socialization practices to conform to the new realities of moshav life (cf. Inkeles 1955; Miller 1967 has described some of the ways in which the younger mothers and fathers in Even Yosef raise their children differently from older villagers).

TABLE 20. *Parent–youth economic solidarity and intergenerational conflict*

Economic solidarity*	Conflict		
	Low	High	Totals
High	10	1	11
Medium	4	7	11
Low	4	9	13
Totals	18	17	35

* High corresponds to step 1 of Table 15 (p. 140). Medium corresponds to step 2, and Low corresponds to steps 3–5.

It will be remembered that a strong OWS on the part of parents is most common in the families characterized by elite status and wealth (p. 97). Not surprisingly, then, the data show that families which are wealthy (and elite) tend to be 'solidary' with greater frequency than the rank and file families of the community. Those who wish to banish 'psychology' from social analysis might argue that the solidarity of the strong OWS families is mainly a function of their wealth. It 'pays' for the boys of those families to be 'on good terms' with their parents while there is no such reward for the youth of the poorer families. While this is undoubtedly another important factor in the intergenerational transmission of OWS, I do not believe that wealth alone can explain the variation in solidarity of family organization, and have presented reasons in detail elsewhere.[1]

[1] Briefly, the argument runs as follows. The migration to Israel and settlement on Even Yosef may be seen as a sort of 'natural experiment' which controlled (equalized) a number of factors that might account for wealth differentials among the families of the community, and allowed the effects of 'OWS' and 'domestic solidarity' on family wealth to become apparent. Thus, there was no difference between the two groups of families in the amount of wealth which they brought from the Gharian, nor were there differences in amount of land they received, or in the credit made available to them. Also, the demographic characteristics of the two sets of families were roughly similar. Rather than wealth 'causing' greater

In summary, I have suggested some mechanisms by which varying orientations to the wider society are transmitted inter-generationally within the family, reproducing (not exactly, of course) this variation in attitudes among the village youth. In the next section, I will consider some of the *consequences* of this variation for the 'adolescent society' of Even Yosef and, ultimately, for the structure of the community as manifest in the behavior of the adults.

THE STRUCTURAL IMPLICATIONS OF ATTITUDINAL VARIATION

The existence of variation in OWS among the village youth has various implications, and those which are emphasized depend upon one's point of view. In terms of the national goals of Israeli society it may be most important to ask – 'What are the determinants of acculturative tendencies among the immigrant youth, and how can they be fostered?' In terms of Even Yosef, though, I wish to consider the effects of attitudinal variation on the structure of the community. My central assertion is that, from a diachronic point of view, the preservation of variability in OWS has the 'function' of insuring that there will be an adequate 'supply' of these orientations in each generation to provide leadership (and followership) for the community. Just as the present day elite are to a great extent descendants of the elite in Tripolitania (p. 100), so, if my thesis is correct, the sons of the present day elite will in large measure be selected as leaders in the future. While a test of this prediction must await the future,[1] there is some insight to be gained by a close study of contemporary adolescent society in Even Yosef.

solidarity, the stronger OWS, and the greater solidarity of the strong OWS families enabled them to take greater material advantage of their new environment (Goldberg 1969*b*).

[1] There is some evidence, however, with regard to second generation continuity in the principles of leadership, from the 'new moshav' settled by 19 young families from Even Yosef (p. 66). This moshav originally consisted of 36 families from Europe (mostly from Hungary), 11 Yemenite families, and 19 Moroccans. The 19 Tripolitanian families were accepted on 'probation' for one year before achieving full moshav membership. During this time they were allowed to send one (non-voting) representative to the moshav committee. The individual they selected fits the traditional picture of the 'sheikh-mazkir'. He had more secular and religious education than the others, and was the son of one of the Misuratan families (i.e. a 'stranger').

If quizzed directly, the youth do not explicitly relate their present day behavior and attitudes to future political roles. They do not concern themselves with village politics, which in any event, is not a salient aspect of daily life in Even Yosef. Many of the village youths cannot name the current members of the moshav committee. Certain boys, in emphasizing their 'modernity', assert that local moshav affairs are of little moment to them. Nevertheless, despite the dissimilarity in the content of the concerns of the adults and the youth, it is possible to discern in the structure of adolescent society in Even Yosef a definite congruence to the structure of the community as a whole.[1]

As mentioned earlier (p. 142), there are three structural features of the community which are replicated in adolescent society: the relative isolation of the group from the environing society, the absence of factions and cliques coupled with an egalitarian ethos, and the importance of a small number of leaders who are more knowledgeable about the wider society than the 'typical' members of the group. Each of these will now be elaborated by reference to comparative material.

Contact with wider society

The youths, of Even Yosef, of course, in many ways have greater contact with the wider society than their parents. They have had more formal education, speak Hebrew better, have travelled around the country somewhat more, partake in modern forms of leisure such as going to the movies, and many have served in the army. On the other hand, as detailed above (pp. 137–8), this contact has been limited, particularly in comparison to urban immigrant youth and the youth on other new moshavim.

For example, in many moshavim there are youths who have completed several years of agricultural boarding school and who, upon returning to their village, have influenced both their own families and their moshav as a whole (Weintraub and Lissak 1964 b: 150–8). To date (1965), this has not occurred in Even Yosef. Another contrast is provided by a new moshav settled by 57 families from Marrakesh (Morocco) which sent 38 students to

[1] Aberle and Naegele (1952), for example, have shown that American middle class parents are only partially aware of the relevance of their sons' activities for future economic roles within society. Similarly, the people of Even Yosef are not cognizant of the implication of adolescent activities for future political roles within the community.

high school in 1963 (Silverstein 1964: 38), in comparison to the 4 students from the 99 families of Even Yosef in the same year.

In this Moroccan moshav, Silverstein (1964: 40, 52) reports, the youth frequently visit outside the village and their dating patterns are similar to those of Western Europe. Both these patterns contrast sharply with Even Yosef. Descriptions of mate selection in Yemenite and Kurdish moshavim are given by Weintraub and Lissak (1964b: 146–7) and Weintraub and Shapiro (1968: 290). With regard to the former they state:

At this age (18) the Yemenite girl is already mature, and knows her own mind as well as her way around. She has been outside the home and has mixed in general society on the one hand, and in the society of boys, on the other. While in the Yemen she saw her bridegroom for the first time usually shortly before the marriage ceremony, here both sexes meet much more freely. In consequence, the prospective pair know each other and are able to estimate their mutual compatibility, and it is usually they themselves who make the choice. Since both the boy and the girl can find employment and leave the house, the parents usually comply with their children's choice.

Were this generalized portrait applied to Even Yosef, it would greatly misrepresent the current mode of choosing a spouse (pp. 141–2).

The youths of the village are aware that many traditions that are rapidly disappearing elsewhere are still maintained in Even Yosef (Goldberg n.d.), and see their village as somewhat 'backward'. This image of backwardness is undoubtedly internalized, in varying degrees, by some of the boys. The 'rural character' of the Even Yosef adolescents is likewise shown in their stereotypes of urban youth. On several occasions Even Yosef boys called my attention to groups of motorcycle-jacketed teenagers in the nearby town who were strolling 'aimlessly' down the street, and referred to them as 'delinquents'. They apparently do not apply that moral judgement to similar behavior, on their own part, in the vicinity of the kiosk of Even Yosef.

Many of the boys express the hope that by serving in the army they will 'learn something', meaning both an occupational skill and a general familiarity with the world outside the village. However, while the army does take them away from the village for several years, it does not seem to permanently alter their orientation to the wider society. Thus, once when I was recording songs that some boys were singing, I was surprised to find that most of the youths who had been in the army had not learned to sing correctly the Israeli national anthem.

Egalitarianism and the lack of cliques

Another way that adolescent society in Even Yosef replicates the communal structure is in its egalitarian ethos ('we all are friends here') which inhibits the formation of cliques. Just as there are no kinship based (or other types) of corporate political (village sub-) groups among the adults, so there are few friendship cliques among the youth. Similarly, in a (non-agricultural) Yemenite community in Israel that is not divided into mutually exclusive kinship groups, research on the youth shows that there are no conspicuous friendship cliques.[1] In contrast, research in two traditional Lebanese communities indicates that lineage affiliation significantly affects the adolescents' choice of friends (Fuller 1961: 62; Williams 1968: 87–90).

Leadership patterns

As indicated above, sociometric data indicate the presence of certain 'stars' who are leaders among the youth by virtue of their stronger orientation to the wider society (p. 144). Table 21 presents data relevant to this hypothesis[2] and shows that those youths with a strong OWS are much more likely to appear as sociometric leaders than those with a weaker OWS. Just as among

[1] See P. Cohen (1962) and Katz and Zloczower (1961). The latter authors, in discussing the lack of cliques among the Yemenite adolescents, state that within the Yemenite community there is a general stress on familial (as opposed to 'universal') values and an overall acceptance of parental authority by the younger generation. This, they suggest, implies that there is little need for extensive social (and intensive psychological) peer-group relationships among the adolescents. One inference from this hypothesis might be that those youth who are more oriented toward the wider society are more likely to be involved in peer-group networks than those who are locally oriented. The data on Even Yosef, however, show no association ($\phi = 0.063$, $n = 32$) between strong OWS and involvement in a reciprocal sociometric choice. When the total sample is partialled by the OWS of the fathers, there remains no association between OWS of the youth and reciprocal sociometric involvement for the sons of the more cosmopolitan fathers. In the case of the weak OWS fathers, however, a slight tendency in the hypothesized direction appears.

[2] Table 21 includes only boys who received one or more sociometric choices (those who received no choices were excluded). The resulting distribution was divided at the median.

the village adults then, the leaders of the male youth serve as cultural intermediaries between the wider society and their more local-oriented peers.

TABLE 21. *Orientation to the wider society of the youths and number of sociometric choices received*

	Number of choices		
OWS	(8–3)	(2–1)	Totals
Strong	8	5	13
Weak	3	11	14
Totals	11	16	27

$\phi = 0.408$; P (exact) < 0.05.

The two-step transmission of culture

The youths with a strong OWS come into greater contact with the world outside of Even Yosef, of course, by definition. In addition these boys visit the nearby town and city more frequently than the other youths. Moreover, they are likely to travel to the city two or three times a month just in order to spend time there, while the other boys go only for some specific purpose, such as to make a purchase or see a movie. On the occasions that youth leaders came to the village, the strong OWS youths attended the activities with much greater frequency than the others. Similarly, these boys spent more of their free time with the ethnographer than did those with the weaker OWS. There are several boys who have considered Hebraicizing their (given or family) names (pp. 43–4, n.2), and one, in fact, has legally done so. All of these boys are in the strong OWS category.

Viewed as a communicative process, the cultural influences which impinge upon those youths who have greater contact with the wider society are, in turn, transmitted by them to their less cosmopolitan peers. For example, in attempting to learn a trade, these boys took the initiative of establishing contacts in the city, or in neighboring settlements. These initial contacts served as links for other youths who imitated the behavior of the inno-vators. Social dancing was first learned by the acculturated youth, who then taught it to their less acculturated comrades (Goldberg n.d.). Similarly, sunglasses worn 'cosmetically', rather than medically, were introduced by the youth who had more contact with the outside, and were then incorporated into the cultural inventory of the youth as a whole. This two-step flow of influence was also observed in the realm of language.

Modern Standard Hebrew contains a traditional word for 'cash' (as opposed to 'check', or 'credit'). However, the loan word *kesh* or *keshmāni* is frequently employed in Israeli vernacular.[1] I had been in Even Yosef for over a year and had never heard the word *keshmāni* until it was once used by one of the more acculturated boys in the village. At that time he asked me if I knew what the word meant, suggesting that he had only recently learned its meaning himself. Within several weeks, *keshmāni* had become a commonplace word in the speech of the youth, and the younger adults, apparently having been introduced by one of the strong OWS sociometric leaders.

The replication of the structure of the community within adolescent society is further indicated by the fact that the more acculturated youth are willing to initiate new forms of behavior, the egalitarian pressures of their peers notwithstanding. By contrast, DeVos (1968: 366–7) cites several instances in which boys, in acculturative contexts, who were personally motivated to adopt new forms of behavior were inhibited from doing so by the leveling criticism of their peers.

In sum, this chapter has attempted to analyze some mechanisms of continuity and change. The community traditionally has been able to cope with a changing environment because of the presence of an elite group with a stronger orientation to the wider society, relative to the majority of the community. The elite, by virtue of their position, are first to come into contact with changing conditions and are also the best equipped to adapt to these changes. Their successful adaptation in turn reinforces their elite position. This mechanism of dealing with change has survived over the generations because the elite families have socialized their

---

[1] Haim Blanc (personal communication) states that the *kesh/keshmāni* variants correspond to communal dialect differences in modern spoken Hebrew. The former variant characterizes the Ashkenazic (European) dialect, while the latter is found in Middle Eastern Israeli Hebrew. This indicates, Blanc suggests, that the boys of Even Yosef, when outside the village, have more contact with Middle Easterners than with Europeans. My own observations and interviews corroborate this conclusion.

children to have similar positive attitudes toward the wider society. On the basis of these demonstrated orientations, the children of the elite are likely to be selected for leadership positions in the succeeding generation. This pattern of leadership selection is prefigured in the structure of adolescent society, where the more acculturated youths are accorded high status and serve to introduce the other youths to new forms of behavior prevalent in the wider society. Finally, this analysis has been made possible by combining structural analysis with attitudinal measurement to elucidate how social-psychological leadership 'resources' are maintained, within the community, over the generations.

7. Some general considerations

A work of scholarship, by tradition, should present some new idea, some innovation. Innovation, according to one anthropological treatise, 'is an intimate linkage or fusion of two or more elements that have not been previously joined in just this fashion...' (Barnett, 1953: 181). This view of the process of change in the ideas held by men dovetails with other social theories which view thought and behavior as progressing through a series of resolutions of distinct (or opposing) beliefs and actions. Accordingly, I find it congenial to discuss whatever contribution the social history of Even Yosef may make to general theory in relation to several general 'bipolar' issues, namely, materialism versus 'mentalism', uniformity and heterogeneity, history as against 'functionalism', and sociology in opposition to psychology.

Theories do not stand or fall on the basis of single cases, so rather than continue the detailed presentation of data, I will indicate which perspectives have made most sense in terms of the data already analyzed. Some speculative interpretations also will be offered, and I will discuss how recourse to biological analogies have helped provide an overview for my interpretation of stability and change in Even Yosef.

In recent years there has been a reactivation of the long-standing debate on the relative importance of *material*, as opposed to *mental*, factors in understanding social life. The latter approach emphasizes the 'rigorous description of indigenous cultural categories' (Goodenough 1969: 332), while the former 'assigns priority to the study of the material conditions of sociocultural life' (Harris 1968: 4). This approach, labeled cultural materialism, claims that an analogue of natural selection is operative in social life, with techno-economic success replacing success in biological reproduction.

In examining this analogy it is important to note that biological evolution is an ongoing, yet long-range process in comparison to the life span of a single individual. Culture change, as well, may be slow and imperceptible, but it also may be rapid and dramatic, as major alterations in sociocultural configurations can occur within a few years. Thus, within a short period of time, a centuries-old community of Jews in Tripolitania removed itself from its technoeconomic (and geographic) environment and 'took root', with apparent viability, in a new material setting.

One aspect of this success story is, of course, the rapid adaptation of the traditional social structure to the technoeconomic realities of moshav life. No one would deny that any workable community does fit into its particular material environment. The claim, however, that 'similar arrangements of labor in production and distribution *call forth* similar kinds of social groupings' (Harris 1968: 4 – emphasis mine) seems misleading in this instance. The traditional social organization of this Jewish community, featuring the political importance of the sheikh, the elite/non-elite distinction, and the emphasis of the nuclear family, indeed seems to have been well adapted to technoeconomic conditions in the Gharian. In addition, however, if my interpretation is correct, these arrangements also fit well into the material framework of the Israeli moshav, which consists of very different techno-economic elements. Moreover, it appears that adaptation to the Israeli situation was made possible, to a significant degree, by the political structure that the Gharian Jews 'brought with them' from Tripolitania. It is difficult to know how these social arrangements 'arose' in the Gharian (if in fact they originated there), but it seems clear that they were not 'called forth' by conditions in Even Yosef, into which they also fit so well.

There is a general point at issue here which is raised by pursuing the analogy between 'culture' and 'genes', as is implied by explanation in terms of natural selection. As far as can be ascertained from biological research, there is no mechanism by which biological entities can bring about genetic changes which would prove adaptive to new environmental circumstances affecting the individual organism or species. That is to say, when changes in the environment exert pressure on living organisms, there is no known way in which these organisms can 'call forth' genetic alterations suitable to the new situation. Rather, species are dependent on genetic mutations, whose production seems to be largely fortuitous, and influenced by factors outside 'the system'.

The implication with regard to culture is that environmental conditions do not 'automatically produce' technoeconomic configurations, which do not, in turn, 'call forth' social arrangements and so on. Rather, the appearance of new cultural forms, more suitable than the old to new conditions, may be largely a function of events outside a specific cultural system. That is, the origin of new 'cultural matter' may stem from individual innovation and/or diffusion. Once new cultural forms are introduced into a community or society, however, their fate may be largely a matter of social selection. The main point here is not to 'refute' cultural materialism, but to stress that it is premature to assign 'primacy' to one aspect of the environment of a cultural system, without, at least, stating with greater precision the meaning of the term primacy, or specifying the mechanisms by which one level of events influences another.

While many may consider the debate over material determinism a forgotten issue, I have, in fact, utilized some parallels between natural history and social history in analyzing the data gathered in Even Yosef. This is done most successfully, it seems, if distinctions are made among various aspects of 'the environment', and attention is focused separately to the economic environment, the political environment and so forth (e.g. Parsons 1961: 36).[1] Thus, the internal structure of the Gharian Jewish community appears to be most immediately related to its political environment. The weak position of the Jews as *dhimmis* (a 'protected' minority) meant that it was adaptive for the community to play down internal cleavages which might have invited a 'divide and rule' policy on the part of the current power. Instead, political quiescence characterized the majority of the Jews, and political interchanges with the environment were concentrated in the hands of the sheikh. This situation of socio-political minority, of course, was by no means unique to the Jews of the Gharian, but has recurred often in both Moslem and Christian environments. Consequently, the political structure of the Gharian Jews is similar to that described for Jewish (and other) minority communities in various times and places.

For example, on the basis of preliminary data from other

[1] A similar point of view is advocated by Morton-Williams (1968: 5–6) who states that 'institutions have a different history from the societies that contain them'.

Tripolitanian Jewish towns, the sheikh was a singularly important political figure elsewhere in the region. Similarly, the 'court Jew' was a familiar political image in many periods of European (Stern 1950) and Middle Eastern history (Fischel 1969). It is thus reasonable to assume that the political structure of the Gharian Jewish community, viewed as a *cultural model* through which political relations between the community and its environment best could be handled, had its (historical) origin outside the community in question. On the other hand, it is not surprising that such a widely diffused structure proved equal to the task of survival in this particular locale as well.

Returning to the general discussion, a further implication of the procedure of distinguishing different levels and aspects of 'the environment' is that it calls for the specification of various 'exchanges' between particular external factors and corresponding relevant subsystems of the community. The appropriateness of an 'exchange' viewpoint is obvious with regard to economic matters, but we may again turn to the political sphere for further elaboration of its wider utility. It is clear, in the traditional situation in the Gharian, that the ruling power provided 'protection' for the Jewish minority, but what political resource(s) did the group in power receive in return? A tentative answer may be given on two levels.

First of all, as suggested by the analogy with the 'court Jew' (above), the literate and commercially skilled Jews provided administrative talents to local rulers and administrators. This was the case in the Gharian during the early part of the previous century (p. 19, and a similar situation has been reported for other 'remote' Jewish communities (Fischel 1944). These administrative talents were particularly valuable because the Jews were a religio-political minority, who were not in a position to supplant the individuals or groups in power. More recently, too, under non-Islamic rule, some of the Gharian Jews were suppliers to the Italian and British military (this was the case in many areas of Tripolitania), a task which would have been accompanied by much more tension, for the European powers, had it been carried out by local Moslems.

At a more symbolic level, it may be claimed that at the same time that the Moslem rulers supplied protection to the Jewish community, the Jews' 'acceptance' of this protection helped legitimate the political power of the group that held it.[1] Although quite different in symbolic content, a similar situation may be seen in the moshav in Israel when the settlement authorities provided vital resources to the new immigrants, while the settlers provided the authorities with their *raison d'être* (Willner 1969).

To summarize the argument thus far, we have maintained that a natural selection approach may be applied usefully to social history, provided that a more refined and differentiated concept of 'the environment' is employed. From this point of view the primary focus of continuity in our case study is made up of the images 'in the minds' of the Gharian Jews which inform the organization of communal political activities. This particular set of cultural symbols (i.e. the community's political structure) has survived in the new social setting of the moshav because it has proved compatible with, and, indeed, helped to shape, the new organizational activities in the Israeli cooperative village. These new interactional patterns, in turn, have survived in, and helped integrate the technoeconomic arrangements of moshav life. To make the biological analogy explicit, we know that the units of biologic intergenerational transmission are the genes, but the immediate environment of genes are the somatic cells and structures, and it is only through these latter 'levels' that genes interact with the environment external to the organism. We shall further allude to the biological model in the ensuing discussion homogeneity and variability.

The description and explanation of variability, as is well known, is central to the concerns of physical anthropology, which sees genetic variation as the 'raw material' of evolutionary selection. An emphasis on variability has recently been advocated by some linguists as well. For example, Weinreich, Labov and Herzog (1968) have argued that the assumption of a completely homogeneous speech community, which has been implied by various linguistic theories, has worked against the development of a theory of language change. These authors advocate the description and analysis of language in terms of structured heterogeneity. Within the tradition of cultural anthropology, as well, two essays,

---

[1] For example, according to Hacohen's account (ms: 81a–b), when the rebel Ghoma conquered the Gharian (during the last century, see pp. 19–20, 23) 'he proclaimed throughout his camp, saying "Guard the honor of the Jews; whosoever does them evil, his blood shall be upon his head".'

published a decade ago (Kaplan 1961; Wallace 1961), both claim that one of the weaknesses of the early culture-and-personality approach was an emphasis on the uniformity of culture patterns, and a neglect of the diversity which may be found even within the simplest society. A concern with variability also grows out of the previous discussion concerning the multiple levels of a community's (or society's) environment.

If the premise is accepted that a community must function within a differentiated environment, then it follows that a variety of internal resources must be available to meet the variegated external demands. Variation may also be viewed as simply stemming from the 'dialectic' of internal differentiation. Thus, for example, if one finds that certain qualities of leadership are required in a given political setting, one should necessarily look for a corresponding, but different (complementary), form of followership (Bateson 1942). With respect to the Gharian Jews, a study only of the attributes and attitudes of the elite clearly would have been misleading, but the same may be said of a study which only formulated an ideal 'typical' rank-and-file villager. Moreover, a statement about the 'average' villager representing a 'mean' of the elite and non-elite would not have shown the attitudinal variation in its relation to the community's social structure. By contrast, our linkage of an attitudinal distribution to a specific social setting, provided, as we have argued, a mechanism whereby the community maintained its structure in spite of external changes. The general point is that the study of internal variation is just as important to understanding 'stability' as it is to the study of 'change', because stable systems, no differently from changing ones, must constantly adapt to an external (variegated) environment. In addition, I would maintain that the perspective of continual adaptation (whether overt change is observed or not) can help bridge the oft-cited gap between historical and functional interpretation.

At the risk of losing the reader's interest (but for the sake of clarity), I will first remark on the concept of function. Among the various ways that this term has been employed in the social sciences, two usages seem to be of particular importance (Inkeles 1964: 34–9). The first is the formal idea that two (or more) sets of phenomena covary systematically. It is hard to see how this idea might be dispensed with in disciplined research. The second meaning, which has been associated with the terms of equilibrium and homeostasis, implies that (at least) one of the sets of (social) phenomena under consideration must stay within defined limits in order for the society or community to perdure. Classically, this notion has been phrased that 'social integration is maintained', while rarely is measurement carried out to indicate the value(s) on a scale of social integration below (or above) which disintegration (or 'over-integration')[1] may be said to occur. Moreover, our earlier discussion implies that thinking about homeostasis solely in terms of the 'overall integration of society' may be too gross a procedure, and that focusing on functioning subsystems within a society, and the specific external factors that interact with that sub-system, may be a more illuminating approach.

In brief, I would argue that it is self-evident that many empirical cases of social stability have been observed, and this legitimizes the search for mechanisms which maintain stability in the face of external change and internal tension. To deny the existence of homeostatic mechanisms in social life is no more warranted than to choose to study only those instances in which they seem to be present. What is clearly needed are the conceptual and methodo-logical tools to distinguish kinds and degrees of social and cultural continuity, including criteria for judging when sociocultural forms have been altered to such a degree that they may be said to have passed away.[2]

With reference to Even Yosef, we have described and analyzed what might be considered a remarkable stability in the community's political structure during the past century, in view of the radical changes in the community's environment. An explanation of this stability has been offered, and some of the main features of the explanation are summarized in diagrammatic form below. Specific arrows in this diagram refer to functional links in the first sense mentioned above, while the diagram in its entirety consists of a homeostatic model. It should be clear that while the model may be

---

[1] The suggestion here is that an 'overly-integrated' society may be one that has become well-adapted to a very specific environment, but may prove to be 'inflexible' when external circumstances change.

[2] For example, in the discussion of the (possible) gradual change in moshav politics from 'autocracy' to 'democracy' (p. 131), we would want to be able to assess the point of transition from one form to another. Ideally, a separate set of measure-ments would be made with regard to the overt behavioral forms, on one hand, and the ideas and values of the actors on the other.

labeled 'functional', it does not assume 'timelessness', and, in fact, was developed to explain historically documented continuity, within the context of change over time. To make this explicit, a representation of sequential time has been included in the chart $(t_0, t_1, \ldots)$, and, as will be discussed, this forces us to consider aspects of the community's internal processes which have not yet been explored.

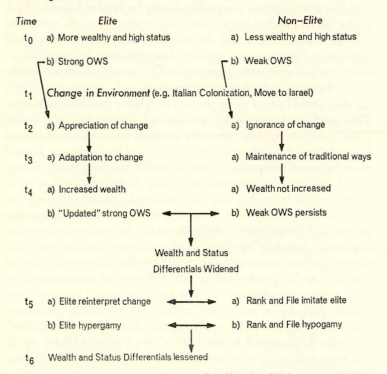

Time	Elite	Non-Elite
t_0	a) More wealthy and high status	a) Less wealthy and high status
	b) Strong OWS	b) Weak OWS
t_1	Change in Environment (e.g. Italian Colonization, Move to Israel)	
t_2	a) Appreciation of change	a) Ignorance of change
t_3	a) Adaptation to change	a) Maintenance of traditional ways
t_4	a) Increased wealth	a) Wealth not increased
	b) "Updated" strong OWS	b) Weak OWS persists
	Wealth and Status Differentials Widened	
t_5	a) Elite reinterpret change	a) Rank and File imitate elite
	b) Elite hypergamy	b) Rank and File hypogamy
t_6	Wealth and Status Differentials lessened	

Figure 7. Diagrammatic representation of the functional links among some factors affecting the community's development over time.

For example, the diagram posits that there is a time (t_4-t_5) during which the community is characterized by a greater differential of wealth between the elite and non-elite, resulting from the elite's meeting the challenge of change, than it was at the base-line time of 'stability' (t_0). This supposition is necessarily implied in the 'two-step' model of acculturative influence (pp. 134–5), unless one imagines the elite/non-elite relationship as two ends of a metal rod in which one end begins to move at the same instant that the other is pulled. Thus, even if the 'return to equilibrium' (t_6) interpretation of the elite/non-elite cultural transmission is correct, one must assume some period of lag during which the elite have 'moved ahead' by coping with the new situation and have thereby increased the gap between themselves and the rank-and-file (t_4).

If this notion seems acceptable, it may be further hypothesized, at the social-psychological level, that during periods when the elite are 'advancing', and the non-elite are not, the latter will experience (and express) greater dissatisfaction with regard to their position within the community. Conversely, the times during which the rank and file are learning from, and 'catching up with', the elite should prove to be periods of relative psychological ease. Thus (and this is very risky speculation), during my 'revisits' to Even Yosef in 1968–9, when the external decor of many houses blatantly declared the newly-won wealth of their owners, I heard more frequent complaints about economic inequity in the village than I had been accustomed to hearing during my earlier, more intensive field trip. This may have reflected a phase[1] of village life in which the gap between the elite and the non-elite had become greater and grown more salient. Similarly the successive, but un-sustained, demands by some of the younger farmers that they receive greater representation on the moshav committee may be seen as periodic dissatisfaction with, followed by acquiescence to, their relative social position. The fact that 'social systems' may exhibit periods of successful coping with external problems, followed by a phase of internal integration and 'pulling together', has been documented in the case of small groups (Bales 1953), and may well apply to communities in relation to their environ-ments.

In general, two of the major criticisms of functionalism, that it is ahistorical and that it ignores conflict, appear to be intertwined. One antidote to these criticisms may be to explicitly plot posited functional interpretations on the axis of time, and 'follow the

---

[1] The use of the word *phase* indicates that the diagram does not imply the existence of a definite *period* when *all* the rank-and-file are dissatisfied with their position vis-à-vis the elite, followed by a period when everyone is satisfied. Similarly, the arrows in the diagram should not be taken to mean that all the elite appreciate and react to change more rapidly than all of the non-elite, as there clearly is variation and mobility in this matter.

arrows wherever they lead', be it to homeostasis or increased tension and change. This procedure, in the case of Even Yosef, has forced the recognition of inherent sources of conflict linked to the presence of intracommunal variability,[1] the very same variability that has been cited as contributing to the community's ability to maintain itself in the face of change. The supposed antithesis between functionalism and (changing or non-changing) history, then, perhaps grows out of the initial omission of time from the functionalist paradigm.[2]

The case of Even Yosef, thus far, has been considered in the light of several anthropological issues. At several points it has been suggested that biological analogies may help elucidate the complex interrelationships of various factors which are frequently cited in sociologic analysis. This will now be illustrated through further elaboration of the discussions pertaining to political and domestic structure, after briefly pointing out some further parallels between genes in biology and culture in behavior.

The basic distinction, in biological discourse, between genotype and phenotype, has several implications for analogical analysis in the realm of behavior. If culture is viewed as the 'genetic component' of observable (phenotypic) behavior, it follows that culture must be understood in its relationship to social, psychological and biological forces that shape behavior. Both culture and genes are the vehicles of the transmission of information, respectively, from the behavioral and biological past. On the negative side, neither genes nor culture are very amenable to direct observation but must be studied by a variety of inferential methods. Most importantly for our discussion, however, is the fact that phenotype and genotype are not isomorphic, and that the genetic make up of an individual is always more complex than might be inferred from the simple classification of his phenotypic characteristics.

In considering the realm of behavior, then, we assume that the symbolic systems (culture) 'in the minds' of individuals and groups,

[1] Functional interpretation has been criticized for ignoring *conflict*, as well as variability, and this criticism is undoubtedly justified. The general lack of conflict in Even Yosef (pp. 108–11), however, keeps us from considering this issue in the present context.

[2] The reader will recall, also, the consideration of several factors related to successful *change* in Even Yosef (and other communities), and the discussion of their (functional) interrelationships (pp. 73–7).

is always more variegated than would be obvious from the straightforward recording of overt behavior. This is the basic reason why, in studying change, it is necessary to collect data on beliefs, values, and so forth, even though these 'ideas' may not be directly expressed[1] in observable action.[2] These various, and often contradictory, idea systems provide the 'raw material' of culture change[3] which may be differentially 'selected for' as the social, psychological and material environments of the symbol systems change. The fact that economic and social changes sometimes rapidly 'call forth' appropriate symbol systems, suggests, using this model, that those symbol systems may have already been present within the overall heterogeneous 'culture pool' of a group. It should thus be clear that the study of individual 'mental' data is complementary, and not in opposition, to the study of material conditions.

Reference was made, earlier, to the recent emphasis in anthropological research on the 'rigorous description of indigenous cultural categories'. In terms of the analogy at hand, this approach is seen as parallel to biological research aimed at 'cracking' the genetic code. The recent approach of ethnographic semantics may be seen, in part, as a descendant of the culture-and-personality tradition in its attempt to systematically understand the *meaning* (cultural) dimension of behavior. This recent effort has turned from psychology to linguistics (another discipline concerned with codes) for conceptual and methodological inspiration. One assumption imported willy-nilly from linguistics, however (for reasons of convenience, perhaps, rather than for theory), is the validity of working with a single informant, or the habit of presenting findings as if they represent what is 'in the mind' of a single typical group member. In doing this, ethnographic semantics often ignores the criticism directed toward culture-and-personality about overlooking the importance of variability. To use the words of Harris (1968: 585) it is, in one sense, 'social psychology shorn of its statistical base'.

[1] The word *expressed* is used as parallel to the concept of *expressivity* in genetics (Stern 1960: 297).
[2] Similarly, Geertz has commented (1967) that 'anthropologists tend to interview intellectuals and observe peasants, and might better *interview peasants* and observe intellectuals...' In the present work we have tried to show the importance of the actors' *awareness* of alternative behaviour patterns (e.g. pp. 4, 41–2, 106–7, 127, 128, 149).   [3] As genes are the 'raw material' of biological change.

The case study of Even Yosef has not had the benefit of new techniques associated with ethnographic semantics, but has relied, instead, on the traditional technology of interviewing and attitude measurement. The data thus gathered, however, are viewed as constituting a sample of the heterogeneous (but structured) pool of (explicit and implicit) 'categories' which, in their totality, comprise the culture of the community under consideration. This pool of cultural 'material' provides the potentiality of adaptation to future (changed or unchanged) environmental conditions. Two specific illustrations from the case at hand should assist in showing the usefulness of this formulation.

To repeat, once more, one of our major findings, the political image of the centrality of a single leader, coupled with the quiescence of communal subgroups, has shown its survival capacity both in the Gharian and in Even Yosef, despite differences in the concrete social interactions that were 'controlled by' this model, and to which this model has had to prove itself fit. This is not to say, however, that other models of political action are not to be found within the community's cultural repertoire. On the contrary, we have emphasized that the awareness of political organization based on competing kin groups could be found within the community's storehouse of ideas both in Tripolitania (p. 42) and in Israel (p. 127). This should be obvious from the fact that, when I asked the questions making up the 'public opinion poll' (p. 122) concerning the importance of the ten Hajjaj brothers, everyone understood perfectly well to what I was alluding, although most did not think that this model of moshav politics was accurate.

If, however, the conditions of settlement and development in Even Yosef had been different from what they were, it is quite possible that the community would have split into factions, as happened in many other Middle Eastern moshavim. In this case the villagers of Even Yosef, too, would have had available to them a social ideology utilizing the idiom of patri-kin relations, to justify their factionalism.

The view that cultural systems contain variant, and even opposing, models of social behavior does not imply that individuals and groups immediately shift their political images as the social reality demands. Rather, to utilize Geertz' phrase (1966: 9), political images constitute both *models of* and *models for* political behavior. Among the Gharian Jews the model of a strong leader with weak subgroups is not simply a reflection of the political reality but is also an arrangement to which positive valuation is attached.[1] Thus, the maintenance of the traditional structure of the community came about not because it fits effortlessly into the new setting, but because of conscious and unconscious strivings on the part of the Gharian Jews to re-establish communal political forms in which they were most comfortable and which they found meaningful. These 'inherited' political forms, then, partially modified the new environment to which they had been transplanted, a modification that was made possible by the flexibility of the moshav framework.[2]

The utility of an internal variation–selection perspective on social change may be illustrated also with regard to domestic organization. Although I do not have exact data, it is clear that the extended family form was more prevalent in the Gharian than it is in contemporary Even Yosef. It has been common to assume in situations where the extended family is widespread, that this reflects a cultural value on patriliny, respect for the father, many sons, and so forth. This assumption, it seems, is analogous to the confusion between phenotype and genotype. The statistical prevalence of the extended family form is indeed related to cultural values, but it is related also to specific economic and social conditions. In particular, if the situation arises where sons are provided with economic opportunities other than continuing in the father's trade (or, working the father's land)[3] they very often choose the new opportunities. This choice also is related to values, in this case the value of economic independence (pp. 111–12). In addition, the psychological tensions generated within the extended family often provide the motivational push for the nuclearization of that family.

In the case of Even Yosef, as has been shown (pp. 139–40), there is variation in the domestic organization among the families of the community and corresponding variation in the psychological relationships between parents and children. We infer that this variation existed in the Gharian as well, and is also linked to

---

[1] This point is discussed at length by Silverman (1969) in dealing, interestingly enough, with another kind of 'transplanted community' in Oceania.

[2] Weingrod (1966: 143–66) stresses *reciprocal change* in the moshav situation, that is, the way the immigrant settlers affected the absorbing society.

[3] See, for example, Rosenfeld's analysis (1958).

variations in values concerning domestic life. The type of variation referred to is akin to what is called by Kluckhohn and
Strodtbeck (1961) the difference between 'lineal' and 'collateral'
value orientations. Thus, while a common overt (phenotypic)
form of the family in the Gharian may have been the extended
family, this observable homogeneity hid, I believe, an underlying
(genotypic) variability. In some of these families (the majority,
I hypothesize), the value orientations called upon to give direction
to family organization were the traditional patriarchal images
commonly associated with Middle Eastern culture. These values
were supported by the social reality in which there were limited
economic opportunities outside the family, and general community pressure for 'obedience' and cohesiveness stemming from
minority group status. Upon the move to Israel, when these
external supports for 'lineal' family structure disappeared, the
fissioning of the extended family followed quite rapidly.

In a minority of families, however, the extended family organization was informed by values which stressed mutual adjustment
and compatibility, rather than the 'sacred' authority of the father.
I recall, again, the family of Rebbi Shmuel (pp. 103–4) in which
the elder males graciously relinquished their decision-making
prerogatives to the younger men who were more knowledgeable
about the moshav situation. The cohesion of this type of family
was due more to the strength of internal ties than it was to the
'props' of external pressure. The move to Even Yosef did not
necessarily eliminate the extended family form in this case. In
other words, this latter (numerically small) variant of values
related to the extended family was able to survive in the new social
setting, while the former (and more common) variant was
'extinguished'.

In conclusion, I hope that I have persuaded the reader that
social analysis can be enriched by considering individual *psychological* variables. While these do represent distinct levels of analysis,
the nature of their interrelations is a perfectly valid, if not crucial,
area of investigation. To argue whether anthropologists should be
studying social categories *or* should be studying material conditions is as naive as attempting to decide whether biology should
inquire into genetic structure *or* should investigate the adaptation
of species to their enironment.

Interviewing the youths and their fathers

After several months of work in Even Yosef, some of the youths, seeing that I was going to be a more or less 'permanent feature' of village life began to approach me on a friendly basis. Thus, rapport with them was established at their own initiative, rather than at mine. This obviated the problem of 'penetrating' a group that was resisting a researcher who had come to 'study them'. The youths who took this initiative were those who were generally more oriented to life outside the village and saw me as a source of information and diversion. There was, in this way, a bias in the relationship of the researcher to the youths. A certain type of youth was 'naturally' attracted to me and the converse was also true. Other boys were just as content to have nothing to do with 'outsiders'. This situation, therefore, called for a strategy of studying a representative sample of the youth and their behavior.

There also were two other reasons why participant observation was only able to provide limited data on the behavior and attitudes of the youth. First of all, the village covers a large area (Figure 5, pp. 57–8) and the youth, during the day-time, are scattered in diverse points in the village. Frequently I would hear of, or observe, certain events which some villagers would not hear about till a day or two later. Of course, the opposite also took place. Thus, I frequently had to rely on reports about events which occurred at the very time I was 'in the village'.

Secondly, there were certain classes of behavior which were kept from the public eye (including my own). One such class of behavior, family conflicts, seemed of particular relevance to research on the acculturation of the youth. In order to systematically collect reports about behavior, and to achieve standardization in eliciting these reports, I decided to conduct interviews among a sample of youth. An interview schedule was also desirable in order to collect data on values and attitudes.

Ideally, an interview, or any assessment instrument, should be administered separately as a pre-test and then again in a final 'test' form. In the field situation this was impractical due to the small number of subjects available. Thus, the pre-testing and testing were not carried out as separate operations, but I modified the interview schedule during the initial interviews till I thought I was obtaining valid and reliable data.

A second interview schedule was administered to the fathers of the youths in the sample. The mean age of these 28 fathers was 52.5 years (median = 52.0), while the average age of the heads of households of all the moshav members was 44.1 (median = 43.9). I do not believe that, for most matters, this difference in age introduces a bias which disallows generalization from this sample to the total adult male population. The reasons which made systematic interviewing of the youth desirable apply equally to the study of their fathers. It is perhaps superfluous to recall that the traditional separation of the sexes within the community accounts for the 'androcentric' bias of this study.

Most of the interviews of the youth were conducted in my own house, several kilometers from Even Yosef. I attempted to have the boys come individually, but many insisted on coming with a friend. Out of 37 (of an ideal 41) interviews administered, 21 were with only the interviewee present and the others were in groups of two and three. The interviews with the young men living on the 'new moshav' were conducted at their homes in that village. On any given item of the interview schedule the number of responses is usually between 30 and 35.

Interviewing some of the youth in groups of two or three does not universally invalidate the results thus obtained. In many instances, such as in questions dealing with background data and with work routines, the results seem perfectly valid. In other instances I was able to compare the responses of the youth with data obtained in other ways. The answers to questions such as 'who are your three best friends?' were clearly influenced by the presence of other boys. However, the fact that an interviewee chose certain friends to accompany him to the interview perhaps indicated that they were, in fact, among his 'best friends'. Questions dealing with family conflict might also have been influenced by the presence of others but I did not find that the youths who were interviewed alone were more willing to talk about conflict with parents than were the youths interviewed with groups. In all instances I insisted that friends leave the room when the picture technique was administered (see Appendix E).

The interviews of the fathers were carried out in their own homes, as the adults did not wish to come to my house. In nine cases out of 25 the interviewee was alone in the room, but in most cases other people were there, usually his wife and children. In most instances the interview was carried out in Hebrew, but in a few cases a younger member of the family had to act as an interpreter from Hebrew to Arabic.

(a)

(b)

Figure 8a and b. Pictures used in eliciting parent–youth conflict story.

With respect to the questions of validity and reliability I was more satisfied with the interviews of the youth than with the interviews of the parents. In both cases there was frequently a lack of motivation to comply with the discipline of an interview schedule. The parents, in particular, were at a loss to understand my switch of roles from a 'non-directive' participant-observer to an interviewer who asked more highly-structured questions.

As was mentioned above, I was particularly interested in eliciting responses on parent–youth conflict, being unable to gather much relevant data by participant observation. The interview, however, was only partially successful in eliciting responses about conflict. Most of the answers were terse, and none of the interviewees showed any interest in elaborating the subject. I therefore attempted to assess the extent of conflict by other techniques, including a projective 'test' fashioned after an instrument used by Parker (1964: 327).

The projective technique was based on a series of pictures, presented to the youths on cards, which depicted situations similar to those common in the village. The boys were asked to tell stories about the cards and to specify the type of interaction going on between the actors in the pictures. The responses were recorded on tape and later translated and transcribed by me into English. Upon returning from the field, I gave two of the pictures (those most closely related to parent–youth conflict), the translated responses, and a set of instructions to two judges. The judges independently scored each of the stories on a three point scale as to the extent of intergenerational conflict reflected in them, and agreed in more than 90% of the cases (the pictures utilized are presented in Figure 8a and b).

The ratings given to the picture-stories, and codings of direct questions about parent–youth conflicts were combined into an overall index of 'intergenerational conflict'. This index gives equal weight to the 'projective' and 'direct interview' measures of conflict which were highly correlated ($\phi = 0.555$, $P < 0.005$). The distribution of 'intergenerational conflict' scores was split at the median for use in the Tables.

The index of 'orientation to the wider society' of the fathers

The orientation to the wider society (OWS) index is based on four variables: (1) farming ability, (2) receipt of a daily newspaper, (3) occupational aspirations for sons, and (4) criticism of the local school (see p. 96). These variables were 'measured' as follows:

Farming ability. The fathers were classified into the categories of 'good farmers' or 'poor farmers' by the agricultural instructor (p. 67).

Receipt of a daily newspaper. The fathers were classified as to whether or not they subscribed to *Hatzofe*, the newspaper of the National Religious Party. Other newspapers rarely reached the village.

Occupational aspirations for sons. Out of 26 fathers interviewed, 13 said they would like their sons to acquire a 'trade' (or 'profession', Hebrew: *miqtzo'a*). These were classified as having 'non-agricultural occupational aspirations'. The 4 fathers who said they wanted their sons to be farmers, or they 'didn't know', were classified as 'not having occupational aspirations "out of" agriculture'.

Criticism of the local school. The rationale of using this as an indicator of a strong orientation toward the wider society is discussed on p. 148. The fathers who expressed criticism of the school were placed in one category, and the fathers who expressed no opinion, or stated that the school was satisfactory were placed in another.

Tables 22 through 27 show the intercorrelations of the variables. The index gives equal weight to each of the four items. The distribution of OWS scores was split at the median for the Tables in the text.

TABLE 22. *Farming ability and criticism of the school*

| Farming ability | Criticism of the school | | |
	Criticizes	Doesn't criticize	Totals
Good	3	9	12
Poor	8	3	11
Totals	11	12	23

$$\phi = 0.477; \quad P < 0.05.$$

TABLE 23. *Farming ability and receiving a newspaper*

| Farming ability | Receives a newspaper | | |
	Yes	No	Totals
Good	8	4	12
Poor	3	10	13
Totals	11	14	25

$$\phi = 0.439; \quad P < 0.05.$$

TABLE 24. *Farming ability of the fathers and the occupational aspirations of these fathers for their sons*

| Farming ability | Occupational aspirations | | |
	Non-agriculture	Agriculture, or 'don't know'	Totals
Good	9	3	12
Poor	3	10	13
Totals	12	13	25

$$\phi = 0.519; \quad P < 0.025.$$

TABLE 25. *Criticism of school and receiving a newspaper*

Criticism of the school	Receives a newspaper		
	Yes	No	Totals
Criticizes	1	11	12
Doesn't criticize	9	3	12
Totals	10	14	24

$\phi = 0.676$; $P < 0.001$.

TABLE 26. *Criticism of school and occupational aspirations for sons*

Criticism of the school	Occupational aspirations for sons		
	Non-agricultural	Agricultural	Totals
Criticizes	1	11	12
Doesn't criticize	11	1	12
Totals	12	12	24

$\phi = 0.833$; $P < 0.001$.

TABLE 27. *Receiving a newspaper and occupational aspirations for sons*

Receives newspaper	Occupational aspirations for sons		
	Non-agricultural	Agricultural	Totals
Yes	8	2	10
No	4	11	15
Totals	12	13	25

$\phi = 0.525$; $P < 0.025$.

Matrix of sociometric choices

The individuals listed in the outside columns chose the individuals listed in the top row. The numbers in the cells (1 through 3) indicate whether the chooser chose the individual as a first, second, or third choice. The numbers in the diagonal, set in bold type, indicate the number of reciprocal choices in which the individual is involved. The column totals indicate the number of choices received by the individuals. If a subject chose someone outside of the sample, it is not indicated in the matrix. Also, subjects who were not interviewed *and* received no choices are not listed here so that the total number of individuals shown is 36.

	Chosen																	
Chooser	01	02	03	04	05	06	07	08	09	10	11	12	13	14	15	16	17	18
01	0	–	–	–	–	–	–	–	–	–	–	–	–	–	–	–	–	–
02	–	0	–	–	–	3	–	–	–	–	–	–	–	–	–	–	–	–
03	–	–	0	–	–	–	–	–	–	–	–	–	–	–	–	–	–	–
04	–	–	–	1	–	–	–	–	–	–	–	2	1	–	–	–	–	–
05	–	–	–	–	3	–	–	–	–	–	–	–	–	–	–	2	–	–
06	–	–	–	–	–	1	–	–	–	–	–	–	–	–	–	–	–	–
07	–	–	–	–	–	–	1	–	–	–	–	2	–	–	–	–	3	–
08	–	–	–	–	–	–	–	0	–	–	–	–	–	–	2	–	–	–
09	3	–	–	–	–	–	1	–	0	–	–	–	–	–	–	–	–	–
10	2	–	–	–	–	–	–	–	–	0	–	–	1	–	–	–	–	–
11	–	–	–	–	–	–	–	–	–	–	0	–	–	–	–	–	–	–
12	–	–	–	–	–	–	1	–	–	–	–	2	–	–	–	–	–	–
13	–	–	–	1	–	–	–	–	–	–	–	–	2	–	–	–	–	–
14	–	–	–	–	–	–	–	–	–	–	–	–	–	0	–	–	–	–
15	–	–	–	–	–	–	–	–	–	–	–	–	–	–	0	–	–	–
16	–	–	–	–	1	–	3	–	–	–	–	–	–	–	–	1	–	–
17	–	–	–	–	–	3	–	–	–	–	–	–	–	–	–	2	0	–
18	–	–	–	–	–	1	–	–	–	–	–	–	–	–	–	–	–	0
19	3	–	–	–	–	–	–	–	–	–	–	–	–	–	–	–	–	0
20	–	–	–	3	–	–	–	–	–	–	–	–	–	–	–	–	–	–
21	2	–	–	–	1	–	–	–	–	–	–	–	–	–	–	–	–	–
22	1	–	–	–	3	–	–	–	–	–	–	–	–	–	–	2	–	–
23	1	–	–	–	–	–	–	–	–	–	–	–	–	–	–	–	–	–
24	–	–	–	3	1	–	–	–	–	–	–	–	–	–	–	–	–	–
25	–	–	–	–	–	–	–	–	–	–	3	–	–	2	–	–	–	–
26	–	–	–	–	2	–	–	–	–	–	–	–	–	–	–	1	–	–
27	–	–	–	–	–	–	–	–	–	–	3	–	–	2	–	–	–	–
28	–	–	–	–	–	2	–	–	–	–	–	–	–	–	–	–	–	–
29	–	–	–	–	–	–	–	–	–	–	–	–	–	–	–	–	–	–
30	–	–	–	–	–	–	–	–	–	–	–	–	–	–	–	–	–	–
31	–	3	–	–	–	2	–	–	–	–	–	–	–	–	–	–	–	–
32	–	–	–	–	–	–	–	–	–	–	–	1	–	–	–	–	–	–
33	–	–	–	–	–	–	–	–	–	–	–	–	3	–	–	–	–	–
34	–	–	–	–	–	2	–	–	–	–	–	3	–	–	–	–	–	–
35	–	–	3	–	–	–	–	2	–	–	–	–	–	–	–	–	–	–
36	–	–	–	–	–	2	–	–	–	–	–	–	–	–	3	–	–	–
Total	6	1	1	2	5	7	3	1	0	0	2	4	3	2	2	4	1	0

	Chosen																	
19	20	21	22	23	24	25	26	27	28	29	30	31	32	33	34	35	36	Chooser
–	–	–	–	–	–	–	–	–	–	–	–	–	–	–	–	–	–	01
–	–	–	–	–	–	–	–	–	2	–	–	–	–	–	–	–	–	02
–	–	–	–	–	–	–	–	–	–	–	–	–	–	–	–	–	–	03
–	–	–	–	–	–	3	–	–	–	–	–	–	–	–	–	–	–	04
–	–	1	–	–	–	–	3	–	–	–	–	–	–	–	–	–	–	05
–	–	–	–	–	–	–	–	–	1	–	–	–	–	–	–	–	–	06
–	–	1	–	–	–	–	–	–	–	–	–	–	–	–	–	–	–	07
–	–	–	–	–	–	–	–	–	–	3	–	–	–	–	–	–	–	08
–	–	2	–	–	–	–	–	–	–	–	–	–	–	–	–	–	–	09
–	–	–	–	–	–	–	–	–	–	–	–	–	–	3	–	–	–	10
–	–	–	–	–	–	–	–	–	–	–	–	–	–	–	–	–	–	11
–	–	–	–	–	–	–	–	–	2	–	–	–	3	–	–	–	–	12
3	–	–	–	–	–	–	–	–	–	–	–	–	–	–	2	–	–	13
–	–	–	–	–	–	–	–	–	–	–	–	–	–	–	–	–	–	14
–	–	–	–	–	–	–	–	–	–	–	2	–	–	–	–	–	–	15
–	–	2	–	–	–	–	–	–	–	–	–	–	–	–	–	–	–	16
–	–	–	–	–	–	–	–	–	–	–	–	–	–	–	–	–	–	17
–	–	–	–	–	–	–	–	–	–	–	–	–	–	–	–	–	–	18
0	–	1	–	–	–	–	–	–	–	–	–	–	–	2	–	–	–	19
–	0	–	–	–	–	2	–	1	–	–	–	–	–	–	–	–	–	20
–	–	0	–	–	–	–	3	–	–	–	–	–	–	–	–	–	–	21
–	–	–	0	–	–	–	–	–	–	–	–	–	–	–	–	–	–	22
–	–	3	2	0	–	–	–	–	–	–	–	–	–	–	–	–	–	23
–	–	2	–	–	0	–	–	–	–	–	–	–	–	–	–	–	–	24
–	–	–	–	–	–	0	–	1	–	–	–	–	–	–	–	–	–	25
–	–	3	–	–	–	–	0	–	–	–	–	–	–	–	–	–	–	26
–	–	–	–	–	–	1	–	0	–	–	–	–	–	–	–	–	–	27
–	–	–	–	–	–	–	–	–	0	–	–	–	–	3	–	–	–	28
–	–	–	–	–	–	–	–	–	–	0	–	–	–	–	–	–	–	29
–	–	–	–	–	–	–	–	–	–	–	0	–	–	–	–	–	–	30
–	–	–	–	–	–	–	–	–	–	–	–	0	–	–	1	–	–	31
–	–	–	–	–	–	–	–	–	2	–	–	–	0	–	–	–	–	32
1	–	–	–	2	–	–	–	–	–	–	–	–	–	0	–	–	–	33
–	–	–	–	–	–	–	–	–	1	–	–	–	–	–	0	–	–	34
–	–	–	–	–	–	–	–	–	–	–	–	–	–	–	–	0	–	35
–	–	–	–	–	–	–	–	–	1	–	–	–	–	–	–	–	0	36
2	0	8	1	1	0	3	2	2	6	1	1	0	1	3	2	0	0	Total

The index of 'orientation to the wider society' of the male youths

The four items used to construct the OWS index of the youths are: (1) attitude toward village endogamy/exogamy, (2) occupational aspirations, (3) Hebrew speaking, and (4) attempting to learn a trade.

Attitude toward endogamy/exogamy. Boys who preferred to marry a village girl were given a 'low' rating; those who answered 'I don't know', or said it did not matter whether a girl came from the village or not, were given a 'medium' rating; and those who preferred to marry girls 'from the outside' were rated 'high'.

Occupational aspirations. Youths who named agriculture as their preference were rated 'low' and youths who named a non-agricultural occupation were rated 'high'.

Hebrew speaking. Each boy was asked to rate himself as to whether he spoke 'mostly Hebrew', 'half Hebrew and half Arabic', or 'mostly Arabic' (see pp. 145–6, n. 2). Each boy also rated his named 'best friends' in the same manner. The scores 3 to 1 were assigned to each of these categories and a mean score was given to each youth from all the ratings made of him (including his self-rating). The mean scores ranged from 1.00 to 3.00. The distribution was divided into three categories and assigned the numerical values of 1 through 3 (low to high Hebrew-speaking).

Attempts to learn a trade. Boys were divided into those who had attempted to learn an 'outside' (non-agricultural) occupation, and those who did not. If a boy had worked consistently in another village, in agriculture, for more than 3 months, he was considered as having attempted to learn non-agricultural skills. If a youth attempted to learn a non-agricultural skill but did not persist at this effort for more than a month, he was considered as not having attempted to learn a non-agricultural skill.

Tables 28 through 33 show the intercorrelations of the variables. The index gives equal weight to each of the four items. The distribution of OWS scores was split at the median for the Tables in the text.

TABLE 28. *Attitude toward village exogamy and occupational aspirations*

Attitude toward village exogamy/endogamy	Occupational aspirations		
	Non-agricultural	Agricultural	Totals
Prefers exogamy	7	1	8
No preference	6	9	15
Prefers endogamy	6	4	10
Totals	19	14	33

$\phi = 0.384$; $P < 0.10$.

TABLE 29. *Attitude toward village exogamy and Hebrew-speaking*

Attitude toward village exogamy/endogamy	Hebrew-speaking*		
	High	Low	Totals
Prefers exogamy	6	2	8
No preference	7	7	14
Prefers endogamy	2	8	10
Totals	15	17	32

$\phi = 0.414$; $P < 0.01$.

* In this table the Hebrew-speaking variable is subdivided into 2 categories so as not to have a 3 × 3 table.

TABLE 30. *Attitude toward village exogamy and the attempt to learn a trade*

Attitude toward village exogamy/endogamy	Attempted to learn a trade		
	Yes	No	Totals
Prefers exogamy	8	0	8
No preference	9	6	15
Prefers endogamy	1	9	10
Totals	18	15	33

$\phi = 0.671$; $P < 0.001$.

TABLE 31. *Hebrew-speaking and occupational aspiration*

| | Occupational aspiration | | |
Hebrew-speaking	Non-agricultural	Agricultural	Totals
High	12	4	16
Medium	1	4	5
Low	7	8	15
Totals	20	16	36

$\phi = 0.391$; $P < 0.10$.

TABLE 32. *Occupational aspiration and attempt to learn a trade*

| Occupational aspiration | Attempted to learn a trade | | |
	Yes	No	Totals
Non-agricultural	15	5	20
Agricultural	5	12	17
Totals	20	17	37

$\phi = 0.456$; $P < 0.10$.

TABLE 33. *Hebrew-speaking and attempt to learn a trade*

| Hebrew-speaking | Attempted to learn a trade | | |
	Yes	No	Totals
High	14	2	16
Medium	2	3	5
Low	4	11	15
Totals	20	16	36

$\phi = 0.581$; $P < 0.005$.

Interaction among the variables of 'orientation to the wider society' of the fathers and of the youths, education and intergenerational conflict

Table 34 consists of partial tables of Table 17 (p. 148) which show the effect of the OWS of the fathers on the relationship between 'education' and 'OWS of the youths'. This latter relationship tends toward $\phi = 0.0$ in both partial tables, suggesting that the relationship between education and OWS of the youths is spurious. The variability in the latter variable can be 'explained' by the OWS of the fathers.

TABLE 34. *OWS of the youths, education, and OWS of the fathers*

	OWS of fathers					
	Strong				Weak	
			OWS of youths			
Education	Strong	Weak	Totals	Strong	Weak	Totals
High	9	0	9	1	3	4
Low	0	0	0	2	9	11
Totals	9	0	9	3	12	15

$\phi = 0.0;$ $\qquad\qquad\qquad \phi = 0.075.$

Table 35 consists of partial tables of Table 18 (p. 150) which show the effect of the OWS of the fathers on the relationship between 'OWS of the youths' and 'intergenerational conflict'. The weak relationship between the two latter variables disappears in the case of the 'strong' OWS fathers, while the expected relationship, between 'acculturation' of the youths and conflict with their parents, appears more strongly in those families where the father has a low OWS score.

In both Tables (34 and 35) the unit utilized is the family, rather than the individual youth, as it is in the Tables from which they are derived (17 and 18 respectively). In Table 34, a mean OWS score, and mean level of education, are used when more than one boy in the sample are from the same family. Similarly a mean 'intergenerational conflict' score is used in Table 35 (see also p. 150, n. 1).

TABLE 35. *Intergenerational conflict, OWS of the youths, and OWS of the fathers*

| | OWS of fathers | | | | | |
| | Strong conflict | | | Weak conflict | | |
OWS of youths	High	Low	Totals	High	Low	Totals
Strong	4	4	8	5	0	5
Weak	0	0	0	5	5	10
Totals	4	4	8	10	5	15

$\phi = 0.0.$　　　　　　$\phi = 0.500.$

Glossary

This section contains explanations of the Arabic and Hebrew terms that appear in the text, and in some instances, references to sources of further information.

'abā. A woolen cloak, usually obtained from Tripoli.

'Abbāsīyya. A resident of Ben'abbās.

Ardilyhūd. Literally: 'land of the Jews'. A Moslem designation of the Jewish hamlet of Tighrinna. Also called Ḥāritilyhūd and Ḥūsh-ilyhūd.

'aila. The term for 'family' in the Jewish dialect of the Gharian, and for 'lineage' in the Moslem dialect.

'arbīt (Hebrew: 'arvīt). The evening prayer.

baqqāl (pl. baqqāla). A traditional grocer.

bēt. The term for 'family' in the Moslem dialect of the Gharian.

besīsa. A festive dish made from roasted wheat and barley, ground with coriandrum and cumin, and mixed with olive oil.

bḥurīm (Hebrew: baḥurīm). Unmarried young men.

dār (pl. diyār). The home of a single family within a cave dwelling.

'edot hamizraḥ. Hebrew: The Middle Eastern ethnic groups in Israel.

ēi. A term of address used by spouses to call the attention of their mate.

esm'i. Same as above.

fqih. A local Moslem religious specialist (cf. Gellner 1969: 286–7).

ftīra. A large, round, flat bread baked in a beehive-shaped oven, open at the top.

gabbāi. The 'treasurer' of the synagogue.

gābīla. A tax paid to the synagogue for having an animal slaughtered.

Ghāina. The residents of the village of Tighrinna.

ḥakham bashi. The Head Rabbi. A term deriving from the organization of Jewish communal life under Ottoman rule. See Hirschberg 1969 (183, 203).

Hamashbir hamerkazi. Hebrew: The cooperative wholesale society of the Histadrut.

ḥamūla. A term used to refer to 'lineage' in Arab villages in Palestine

(Cohen 1965), and more recently applied to quasi-kinship factions in Middle Eastern immigrant communities in Israel.

Ḥāritilyhūd. Jewish quarter. See Arḍilyhūd.

ḥāshim. Shame or embarrassment.

Hatzofeh. Hebrew: The daily newspaper of the National Religious Party in Israel.

hīkhal (Hebrew: hēkhal). The cabinet in which the Torah-scrolls are kept in the synagogue.

hillūla. A Celebration. Usually refers to the celebration on the anniversary of the death of the mystic Shim'on Bar Yoḥai. Also called hillūlit rebbi shim'ūn, or hillūla gdūla.

Histadrut. Histadrut Haklalit shel Ha'ovdim Ha'ivrim B'eretz Yisrael. The General Federation of Jewish Workers in Israel. See Eisenstadt (1967: 38–40, passim) and Willner (1969: 75–8).

Hosha'na rabba. Hebrew: The seventh day of the festival of Tabernacles when special hymns are read during processions in the synagogue.

ḥush (pl. ḥiyāsh). A cave-dwelling usually containing room for several (up to eight) nuclear families.

Ḥūshilyhūd. Literally: 'dwelling of the Jews'. See Arḍilyhūd.

ibī'ushrī. Literally: sells and buys. A small-scale merchant or peddler.

kaymakam. Under Ottoman rule, the official in charge of the Gharian (Cachia 1945: 76). His headquarters were in the fort just outside of Gharian-town.

kesh or keshmāni. A modern (non-'standard') Hebrew term for 'cash' (p. 158).

khamsīn. Literally: fifty. The fifty day period from Passover to Pentecost.

kibbutz. A collective agricultural settlement in Israel. See Weintraub et al. (1969) and Willner (1969: 41–60).

kibbūr. Hebrew: kippur. The Day of Atonement (Leviticus 23: 26–32 and Numbers 29: 7–11). See The Jewish Encyclopedia (Vol. 2: 284 f., s.v. Atonement, day of).

leqeṭ. The Biblical injunction not to collect the gleanings while harvesting, so that these may be gathered by the poor (Leviticus 19: 9).

MAPAI. Hebrew acronym from Mifleget Po'alei Eretz Yisrael. The Workers Party of Israel. The major party in Israel, recently merged within the Israel Labor Party.

ma'abara. Hebrew: A transit camp. These were established in 1950 to receive and settle members of the mass immigration. See Shuval (1963).

maḥanei 'olim. Hebrew: Immigration Camps set up to house the arrivals to Israel during the initial phase of mass immigration reception.

mazkir pnīm. Hebrew: Internal secretary. The administrative position formally in charge of internal moshav matters. The scope of this secretary's responsibilities varies widely from village to village.

Meqorot. The Water Company of the holding company of the Histadrut.

minḥa. The afternoon prayer.

miqwa. A ritual bath. Used most often by women after each menstrual period, and also by men on certain ritual occasions.

miṣwa (pl. miṣwūt). A religious commandment. A general obligation to do good. A ritual honor in the synagogue. The merit of performing a ritual or moral act.

moshav 'ovdīm. Hebrew: A workers' moshav (cooperative small-holder's village). For the distinctions among the various types of moshavim, see Willner (1969: 42–4, 87–8) and Weintraub *et al.* (1969).

muhīl (Hebrew: mohel). A ritual circumcisor.

nsībi. Male 'affine'. For the list of kintypes see p. 106.

Osmanli. Ottoman.

Po'el Mizraḥi. The Mizraḥi (Merkaz Ruḥani = Spiritual Center) Workers' Party. A religious socialist party.

qadīsh. A prayer sanctifying God's name and calling for His world redemption. Various versions of the prayer are utilized on many occasions in Jewish liturgy, including times of memorialization of deceased relatives (see *The Jewish Encyclopedia*, Vol. 7: 401 f., *s.v. Kaddish*).

qbīla (pl. qabail). In literary Arabic: tribe; in spoken Tripolitanian Arabic: a village.

qmīja. A long white shirt worn by men.

rebbi. A title accorded to minor religious specialists in Tripolitania, such as a mohel, shoheṭ, synagogue school teacher, prayer leader and so forth. A rebbi does not have the power of legal decision possessed by a Rabbi.

Rebbi Shim'ūn Bar Yūḥay. Rabbi Shim'on Bar Yohāi. See pp. 83, 85.

rūshshana (Hebrew: Rosh Hashshana). The Solemn New Year (*The Jewish Encyclopedia*, Vol. 9: 254 f., *s.v. New Year*).

ṣaḥab. A Moslem 'friend' of a Jewish merchant or artisan with whom the Jew has long-standing social and economic ties. See p. 18.

semmās (Hebrew: shammash). Caretaker or sexton of the synagogue.

shalīaḥ kūllīl (Hebrew: shalīaḥ kollel). The emissary of a religious institution in Palestine who travelled and collected funds from Jewish communities throughout the diaspora.

shara' rebbi shmuīl. The 'street' where the oil press, the mill and other buildings owned by Rebbi Shmuel stood (see pp. 31–2). Called by the Moslems mṭraḥ rebbi shmuīl (the 'place' of Rebbi Shmuel), a term that might imply a derogatory reference to the nearby refuse dump (see map, pp. 14–15).

shari'a. The Body of Moslem law. The Italian Administration provided for 'Sciaritic courts' for Moslems, and 'Rabbinic courts' for Jews in matters of religious and tribal traditions, property, family rights and so forth (Italian Library of Information 1940: 33–4).

sheikh. The head of the Jewish community. The head of a Moslem community (village) was known as shekh elqbīla.

shevet̤. Hebrew: tribe.

shuḥīt̤ (Hebrew: shoḥet̤). A ritual slaughterer.

siman t̤ov. Hebrew: A good sign. A conventionalized 'blessing' utilized on many occasions both verbally and in writing.

sokhnut. Hasokhnut Hayehudit Le-eretz Yisrael. The Jewish Agency for Israel. See Willner (1969: 227–52) and Weingrod (1966: 24–5, 159–65 and passim).

sukka. Hebrew: A ritual booth constructed on the festival of Tabernacles (*The Jewish Encyclopedia*, Vol. 11: 656 f., *s.v. Tabernacles, Feast of*). Also, the festival of Tabernacles in the dialect of the Gharian Jews.

surwāl. Tripolitanian trousers.

tājir (pl. tujjār). Large-scale merchants who had connections with the city of Tripoli and other communities.

t̤awwāf (pl. t̤awwāfa). An itinerant peddler or tinker.

tfillīn (Hebrew: tefillīn). The phylacteries worn by males during morning weekday prayer. A boy normally starts to wear phylacteries at age 13 (religious majority), hence the celebration of this transition is also called tfillīn by the Gharian Jews.

Tnuva. The cooperative agricultural marketing society of the Histadrut.

T̤rabūlsi. A man from the city of Tripoli (p. 86).

tūqī'a. A man who sounds the ritual ram's horn of Rosh Hashshana (*The Jewish Encyclopedia*, Vol. 11: 30 f., *s.v. Shofar*).

'ūmer. Hebrew: 'omer. The fifty day period between the festivals of Passover and Pentecost. Also known as khamsīn among the Gharian Jews.

Yhūd ben'abbās. The Jewish hamlet of Ben'abbās. A designation utilized by the Moslems.

zdād. A long (about 5 meters), rectangular, colored sheet which, when wrapped around the body, and over the head, serves as an outer garment for women.

zghār. Sons or children.

Bibliography

Aberle, D. and Naegele, K. 1952. 'Middle Class Fathers' Occupational Role and Attitudes toward Children.' *American Journal of Orthopsychiatry* 22: 366–78.

Adams, R. 1959. *A Community in the Andes: Problems and Progress in Muquiyauyo*. Seattle, University of Washington Press.

Addadi, Avraham Haim. 1865. 'Quntreis Makom Shenahagu' (it was customary in this place). In *Vayiqra Avraham*. Leghorn, E. Ben Amozaz & Co.

Africanus, Leo (Giovanni Leone *or* Al-Hassan Ibn Mohammed Alwezaz Al-Fasi). 1847. *The History and Description of Africa and of the Notable Things therein Contained*. London, Works of the Hakluyt Society, Vols. 92–4.

Agar, Herbert. 1960. *The Saving Remnant: An Account of Jewish Survival*. New York, Viking Press.

Agostini, Enrico de. 1917. *Le popolazioni della Tripolitania: notizie etniche e storiche*. Tripoli.

Alliance Israélite Universelle. 1902. 'Les Israelites de la Tripolitaine.' *Revue des Ecoles de l'Alliance Israelite Universelle* 7: 41.

Anderson, T. R. and Zelditch, M. Jr. 1968. *A Basic Course in Statistics: with sociological applications*. New York, Holt, Rinehart and Winston.

Attal, Robert. 1964. 'A Bibliography of Publications concerning Libyan Jewry.' *Sefunot: Annual for Research on the Jewish Communities of the East* (Jerusalem). 9: 383–98.

Avidor, Moshe. 1960. 'The General Education System.' In M. Smilanski, S. Weintraub and Y. Hanegbi, eds., *Child and Youth Welfare in Israel*. Jerusalem, Szold Institute.

Bales, F. 1953. 'The Equilibrium Problem in Small Groups.' In T. Parsons *et al.*, eds., *Working Papers in the Theory of Action*. Glencoe, The Free Press.

Barnett, H. 1953. *Innovation: The Basis of Cultural Change*. New York, McGraw-Hill.

Barth, Henry. 1857. *Travels and Discoveries in North and Central Africa*. Vol. 1. New York, Harper & Bros.

Bateson, G. 1942. 'Morale and National Character.' In G. Watson, ed., *Civilian Morale*. Boston, Houghton-Mifflin.

Benedict, R. 1949. 'Child Rearing in Certain European Countries.' *American Journal of Orthopsychiatry* 9: 342–50.

Benjamin, Israel Joseph. 1859. *Eight Years in Asia and Africa*. Hanover, 238–45.

Ben-David, J., ed. 1964. *Agricultural Planning and Village Community in Israel. Arid Zone Research 23*. Paris, UNESCO.

Bensimon, D. 1969. 'L'intégration économique des immigrants nord-africaines en Israël et des Juifs nord-africaines en France.' *Revue Francaise de Sociologie* 10: 491–514.

Bensimon-Donath, D. 1968. *Évolution du Judaïsme Marocain sous le Protectorate français: 1912–56*. Paris, Mouton.

Ben-Zvi, Yitzhaq. 1964. 'The Travels of an Emissary of Safed: by Rabbi Ya'aqov Siqli Hakohen.' *Otzar Yehudei Sefarad* 7: 77–86. (In Hebrew.)

Blake, G. 1968. *Misurata: a market town in Tripolitania*. Research Papers 9, Durham, Department of Geography, Durham Colleges in the University of Durham.

Brandenburg, E. 1911. 'Die Troglodyten des Djebel Garian.' *Oriental-ische Literaturzeitung* 14: 1–14.

Cachia, A. J. 1945. *Libya under the Second Ottoman Occupation (1835–1911)*. Tripoli, Government Press.

Cesaro, Antonio. 1939. *L'Arabo parlato a Tripoli*. Rome.

Chance, N. 1960. 'Culture Change and Integration: An Eskimo example.' *American Anthropologist* 62: 1028–44.

Chouraqui, A. 1968. *Between East and West: A history of the Jews of North Africa. Translated from the French by M. M. Bernet*. Philadelphia, Jewish Publication Society of America.

Cohen, Abner. 1965. *Arab border-villages in Israel: A Study of Continuity and Change in Social Organization*. Manchester, Manchester University Press.

Cohen, E. 1968. '"Social Images" in an Israeli Development Town.' *Human Relations* 21: 163–76.

Cohen, P. 1962. 'Alignments and Allegiances in the Community of Shaarayim in Israel.' *Jewish Jn'l. of Sociology* 4: 14–38.

Colòsimo, Gaspare. 1917. 'Lo statuto della Communita di Tripoli.' *Vessillo Israelitico* 65: 161–71.

Comunità Israelitica della Tripolitania. 1943. *Relazione morale-economica dell'esercizio 1943*. Tripoli.

Coon, C. S. 1958. *Caravan: The Story of the Middle East*. New York, Henry Holt & Co.

Daniels, Clifton. 1945. 'Seventy-four Tripolitan Jews Slain in Arab Riots.' *New York Times*, November 8.

Darin-Drabkin, H. 1962. *Patterns of Cooperative Agriculture in Israel.* Tel Aviv, Dep't. for International Cooperation, Ministry of Foreign Affairs.

Deshen, S. 1965. 'A Case of Breakdown of Modernization in an Israeli Immigrant Village.' *Jewish Jn'l. of Sociology* 7: 63–91.

1966. 'Conflict and Social Change: The Case of an Israeli Village.' *Sociologia Ruralis* 6: 31–55.

1970. 'On Religious Change: The Situational Analysis of Symbolic Action.' *Comparative Studies in Society and History* 12: 260–74.

Despois, J. 1935. *La Colonisation Italienne en Libye: Problèmes et Méthodes.* Paris, Larose-Editeurs.

De Vos, G. 1968. 'Achievement and Innovation in Culture and Personality.' In E. Norbeck, D. Price-Williams and W. McCord, eds., *The Study of Personality: An Interdisciplinary Appraisal.* New York, Holt, Rinehart and Winston, pp. 348–70.

Duvdvani, B. 1960. 'Episodes from the Ingathering of the Libyan Exile.' In F. Zuaretz *et al.*, eds., *Yahadut Luv* (Libyan Jewry). Tel Aviv, Vaad Kehilot Luv Beyisrael, pp. 297–316 (Hebrew).

Eisenstadt, S. N. 1954. *The Absorption of Immigrants.* London, Routledge and Kegan Paul.

1967. *Israeli Society.* New York, Basic Books.

Elmaleh, Avraham. 1943. 'Among the Cave-dwellers of Tripolitania.' *Hed Hamizrah* (Jerusalem) Vol. 2, no. 11 (18): 5, no. 12 (19): 8–9 (Hebrew).

Evans-Pritchard, E. 1940. 'The Nuer of the Southern Sudan.' In M. Fortes and E. Evans-Pritchard, eds., *African Political Systems.* London, Oxford University Press.

Féraud, L. C. 1927. *Annales Tripolitaines.* Paris and Tunis, Librarie Vuibert.

Firth, R. 1951. *Elements of Social Organization.* London, Watts.

1954. 'Social Organization and Social Change.' *Jn'l. of the Royal Anthropological Institute of Gt. Britain and Ireland* 84: 1–20.

Fischel, W. 1944. 'The Jews of Kurdistan 100 Years Ago.' *Jewish Social Studies* 6: 195–226.

1969. 'Introduction.' In *Jews in the Economic and Political Life of Medieval Islam.* New York, Ktav Publishing House.

Fortes, M. 1949. *The Web of Kinship among the Tallensi.* London, Oxford University Press.

Foster, G. 1965. 'Peasant Society and the Image of Limited Good.' *American Anthropologist* 67: 293–315.

Frankenberg, R. 1957. *Village on the Border: a social study of Religion, Politics and Football in a North Wales Community.* London, Cohen and West.

Fuller, A. 1961. *Buarij: Portrait of a Lebanese Muslim Village.* Harvard

Middle Eastern Monographs 6. Cambridge, Harvard University Press.

Geertz, C. 1966. 'Religion as a Cultural System.' In M. Banton ed., *Anthropological Approaches to the Study of Religion*. London, Tavistock, pp. 1–46.

—— 1967. *Discussion of a Symposium on 'Local Expressions of Islam'*. Chicago, Middle East Studies Association Annual Meeting, December.

Gellner, E. 1969. *Saints of the Atlas*. Chicago, University of Chicago Press.

Gluckman, M. 1963. 'Gossip and Scandal.' *Current Anthropology* 4: 307–16.

Goffman, E. 1957. 'Status Consistency and Preference for Change in Power Distribution.' *American Sociological Review* 22: 275–81.

Goitein, S. D. 1955. 'Portrait of a Yemenite Weaver's Village.' *Jewish Social Studies* 17: 3–26.

Goldberg, H. 1965. *The Internalization of Ethnic Attitudes in a Tripolitanian Moshav in Israel*. Paper read at the 64th Annual Meeting of the American Anthropological Association, Denver.

—— 1967a. 'FBD Marriage and Demography among Tripolitanian Jews in Israel.' *Southwestern Jn'l. of Anthropology* 23: 176–91.

—— 1967b. 'Patronymic groups in a Tripolitanian Jewish Village: Reconstruction and Interpretation.' *Jewish Jn'l. of Sociology* 9: 209–26.

—— 1968. 'Elite Groups in Peasant Communities: A comparison of Three Middle Eastern Villages.' *American Anthropologist* 70: 718–31.

—— 1969a. 'Egalitarianism in an Autocratic Village in Israel.' *Ethnology* 8: 54–75.

—— 1969b. 'Domestic Organization and Wealth in an Israeli Immigrant Village.' *Human Organization* 28: 58–63.

—— 1970. 'From Sheikh to Mazkir: Structural Continuity and Organizational Change in the Leadership to a Tripolitanian Jewish Community.' *Folklore Research Center Studies*, Vol. 1. The Magnes Press. The Hebrew University: 29–41.

—— 1971. 'Ecologic and demographic aspects of rural Tripolitanian Jewry: 1853–1949.' *International Jn'l. of Middle East Studies* 2: 245–65.

—— n.d. 'Culture Change in an Israeli Immigrant Village: How the Twist came to Even Yosef.' *Middle Eastern Studies* (forthcoming).

Goodenough, W. 1969. 'Frontiers of Cultural Anthropology: Social Organization.' *Proceedings of the American Philosophical Society* 113: 329–35.

Great Britain. 1920. *A Handbook of Libya*. London, Geographical Section of Naval Intelligence Division, Naval Staff, Admiralty.

Guweta', A. 1960a. 'The Jewish Community of Tripoli and its

Institutions.' In F. Zuaretz *et al.*, eds., *Yahadut Luv* (Libyan Jewry). Tel Aviv, Vaad Kehilot Luv Beyisrael: 20–5 (in Hebrew).

1960*b*. 'The Bushaif Synagogue.' In F. Zuaretz *et al.*, eds., *Yahadut Luv* (Libyan Jewry). Tel Aviv, Vaad Kehilot Luv Beyisrael: 123–5 (in Hebrew).

Hacohen, Mordechai. n.d. *Higid Mordechai* (Mordechai Narrated). Ms. no. 8° 1292, National and University Library, Jerusalem.

1969. 'Letters to N. Slouschz.' *Genazim: Collections concerning the modern history of Hebrew Literature* III. Tel Aviv, Masada: 45–90 (in Hebrew).

Ḥakmon, Y. 1960. 'In the Exile of Jado.' In F. Zuaretz *et al.*, eds., *Yahadut Luv* (Libyan Jewry). Tel Aviv, Vaad Kehilot Luv Beyisrael: 197–9 (in Hebrew).

Halpern, B. 1961. *The Idea of the Jewish State*. Cambridge, Harvard University Press.

Harris, M. 1968. *The Rise of Anthropological Theory: A History of Theories of Culture*. New York, T. Crowell.

Hillery, G. 1971. 'Freedom and Social Organization: A Comparative Analysis.' *American Sociological Review* 36: 51–65.

Hirschberg, H. Z. (J. W.). 1965*a*. 'Tripolitania.' In *A History of the Jews of North Africa: From Antiquity to Our Time* (2 Vols.); Vol. II: *From the Ottoman Conquests to Modern Times*. Jerusalem, Bialik Institute: 173–206 (in Hebrew).

1965*b*. 'An Evil and Bitter Experience of the People of the Maghreb.' *Bar-Ilan University Decennial Collection*. Ramat-Gan, Bar-Ilan University: 415–79 (in Hebrew, English summary).

1969. 'The Oriental Jewish Communities.' In A. J. Arberry, ed., *Religion in the Middle East: Three Religions in Concord and Conflict*, Vol. I. Cambridge, Cambridge University Press: 119–225.

Inkeles, A. 1955. 'Social Change and Social Character: The Role of Parental Mediation.' *Jn'l. of Social Issues* 11: 12–23.

1964. *What is Sociology: An Introduction to the Discipline and the Profession*. Englewood Cliffs, Prentice-Hall.

Ish, S. D. H. 1886. 'Tripolitania in Africa.' *Knesset Yisrael* (Warsaw) 1: 730–5 (Hebrew).

Italian Library of Information. 1940. *The Italian Empire: Libya*. New York, Italian Library of Information.

Italy, Istituto Centrale di Statistica. 1935. *VII Censimento generale della popolazione, 21 Aprile, 1931; Vol.* v, *Colonie e possedimenti*. Rome.

1939. *VIII Censimento generale della popolazione, 21 Aprile, 1936; Vol.* v, *Libia, Isole dell'Egeo–Tientsin*. Rome.

Jacobs, Milton, 1956. *A Study of Stability and Change: The Moroccan Jewess* (Abstract of a Dissertation). Washington, D.C., Catholic University of America Press.

Jewish Encyclopedia, The. 1901. New York, Ktav Publishing House.

Joffe, N. 1953. 'Non-reciprocity among East European Jews.' In M. Mead and R. Metraux, eds., *Studying Culture at a Distance.* Chicago, University of Chicago Press: 386–9.

Kaplan, B. 1961. 'Editor's Epilogue: A Final Word.' In *Studying Personality Cross-Culturally.* New York, Harper and Row.

Katz, E. 1957. 'The Two-Step Flow of Communication: An Up-to-date Report of an Hypothesis.' *Public Opinion Quarterly* 21: 61–78.

—— and A. Zloczower. 1961. 'Ethnic Continuity in an Israeli Town, II: Relations with Peers.' *Human Relations* 14: 309–27.

Khadduri, M. 1963. *Modern Libya: A Study in Political Development.* Baltimore, Johns Hopkins Press.

Khuja, Mahmud. 1960. 'Garian Town.' In S. G. Willimot and J. I. Clarke, eds., *Field Studies in Libya.* Research Papers 4. Durham, Dep't. of Geography, Durham Colleges in the University of Durham, pp. 120–4.

Kimche, Jon. 1948 *a.* 'Tripolitanian Jewry's Inexorable Decline.' *Jewish Chronicle* (London), No. 4117 (March 19), p. 11.

—— 1948 *b.* 'The Oldest Jewish Underground.' *Jewish Chronicle* (London), No. 4118 (March 26), p. 11.

Kleinlerer, D. 1929. 'Cave-Dwellers of North Africa: A Visit among the Picturesque Inhabitants of Djebel Gharian.' *The Jewish Tribune* (New York) Vol. 94, no. 22 (May 31): 1, 4.

Kluckhohn, F. and Strodtbeck, F. 1961. *Variations in Value Orientations.* Evanston, Row Peterson.

Kushner, G. 1971. *The Administered Community: Immigrants from India in Israel.* Tucson, The University of Arizona Press (in the Press).

Landecker, W. 1963. 'Class Crystallization and Class Consciousness.' *American Sociological Review* 28: 219–29.

Landshut, S. 1950. 'Libya.' In *Jewish Communities in the Muslim Countries of the Middle East.* London, Jewish Chronicle: 87–92.

Lerner, D. 1958. *The Passing of Traditional Society: Modernizing the Middle East.* Glencoe, Free Press.

Lévi-Strauss, C. 1964. *Tristes Tropiques.* New York, Atheneum.

Lewis, B. 1968. *The Emergence of Modern Turkey.* London, Oxford University Press.

Libya, Government of the Kingdom of. 1959. *General Population Census of Libya, 1954: Report and Tables.* Tripoli, Department of Census and Statistics, Ministry of the National Economy.

Linton, R. 1936. *The Study of Man.* New York, Appleton-Century.

Lyon, G. F. 1821. *A Narrative of Travels in North Africa in the Years 1818, 1819 and 1820.* London, John Murray.

Malka, E. 1952. *Essai sur la condition juridique de la femme juive au Maroc.* Paris, Librarie Generale de Droit et de Jurisprudence.

Marmorstein, E. 1969. *Heaven at Bay: The Jewish Kulturkampf in the Holy Land*. London, Oxford University Press.

Matras, J. 1965. *Social Change in Israel*. Chicago, Aldine.

Mead, M. 1956. *New Lives for Old*. New York, William Morrow.

Miller, Louis. 1967. 'A Study of Socio-cultural Change and Changes in Child-rearing Practices among Libyan Jews in Israel.' *International Understanding*, Vol. 4: 19–26.

Minkovitz, M. 1967. 'Old Conflicts in a New Environment: A Study of a Moroccan Atlas Mountain Community Transplanted to Israel.' *Jewish Jn'l. of Sociology* 9: 191–208.

Moore, W. and Feldman, A., eds. 1960. *Labor commitment and Social Change in Developing Areas*. New York, Social Science Research Council.

Morag, Shlomo. 1963. *The Hebrew Language Tradition of the Yemenite Jews*. Jerusalem, Academy of the Hebrew Language. (In Hebrew.)

Morton-Williams, P. 1968. 'The Fulani Penetration into Nupe and Yoruba in the Nineteenth Century.' In I. M. Lewis, ed., *History and Social Anthropology*. London, Tavistock: 1–24.

Nash, M. 1958. *Machine Age Maya: The Industrialization of a Guatemalan Community*. Memoirs of the American Anthropological Association 87.

Norris, H. T. 1953. 'Cave Habitations and Granaries in Tripolitania and Tunisia.' *Man* (Old Series) 53: 82–5.

Ohel, Mila. 1955. *Gesher* (Bridge). Tel Aviv, Association of Hebrew Writers and Dvir.

1962. *Ish Nidham* (Overwhelmed). Jerusalem.

Parker, S. 1964. 'Ethnic Identity and Acculturation in Two Eskimo Villages.' *American Anthropologist* 66: 325–41.

Parsons, T. 1953. 'A Revised Analytical Scheme to the Theory of Social Stratification.' In R. Bendix and S. Lipset, eds., *Class, Status and Power: A Reader in Social Stratification*. Glencoe, Free Press.

1961. 'An Outline of the Social System.' In T. Parsons *et al.*, eds., *Theories of Society*. Glencoe, Free Press: 30–84.

Perlzweig, M. 1949. 'Statement on Behalf of the Jewish Community of Tripolitania to the Political Committee of the United Nations General Assembly.' *Congress Weekly* 16, no. 18: 15–16.

Peters, E. 1960. 'The Proliferation of Segments in the Lineage of the Bedouin of Cyrenaica.' *Jn'l. of the Royal Anthropological Institute of Gt. Britain and Ireland* 90: 29–53.

Plath, D. 1964. 'Where the Family of God is the Family: The Role of the Dead in Japanese Households.' *American Anthropologist* 66: 300–17.

Raccah, Gabriele di Vittoria. 1938. 'Le comunita della Libia: Garian.' *Israel* (Florence and Rome) 23, nos. 44–5: 6–7.

Redfield, R. 1950. *A Village that Chose Progress: Chan Kom Revisited*. Chicago, University of Chicago Press.

Rejwan, Nissim. 1964. 'Israel's Communal Controversy: an Oriental's Appraisal.' *Midstream* 10, no. 2: 14–26.

Rennel, F. 1948. *British Military Administration of the Occupied Territories of Africa: 1941–1947*. London, His Majesty's Stationery Office.

Roe, Anne. 1953. *A Psychological Study of Eminent Psychologists and Anthropologists, and a comparison with Biological and Physical Scientists*. Psychological Monographs: General and Applied, Vol. 67, no. 2.

Rohlfs, Gerhard. 1874. *Quer Durch Afrika: Reise Vom Mittelmeer Nach Dem Tschad-See Und Zum Gulf Von Guniea*. Leipzig, F. A. Brockhaus.

Rosenfeld, H. 1958. 'Processes of Structural Change within the Arab Village Extended Family.' *American Anthropologist* 60: 1127–39.

Samuel, E. 1960. 'The Ottoman Legacy to Israel.' *Jewish Jn'l. of Sociology* 2: 219–35.

Shilon, Meir. 1960. 'The Immigration from Libya.' In F. Zuaretz *et al.*, eds., *Yahadut Luv* (Libyan Jewry). Tel Aviv, Vaad Kehilot Luv Beyisrael: 317–21 (in Hebrew).

Shokeid (Minkovitz), M. 1968. 'Immigration and Factionalism: An Analysis of Factions in Rural Israeli Communities of Immigrants.' *British Jn'l. of Sociology* 19: 385–406.

Shuval, J. 1962. 'Emerging Patterns of Ethnic Strain in Israel.' *Social Forces* 40: 323–30.

1963. *Immigrants on the Threshold*. New York, Atherton.

Silverman, M. 1969. 'Maximize Your Options: A Study in Values, Symbols and Social Structure.' In R. Spencer, ed., *Forms of Symbolic Action. Proceedings of the 1969 Annual Spring Meeting of the American Ethnological Society*, Seattle: 97–115.

Silverstein, Roberta. 1964. Acculturation in a Moshav Olim: A Study of three Generations of Moroccan Immigrants in a Cooperative Settlement in Israel. Minneapolis, unpublished M.A. Thesis, University of Minnesota.

Slouschz, Nahum. 1908. 'La Tripolitaine sous la Domination des Karamanli.' *Revue du Monde Musulman* 6: 58–84, 211–32, 433–53.

1926. 'In the Mountains of Libya.' *Reshumot* (Tel Aviv) 4: 1–76 (Hebrew).

1927. *Travels in North Africa*. Philadelphia, Jewish Publication Society of America.

Smith, D. H. and Inkeles, A. 1966. 'The O M Scale: A Comparative Socio-Psychological Measure of Individual Modernity.' *Sociometry* 29: 353–77.

Stern, C. 1960. *Principles of Human Genetics*. San Francisco, Freeman & Co.

Stern, S. 1950. *The Court Jew: A Contribution to the History of the Period of Absolutism in Central Europe.* Philadelphia, Jewish Publication Society of America.

Suter, Karl. 1964. 'Die Wohnhöhlen und Speicherburgen des tripolitanisch-tunesischen Berglandes.' *Zeitschrift für Ethnologie* 89: 216–75.

Thwaite, A. 1969. *The Deserts of Hesperides: an Experience of Libya.* New York, Roy Publishers.

Vogt, E. 1965. 'Structural and Conceptual Replication in Zinacantan Culture.' *American Anthropologist* 67: 342–53.

Wallace, A. 1961. *Culture and Personality.* New York, Random House.

Watson, J. and Samora, J. 1954. 'Subordinated Leadership in a Bicultural Community: An Analysis.' *American Sociological Review* 19: 413–21.

Weingrod, A. 1962. 'Reciprocal Change: A Case Study of a Moroccan Immigrant Village in Israel.' *American Anthropologist* 64: 115–31.

1965. *Israel: Group Relations in a New Society.* New York, Praeger.

1966. *Reluctant Pioneers: Village Development in Israel.* Ithaca, Cornell University Press.

and Minkovitz, M. 1963. 'The Absorption of the Second Generation in Immigrant Moshavim.' *Megamot* (Jerusalem) 12: 363–72 (in Hebrew with English summary).

Weinreich, U., Labov, N. and Herzog, M. 1968. 'Empirical Foundations for a Theory of Language Change.' In W. Lehmann, ed., *Directions for Historical Linguistics: A Symposium.* Austin, University of Texas Press: 97–188.

Weintraub, D. 1964. 'A Study of New Farmers in Israel.' *Sociologica Ruralis* 4: 3–51.

and Bernstein, F. 1966. 'Social Structure and Modernization: A Comparative Study of Two Villages.' *American Jn'l. of Sociology* 71: 509–21.

and Lissak, M. 1964a. 'Physical and Material Conditions in the New Moshav.' In J. Ben-David, ed., *Agricultural Planning and Village Community in Israel. Arid Zone Research 23.* Paris, UNESCO: 102–28.

and Lissak, M. 1964b. 'Social Integration and Change.' In J. Ben-David, ed., *Agricultural Planning and Village Community in Israel. Arid Zone Research 23.* Paris. UNESCO: 129–59.

Lissak, M. and Azmon, Y. 1969. *Moshava, Kibbutz and Moshav: Patterns of Jewish Rural Settlement and Development in Palestine.* Ithaca, Cornell University Press.

and Parness, T. 1968. 'Rural life, Orientation to Change, and Modernization: A Pilot Study of Farm Youths in Israel.' *Rural Sociology* 33: 285–99.

Weintraub, D. and M. Shapiro. 1968. 'The Traditional Family in Israel in the Process of Change-Crisis and Continuity.' *British Jn'l. of Sociology* 19: 284–99.

Weitz, R. 1967. 'The Ethnic Factor in the Development of Rural Settlements in Israel.' *Sociologia Ruralis* 7: 130–55.

and Rokach, A. 1968. *Agricultural Development: Planning and Innovation An Israeli Case Study.* New York, Praeger.

Williams, J. 1968. *The Youth of Haouch El Harimi: A Lebanese Village. Harvard Middle Eastern Monographs 20.* Cambridge, Harvard University Press.

Willner, D. 1956. 'Problems involved in the Establishment of Cottage Industries in Immigrant Cooperative Settlements.' *Megamot* (Jerusalem) 7: 274–85 (in Hebrew with English summary).

1962. 'Jews in the High Atlas Mountains of Morocco: A Partial Reconstruction.' *Jewish Jn'l. of Sociology* 4: 207–41.

1969. *Nation Building and Community in Israel.* Princeton, Princeton University Press.

Wolf, E. 1956. 'Aspects of Group Relations in a Complex Society: Mexico.' *American Anthropologist* 58: 1065–78.

Zenner, W. 1963. 'Ambivalence and Self-Image among Oriental Jews in Israel.' *Jewish Jn'l. of Sociology* 5: 214–23.

1965 a. 'Memorialism – Some Jewish Examples.' *American Anthropologist* 67: 481–3.

1965 b. 'Saints and Piecemeal Supernaturalism among the Jerusalem Sephardim.' *Anthropological Quarterly* 38: 201–17.

Zionist Organization, Executive and Executive of the Jewish Agency. 1960. *The Agricultural Settlement Department. Reports submitted to the Twenty-fifth Zionist Congress, Jerusalem.*

Zuaretz, F., Guweta', A., Shaked, Tz., Arbib, G. and Tayar, F., eds., 1960. *Yahadut Luv* (Libyan Jewry). Tel Aviv, Vaad Kehilot Luv Beyisrael.

Zuaretz, F. (B. Y.). 1960. ''*Im Hapereq'* (Introduction). In F. Zuaretz *et al.*, eds., *Yahadut Luv* (Libyan Jewry). Tel Aviv, Vaad Kehilot Luv Beyisrael: 291–3.

Zuaretz, M. and Rubin, Y. 1960. 'The History of Zionism in Libya.' In F. Zuaretz *et al.*, eds., *Yahadut Luv* (Libyan Jewry). Tel Aviv, Vaad Kehilot Luv Beyisrael: 129–41.

Index